PRAISE FOR *TEN TYPES OF INNOVATION*

"I have long admired the innovation work of Larry Keeley and am thrilled that he has shared his concepts, insights, and experience with the world in his terrific book. *Ten Types of Innovation* is a must-read for any manager seriously interested in building an innovation culture rather than waiting around hoping for the next immaculate conception."
—**Roger L. Martin**, Dean, Rotman School of Management

"Innovation is not for amateurs and most meaningful developments are not accidents. Great innovators follow disciplined approaches and Larry Keeley outlines an evidence-based methodology which takes innovation well beyond product tweaking. At Mars we are leveraging sophisticated innovation techniques and creating hard to copy, distinctive propositions which we know will delight our consumers and will remain relevant over time. *Ten Types of Innovation* provides great frameworks to help you rethink the role innovation plays in your business and will raise the quality of the innovation dialogue from a black art to a serious science."
—**Ralph Jerome**, VP of Corporate Innovation, Mars, Inc.

"*Ten Types of Innovation* will become the indispensable 'how to do it' textbook of disruptive innovation, providing an executable roadmap for transformative change in any industry."
—**Dr. Nicholas F. LaRusso**, Medical Director, Mayo Clinic Center for Innovation

"When innovation is defined only as a new product or service, this view ignores a larger, integrated process that must function seamlessly for optimal value creation. *Ten Types of Innovation*, by contrast, captures the entire innovation ecosystem, from essential organizational structures and processes to critical aspects of the product or service being introduced. Equally important, the book explores diverse elements of innovation's impact on the total customer experience. It distills three decades of innovation research into an action-oriented framework, offering a comprehensive map to guide creative teams as they venture into challenging new territory."
—**Dipak C. Jain**, Dean, INSEAD

"Doblin helped us achieve our goal to continuously and successfully introduce transformational innovations to our customers. *Ten Types of Innovation* provides the insights necessary to get you started on your innovation journey."
—**Curt Nonomaque**, President and CEO, VHA

TEN TYPES OF INNOVATION

TEN TYPES OF INNOVATION

THE DISCIPLINE OF BUILDING BREAKTHROUGHS

LARRY KEELEY

RYAN PIKKEL, BRIAN QUINN, HELEN WALTERS

WILEY

PART FOUR
SPOT THE SHIFTS
SEE THE CONDITIONS THAT BIRTH BREAKTHROUGHS

Innovations that change industries can seem like they come out of nowhere. In fact, you can see the early warning signals that reveal when big changes are needed—and then seize on them.

PART FIVE
LEADING INNOVATION
USE BETTER PLANS TO BUILD BREAKTHROUGHS

Sophisticated innovations share similar components at their core. By deconstructing and distilling the work of successful innovations, the building blocks for new concepts emerge.

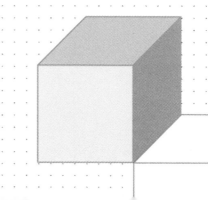

PREFACE
ON INNOVATING EFFECTIVELY

In the middle of August in 2012, Congressional approval rating hit an all time low.[1] This is saying something—the same figure has been less than impressive in earlier eras. Yet the United States Congress isn't the only institution with lukewarm support. People expect very little good news about the wars being fought (whether in Iraq, Afghanistan, or on Terror, Drugs, Poverty, or Ignorance). The promising Arab Spring has given way to a recurring pessimism about progress. Gnarly health problems are on a tear the world over—diabetes now affects over eight percent of Americans—and other expensive disease conditions such as obesity, heart disease, and cancer are also now epidemic. The cost of education rises like a runaway helium balloon, yet there is less and less evidence that it nets the students a real return on their investment. Police have access to ever more elaborate statistical models of crime, but there is still way too much of it. And global warming steadily produces more extreme and more dangerous conditions the world over, yet according to about half of our elected "leaders," it is still, officially, only a theory that can conveniently be denied.

And yet...

We steadily expect more from our computers, our smartphones, apps, networks, and games. We have grown to expect routine and wondrous stories of new ventures funded through crowdsourcing. We hear constantly of lives around the world transformed because of Twitter or Kahn Academy or some breakthrough discovery in medicine. Esther Duflo and her team at the Poverty Action Lab at MIT keep cracking tough problems that afflict the poor to arrive at solutions with demonstrated efficacy, and then, often, the Gates Foundation or another philanthropic institution funds the transformational solution at unprecedented scale.

Storytelling is in a new golden age—whether in live events, on the radio, or in amazing new television series that can emerge anywhere in the world and be adapted for global tastes. Experts are now everywhere, and shockingly easy and affordable to access. Indeed, it seems clear that all the knowledge we've been struggling to amass is steadily being amplified and swiftly getting more organized, accessible, and affordable—whether through the magic of elegant little apps or big data managed in ever-smarter clouds or crowdfunding sites used to capitalize creative ideas in commerce or science.

One way to make sense of these opposing conditions is to see us as being in a time of radical transformation. To see the old institutions as being challenged as a series of newer, more agile ones arise. In

1 This depressing statistic comes to you courtesy of Gallup. See the back of the book for extensive links to additional notes and research data.

2 One elegant recent book that posits such a theory with far more elaboration is *Too Big to Know* by David Weinberger, one of the authors of the earlier and perennially interesting *The Cluetrain Manifesto*.

3 This allowed us to be one of the first consulting firms in the world with a full-time social science research unit. Ours was initially pioneered by the brilliant cultural anthropologist Dr. Rick E. Robinson, who went on to cofound (along with John Cain) the seminal research firm, e-Lab.

4 This leading graduate school was the first in the United States to issue PhD degrees in design.

history, such shifts have rarely been bloodless, but this one seems to be a radical transformation in the structure, sources, and nature of expertise.[2] Indeed, among innovation experts, this time is one like no other. For the very first time in history, we are in a position to tackle tough problems with ground-breaking tools and techniques.

WHAT DO YOU DO WHEN THE PROBLEMS ARE REAL, THE STAKES ARE HIGH, TIME IS SHORT, AND ABSTRACT ANSWERS ARE INADEQUATE?

That is what we've written this book to address: how you can innovate effectively. How you can get the future to show up just slightly ahead of its regularly scheduled arrival. How you can give teams that can't afford to fail the robust methods they need to succeed—whether the problem they are tackling is small or large, trivial or epic.

Part of the innovation revolution is rooted in superior tradecraft: better ways to innovate that are suited for tougher problems. Yet most teams are stuck using goofy techniques that have been discredited long ago. This book is part of a new vanguard, a small group of leading thinkers who see innovation as urgent and essential, who know it needs to be cracked as a deep discipline and subjected to the same rigors as any other management science.

OUR JOURNEY TO THIS BOOK

Ten Types of Innovation has had a long gestation period. Broadly stated, it codifies, structures, and simplifies three decades of work from a consulting firm in Chicago, Doblin, which I cofounded along with the brilliant design methodologist Jay Doblin. From its inception in 1980, Doblin has asked one pervasive, deceptively simple-seeming question: "*How do we get innovation to succeed instead of fail?*"

Over the years we have kept three important dimensions in dynamic tension. We have a theoretical side, where we ask and seek real answers to tough questions about innovation. Simple but critical ones like, "Does brainstorming work?" (it doesn't), along with deep and systemic ones like, "How do you really know what a user wants when the user doesn't know either?"[3] We have an academic side, since many of us are adjunct professors at Chicago's Institute of Design,[4] and this demands that we explain our ideas to smart young professionals in disciplined, distinctive ways. And third, we have an applied side, in that we have been privileged to adapt our innovation methods to many of the world's leading global enterprises and start-ups that hanker to be future leading firms.

From the beginning, Doblin has itself been interdisciplinary, mixing social sciences, technology, strategy, library sciences, and design into a frothy admixture that has always tried to blend both *analysis*, breaking tough things down, with *synthesis*, building new things up. Broadly, we think any effective innovation effort needs plenty of both, stitched together as a seamless whole.

The heart of this book is built around a seminal Doblin discovery: that there are (and have always been) ten distinct types of innovation that need be orchestrated with some care to make a game-changing innovation. If you stick with the book, you'll read about that soon enough. What you need to know now, at the outset, is that this is not just one thin discovery. Along with the framework itself, we also describe what you should do to surround this better way of innovating with even more robust protocols and processes.

OUR AUTHORING TEAM

It is an axiom in writing that when you have a bunch of authors the resulting work is likely to be a compromised hash. Any movie you see with a whole string of screenwriters listed is unlikely to be brilliant. But at Doblin we do nearly everything in teams. This stems from the unique nature of innovation itself: no individual can possibly know enough all by himself or herself to crack tough innovation challenges, and the best teams have many different disciplines involved. So too with this book. It may help you to know

the roles each of us played and thus better glimpse what kinds of contributions go into any complex synthesis.

As the long-time president of Doblin, I have pioneered many ideas and methods at the core of innovation effectiveness, including the Ten Types. I have dedicated my entire professional career to thinking about how to create appropriate tools and techniques — and about how our clients can most effectively use them in practice. I have spent more than 30 years learning and thinking about what makes innovation succeed or fail. As the principal author of the text, I am responsible for the basic arguments throughout, and the system of ideas here either succeeds or fails because of me.

Ryan Pikkel has an advanced degree in innovation skills from the Institute of Design and is himself a skilled designer. He managed the collaboration with a deep and talented team from our colleagues at Pentagram and he worked to ensure that every page in the book is as clear, concise, and accessible as possible. He is also personally responsible for the creation of the incredible Innovation Tactics Cards, which now permit us to codify and deconstruct any valuable innovation — or to help you to build one of your own with the help of robust, reusable modules.

Brian Quinn was for many years a traditional strategist, who left consulting to become a screenwriter, and then returned to the field — but only on the condition that he could focus on solving innovation problems for clients. This makes him one of the rare individuals who really can integrate most of the necessary components for innovation effectiveness — and he has done so repeatedly and reliably for several of our largest clients. His voice in the book has been crucial in helping to make the ideas more actionable for firms that need to innovate.

Helen Walters was the innovation and design editor at *Bloomberg Businessweek*. She has built an amazing personal network of practitioners and practices the world over. Of course, as a journalist, she values telling clear stories with solid facts and getting details right — an indispensable skill for a book with tales on every page.

Finally, our work was materially aided by Bansi Nagji. While he was not an author of this book, he played a role in refreshing and advancing the Ten Types of Innovation. More broadly, Bansi made innovation a strategic priority at Monitor and continues to do so today as a leader in Monitor Deloitte. The team is grateful for his support.

None of this may matter to you as a reader, since the book stands or falls as a unified whole. It mattered a very great deal to us as a team, though. We wanted to make a book that would reveal the whole, remarkable, and important emerging discipline of innovation, because so many people now see the urgent need to innovate. They sense that old ideas and structures must give way. They imagine that newer, better futures are out there, lurking in the loaming, just out of reach.

Well, reach for them, we say.

Start here. Start now. Foment your very own revolution.

We'll show you how.

Larry Keeley
Chicago, 2013

WE DISCOVERED THE TEN TYPES OF INNOVATION IN 1998.
THIS BOOK EXPLAINS WHAT WE HAVE LEARNED SINCE.

Innovation mostly fails. It doesn't need to.
You shouldn't let it.

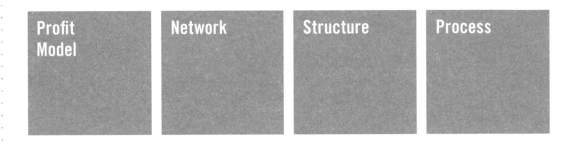

| Profit Model | Network | Structure | Process |

Innovation almost never fails due to a lack of creativity.
It's almost always because of a lack of discipline.

The most certain way to fail is to focus only on products.
Successful innovators use many types of innovation.

Successful innovators analyze the patterns of innovation in their industry.
Then they make conscious, considered choices to innovate in different ways.

Product Performance	Product System	Service	Channel	Brand	Customer Engagement

Innovations can be broken down and analyzed.
When you do so, you will learn why most fail and a few succeed.

Innovations can be built up systematically.
Doing so increases your odds of success exponentially.

We know you might be skeptical now. Suspend your disbelief for the moment. After spending some time with this book and applying its concepts to your work, we believe you'll see these assertions as emerging laws of innovation.

PART ONE

INNOVATION

A NEW DISCIPLINE IS LEAVING THE LAB

Now and then a new science emerges that radically changes how a field is conducted. This is precisely what is occurring now in the modern practice of innovation. But beware: myths are abundant and are exceptionally hard to eradicate.

CHAPTER 1
RETHINK INNOVATION
ERADICATE LORE, SUBSTITUTE LOGIC

When it comes time to innovate, even executives who deeply appreciate the discipline that modern management science has produced in finance, marketing, or logistics seem willing to tolerate all sorts of nonsense.

Too often, innovation is reduced to a series of brainstorming sessions, where facilitators proclaim things like, "Hey, there's no such thing as a bad idea!" (Actually, there really is such a thing as an indisputably bad idea.) Or innovation may be separated from the rest of the enterprise in a special lab or unit, a thin effort to quarantine the crazies. There, we feel like it's only proper to crank up the creativity. We put people in a room, festoon the tables with toys, Nerf balls and guns, Post-it Notes, markers, and fun foods— all because innovation is supposed to be playful. Our use of sticky notes and black Sharpie markers has become almost fetishistic,[1] one of the many rituals in our collective cult of innovation.

Here's the problem—evidence shows that such techniques do not actually lead to better outcomes. A number of years ago, we researched innovation efforts in industries such as manufacturing and services. A full 95% of these efforts failed. A glance around at the state of contemporary innovation suggests we've gotten a

little better, but still do plenty of things that are more grounded in hope or habit than evidence. This is unacceptable. We are overdue for a revolution in the way innovation is diagnosed, developed, fostered, de-risked, launched, and amplified.

Our ambition is to make innovation a systematic approach, moving the field from a mysterious art to more of a disciplined science. The Ten Types of Innovation is part of the foundation of that ambition. We know we are not working on anything as fundamental as the Human Genome Project nor as empirically proven as the periodic table (though we were inspired by the latter). The last thing we are trying to do is to shroud innovation with a different cloak. We use scientific analogies throughout this book to help illustrate our ambition rather than mirror our claims.

Nonetheless, our work over the decades has shown us that using the Ten Types of Innovation demonstrably increases your innovation hit rates. It will help you generate innovations that earn disproportionate returns and that are more difficult for competitors to copy. Sure, it's not foolproof. Innovation depends on many factors we couldn't possibly account for in one book (or actually *any* book). We can't promise that you won't run into

1 Flip through the pages of the innovation books and articles on your shelves, and count how many of them contain images of Post-it Notes with various scribblings. We've been just as guilty of it at times, but the trappings now seem to attract more attention than their results.

2 Welch made this comment mere months after GE topped *BusinessWeek*'s list of Top 100 Companies in Market Value for the second year in a row.

problems and we can't guarantee success (and anyone who does so is a huckster and a charlatan). But we are convinced that by thinking about innovation in a more systemic way, you improve your chances of building breakthroughs.

If you're reading this book, you probably agree that the world needs more innovation now than ever before. We are going through one of the most intense periods of change our small blue planet has ever seen. During such times, the ability to innovate—to evolve, adapt, and improve—is indispensable. Indeed, in the midst of commercial globalization, shifting cultural and social norms, and increasing scarcity of natural resources, our continued success as a species may depend on it.

For enterprises, this means that companies must innovate in order to survive and thrive. Nothing lasts forever, and many companies that make a splash with one innovation fail to follow up on their success. As Jack Welch, the former CEO of General Electric, famously commented in December 1997, "I take absolutely no comfort in where we are today."[2] Meaning that if you aren't moving faster than the rest of the marketplace, you're already dead; you just haven't stopped breathing yet.

Even companies with dominant positions can find themselves overtaken by firms playing by different rules. Once-mighty Kodak enjoyed a storied history before declaring bankruptcy in 2012. What's sobering is that its executives were not, as conventional wisdom would have it, blindsided by the emergence of digital technology. Indeed, they were primary pioneers of the digital photography field. But, as is so often the case, these "new" areas were small and easily dismissed—while sales of photo and cinema film paid all the bills.

This relentless imperative for more effective innovation is our reason for existence. This imperative has driven us over the last 30 years to study what works—to analyze innovation successes and look for patterns in their inputs and precursors. It has called for us to demystify our work as innovators and document, as plainly as possible, our practices and their outcomes. It has demanded that we establish a nuanced and precise taxonomy for innovation in all its forms and permutations. We share all of this so that we can all speak a more common and useful language. Our goal here is to codify and clarify what, in our experience, makes innovation work instead of fail.

DEFINING INNOVATION

Through overuse, misuse, hype, and enthusiasm, the word *innovation* has essentially lost its meaning. We often confuse the outcome and the process, and we describe everything in breathless terms, whether it is a modest product extension or a market-creating breakthrough. The definitions we show here help establish a nuanced understanding of what innovators actually do.

3 To understand this point with far greater subtlety, read the seminal article technologist Bill Buxton originally published in *BusinessWeek* in January 2008. Called "The Long Nose of Innovation," it shows how most breakthrough innovations tend to be built off technical advances that have likely been working their way up through laboratories for decades.

1 **INNOVATION IS NOT INVENTION**

Innovation may involve invention, but it requires many other things as well — including a deep understanding of whether customers need or desire that invention, how you can work with other partners to deliver it, and how it will pay for itself over time.

2 **INNOVATIONS HAVE TO EARN THEIR KEEP**

Simply put: innovations have to return value to you or your enterprise if you want to have the privilege of making another one some day. We like to define viability with two criteria: the innovation must be able to sustain itself *and* return its weighted cost of capital.

3 **VERY LITTLE IS TRULY NEW IN INNOVATION**

Biologist Francesco Redi established the maxim: "Every living thing comes from a living thing." Too often, we fail to appreciate that most innovations are based on previous advances. Innovations don't have to be new to the world — only to a market or industry.[3]

4 **THINK BEYOND PRODUCTS**

Innovations should be about more than products. They can encompass new ways of doing business and making money, new systems of products and services, and even new interactions and forms of engagement between your organization and your customers.

INNOVATION[1] IS THE CREATION OF A VIABLE[2] NEW[3] OFFERING.[4]

1 **KNOWING WHERE TO INNOVATE IS AS IMPORTANT AS KNOWING HOW TO INNOVATE**
Striking oil or mining lithium depends far more on knowing where to dig than on the digging itself. Identify the right innovation opportunities and be very clear about the nature of the innovation you intend to create before you begin a project.

INNOVATING REQUIRE THE PROBLEMS THAT MOVING THROUGH TH TO DELIVER⁴ ELEGANT⁵

[2] TACKLE THE HARDEST PROBLEMS FIRST

Don't look for low-hanging fruit. Instead, target big, gnarly problems with no easy answer. This isn't about what's easy for you; it's about solving deep problems for your customers. When innovating, focus on the hardest parts of a concept you have to get right. The easy stuff can wait until later.

[3] REFUSE INCOMPLETE ANSWERS

Having embraced big challenges, be patient and work to create comprehensive solutions. Look for ways to resolve tensions instead of defaulting to trade-offs. This requires you to be comfortable with ambiguity and to wait for the answers to emerge.

[4] IT DOESN'T COUNT UNTIL IT'S IN THE MARKET

You haven't finished the process of innovating until you bring the offering to market and you're getting revenue for it. Or, for social or government contexts, you have helped your stakeholders in a new and better way that can sustain itself over time.

[5] TURN COMPLEXITY INTO SIMPLICITY

It's easy to take something simple and make it complex: politicians and lawyers seem to do it for a living. Yet very few innovations are championed for their intricacy. Most are known for bringing elegance and simplicity to even the thorniest problems.

S IDENTIFYING [1] MATTER [2] AND EM [3] SYSTEMATICALLY SOLUTIONS.

WHY YOU NEED TO READ THIS BOOK. YES, YOU.

We celebrate the talented innovators of our times, whether Thomas Edison or Steve Jobs—but too often we draw the conclusion that innovation success depends on supremely talented individuals. Actual evidence points elsewhere. It turns out disciplined teams using effective methods get results that are 10, even 20 *times* better than current global norms.

Innovation is a team sport, and it's not the domain of the rare genius or the chosen few. Anyone can (and should) learn to innovate and, with practice, anyone can become better at innovating. Simply put, there is no longer an excuse not to innovate.

Executives need to understand that not only *can* they expect innovation from anyone in their organization—they are doing themselves and their company a disservice if they *don't* do so. The most innovative organizations rely on systems of individuals and teams working across functions in their organizations. Innovation isn't the work of only scientists, engineers, or marketers; it's the work of an entire business and its leadership.

We've used the Ten Types with firms large and small since we first developed the framework in 1998. The most cursory experience our clients will have with the framework goes something like this: we run a workshop for a development team. These are busy people. Often, they resent being pulled out of their regular lives in order to talk to innovation consultants who surely know nothing about their business. Mutters abound; "Where do workshops ever go, anyway?"

Then we get down to it. Sure, some Post-it Notes are involved, but we pair these with structured, prescriptive worksheets that help everyone in the room know what to do to produce *one great concept,* not hundreds of bad ones. Inevitably, the mood in the room changes. Smartphones are put down. Voices become animated. Questions become more pointed and pertinent to the team's current challenges. The discussion shifts from product features and functionality to business systems, platforms, and experiences. The framework is used to deconstruct other innovations and inspire new breakthroughs. The sessions end with teams believing—and then proving through implementation—the innovations they have designed will succeed.

The Ten Types isn't a panacea. But it's a big leap forward toward more rigorous and reliable innovation.

A new discipline of innovation is emerging today because:

Companies need new discoveries and strategies to drive growth and survival.

Efficiency is no longer enough. Organic growth is critical to achieve breakthrough results.

The pace of change requires greater flexibility and innovation effectiveness.

Innovation successes are now expected (and demanded) by customers and analysts.

THE ELEMENTS OF INNOVATION: A MODULAR SYSTEM THAT REPLACES MYTHS WITH METHODS

Scientists make a critical distinction between discovery and invention. Simply put, a discovery is true, whether you know it or not. An invention doesn't exist until a person or a team conceives and builds it.

Take a couple of hydrogen atoms and bond them to an oxygen atom and you are going to get a water molecule. Every time: no mystery, no magic. This has been true since long before humans occupied our world. In such a case, the challenge is to discover this structure, its mechanisms and its properties—to know that it turns to a solid at 0°C and that it becomes a gas at 100°C, on and on.

In the nineteenth century, the Russian scientist Dmitri Mendeleev noticed that the properties of some molecules tended to recur, that there was some weird pattern involved. At that time, there were 65 known elements, the building blocks of chemistry, each one with distinct properties. Mendeleev was in the habit of taking cards marked with the names of these different materials and using them to play "chemical solitaire" on long train rides. His obsession with finding how these materials related to one another caused him to author the first actual periodic table in 1869. This is where we first got the notion that elements could be structured to organize and explain their relative weights and behavioral properties. The rows and columns revealed that copper behaved much like silver, but not at all like sodium or sulfur. The table helped to explain the real nature of how the world works.

As it happens, Mendeleev didn't know about a whole bunch of items that were later crucial for rounding out our modern understanding of the elements. He had no noble gases, for instance: no helium, neon, argon, krypton, and the like. But Mendeleev sensed that there were missing elements that logically had to be there, so he left spaces for them. Whole new columns could be added to the system without disturbing its core structure.

What is particularly useful in this story is that the early sketch of the periodic table was so insightful that it both guided and accelerated the real progress in chemistry for the next 150+ years. It provided the scaffolding for pragmatic discovery, laying out the basics of what should be. A truly elegant theory gets things right enough to foster faster progress—from many people, only loosely organized. Mendeleev's periodic table of the elements has been enduring—it is one of the quintessential examples of scientists taking something tough and making it brilliant, simple, and elegant.

Left: Early drafts of the Ten Types during the discovery process in 1998.

Below: The original structure and categorization of the Ten Types of Innovation, used from 1998–2011.

It made it easier for chemists to understand the world and do hard things reliably. And it made us think about trying to create something similar for the world of innovation.

THE DISCOVERY OF THE TEN TYPES OF INNOVATION

In 1998 we decided to see what, if anything, successful innovations had in common. In doing so, our goal was to see if we might create a version of the periodic table of the elements for innovation.

We gathered up nearly 2,000 examples of the then best innovations: Dell's computer business; Toyota's production system; Gillette's shaving business; oversized tennis racquets from Prince; the way you could step out of your Hertz rental car and get a receipt instantly from someone using a gizmo hanging from his belt; and many others. We even included historical successes, such as the Ford Model T and the US national highway system (yes, that was once innovative, not just snarled with traffic).

Then, we analyzed everything and broke down the innovations using pattern recognition and complexity management techniques. We worked to demystify our own work as innovators. And we labored to

document our practices and their outcomes. In 2011, we undertook a similar effort to test and refresh our analysis, to check that our work was still valid in the very different business environment.

From all of this empirical analysis emerged the framework that forms the heart of this book. Some combination of the Ten Types of Innovation is reliably used in any successful offering, and the framework forms our version of the Periodic Table. The tactics we introduce to you later in the book are our chemical elements, which can be usefully combined to form winning innovation plays.

Our hope is that this is a framework that anyone can usefully employ, from chief executive to management trainee, from any industry, and from any company, large or small. It provides a way to understand the complexities of modern business, presented in what we hope you'll find to be a simple and straightforward manner.

THE DISCIPLINE OF BUILDING BREAKTHROUGHS

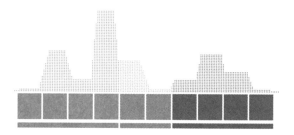

At the heart of the book is our discovery: all great innovations, throughout history, comprise some combination of ten basic types organized within three categories. This is our Periodic Table.

Part Two will make the Ten Types come alive as we describe each one and share many practical and graphic examples of them in action. Part Three helps demonstrate our core philosophy: that innovation is about more than products, and using multiple types in parallel can help produce stronger, more defensible outcomes.

You can use the Ten Types to help your innovation efforts in many ways. It can be a *diagnostic tool* to assess how you're approaching innovation internally, it can help you to analyze your competitive environment, and it can reveal gaps and potential opportunities for doing something different and upending the market.

Part Four shows you how to use the Ten Types to systematically spot opportunities for shifts.

4   We and others continue to discover new tactics. We're always working to make sure our collection is complete— see the latest list at tentypesofinnovation.com.

As of 2013, there are over 100 innovation tactics — specific, known ways you can use the Ten Types of Innovation.[4] These are like the elements that bond together to form molecules; you can use them to construct the breakthroughs that will help you make a real impact on your industry.

Part Five catalogues all the tactics. Here we show you how to mix and match these techniques to create sophisticated innovations.

Innovation is a team sport. In fact, an organization that depends on individual innovators alone is destined to fail. Understanding how you can wire innovation into your organization — and build a robust internal innovation capability — is an imperative for any firm doing business in today's dynamic world.

Part Six breaks it down for you, detailing what you (and your leaders) must do in order to achieve what was once unthinkable: mastery of innovation as a discipline, not a hope or phenomenon.

TEN TYPES OF INNOVATION

THE BUILDING BLOCKS OF BREAKTHROUGHS

At the heart of any new discipline there often lies a simple, organizing system — an underlying structure and order governing what works and what fails. This is what the Ten Types framework brings to innovation. Consciously understanding it makes innovation easier and more effective.

CHAPTER 2
THE TEN TYPES

AN OVERVIEW

The Ten Types framework is simple and intuitive. It is a useful tool you can use both to diagnose and enrich an innovation you're working on, or to analyze existing competition. It makes it especially easy to spot errors of omission — missing dimensions that will make a concept stronger.

The Ten Types framework is structured into three color-coded categories. The types on the left side of the framework are the most internally focused and distant from customers; as you move toward the right side, the types become increasingly apparent and obvious to end users. To use a theatrical metaphor, the left of the framework is backstage; the right is onstage.

Several lessons will emerge from the Ten Types throughout this book — including how to use the framework as a way to identify opportunities, and how to use it to construct sophisticated, defensible innovations.

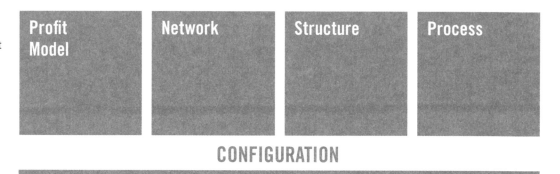

Profit Model   Network   Structure   Process

CONFIGURATION

These types of innovation are focused on the innermost workings of an enterprise and its business system

This is not a process timeline, nor does it imply sequencing or hierarchy amongst the types. Any combination of types can be present in an innovation, and innovators can start by focusing on any type in the framework.

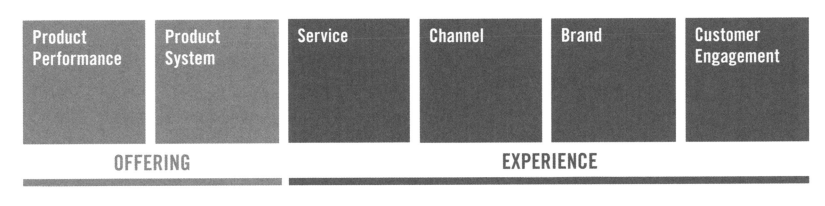

| Product Performance | Product System | | Service | Channel | Brand | Customer Engagement |

OFFERING   **EXPERIENCE**

These types of innovation are focused on an enterprise's core product or service, or a collection of its products and services

These types of innovation are focused on more customer-facing elements of an enterprise and its business system

CHAPTER 3
PROFIT MODEL
HOW YOU MAKE MONEY

Innovative profit models find a fresh way to convert a firm's offerings and other sources of value into cash. Great ones reflect a deep understanding of what customers and users actually cherish and where new revenue or pricing opportunities might lie. Innovative profit models often challenge an industry's tired old assumptions about what to offer, what to charge, or how to collect revenues. This is a big part of their power: in most industries the dominant profit model often goes unquestioned for decades.

Common examples of profit model innovations include *premium prices*, where companies figure out how to charge more for their offering than competitors do, or *auctions*, where the market sets the price for goods. The ideal profit model will vary widely by context and industry. A new entrant may design its profit model to make it easy for customers to try and adopt its products (say, *metered use*), while the incumbent may counter with models that make it difficult for existing customers to switch (say, *subscriptions*). One constant: to succeed, profit models — perhaps more than any other type of innovation — must align with a company's overarching strategy and innovation intent.

If you work for a non-profit or governmental agency, you might feel that this type of innovation clearly doesn't apply to you. It does, but the terminology may need a tweak or two. Perhaps you might think of it instead as a "value model," or how you sustain your organization and create value for constituents. The same principles and tactics are useful, even if maximizing financial returns isn't the objective.

?

How to spot potential Profit Model innovations:

Does the company make money in ways that are different from competitors or industry norms (for example, selling a service when everyone else sells products)?

Are margins (particularly gross margins) significantly higher or lower than those of competitors? Are there substantial differences in variable or fixed costs?

Are there interesting differences between who uses the offering and who pays for it? Does the company have multiple revenue streams from different constituencies?

Does the business generate cash quickly (or immediately)? Are working capital requirements low (or even negative)?

PROFIT MODEL INNOVATION STORIES

GILLETTE

The "razor and blades" profit model has been celebrated for years and adapted to countless other industries, from printers and cartridges to capsule coffee. The gist is simple—create an installed base by selling the enduring part of the system at low cost (or even a loss), and then enjoy recurring revenue by selling the disposable parts at a premium.

As Randal C. Picker noted, Gillette initially used the opposite profit model—charging a premium for the razor handle and selling the blades cheaply.[1] This had the effect of teaching consumers that they could dispose of the blades rather than sharpening and reusing them, which was the norm at the turn of the twentieth century. Only when Gillette's patent

expired in 1921,[2] Picker added, did the company flip its profit model to monetize its healthy installed base of shavers. This is an example of evolving the profit model from driving adoption to extending the product lifecycle—a vital component of business model–driven innovation, which we'll discuss later.

Lately, the razor industry has been stuck in a product innovation arms race—two blade cartridges supplanted by three blades, then four, then five… perhaps when 10-blade razors arrive, they'll slice off the follicles themselves and we'll be done with shaving altogether. But until then, Gillette, now a part of Procter & Gamble,[3] has returned to its roots with P&G's acquisition of The Art of Shaving.[4] As Jessica

Wohl reported for Reuters, that brand's razors can use standard Gillette cartridges; the cheapest handle sells for less than $100 while the most expensive go for as much as $500.[5] What's old is new again.

1 "The Razors-and-Blades Myth(s)" by Randal C. Picker (Chicago: University of Chicago Law School, September 13, 2010); http://tentyp.es/Oam1lF.

2 King C. Gillette's original patent application for "razors of the safety type" is a fascinating read: http://tentyp.es/SBULnb.

3 P&G bought Gillette for $57 billion in 2005, as widely reported by the likes of CNN Money: http://tentyp.es/VQYYr5.

4 P&G acquired The Art of Shaving in 2009, as reported in "P&G Buys Art of Shaving Retail Stores," Ad Age, June 3, 2009: http://tentyp.es/Z5Vcv6.

5 Jessica Wohl wrote "P&G in Upscale Retail Game with The Art of Shaving," Reuters, December 24, 2009: http://tentyp.es/12S45Jw.

GEISINGER

ProvenCare, a system of care for coronary artery bypass grafts (CABGs), uses a bold profit model: for a single fee it guarantees a healthy CABG patient 90 days post-procedure. If there are any complications within that window, Geisinger covers the entire cost of follow-up care. This is a non-trivial guarantee; before this system, such complications had occurred 38% of the time, on average.

HILTI

Headquartered in Liechtenstein, Hilti's core business is in power tools for the construction business. Hilti Tool Fleet Management was developed to help protect contractors from the hidden costs of owning tools, including unscheduled downtime and theft. For a monthly fee, Hilti will loan replacement tools when necessary, offer upgrades when available, and cover any repairs that are needed. The program helps streamline time on site for contractors—and has provided a recurring stream of revenue for Hilti.

NEXT RESTAURANT

Diners buy advance tickets to the restaurant brainchild of Chicago chef, Grant Achatz. By getting customers to pay upfront for their meals, Next earns interest on working capital and limits the risk of empty tables or no-shows (an endemic problem in this business). Next's second trick: to price tickets not according to how much diners eat, but when they visit. Tickets during the dinner rush include a peak hour premium, while those for off-hours seating cost less.

SCHIBSTED MEDIA GROUP

The Norwegian online classified company FINN.no allows users to place any ads for free while paying a premium for preferred placement. For instance, customers could pay a fee to guarantee more prominent position on the website or to cross-post their listings in other newspapers within the Schibsted media family.

CHAPTER 4

NETWORK

HOW YOU CONNECT WITH OTHERS TO CREATE VALUE

In today's hyper-connected world, no company can or should do everything alone. Network innovations provide a way for firms to take advantage of other companies' processes, technologies, offerings, channels, and brands — pretty much any and every component of a business. These innovations mean a firm can capitalize on its own strengths while harnessing the capabilities and assets of others. Network innovations also help executives to share risk in developing new offers and ventures. These collaborations can be brief or enduring, and they can be formed between close allies or even staunch competitors.

Open innovation approaches such as prizes or crowdsourcing are particularly emblematic of how interconnected we all are today, and have helped companies to enlist a chosen few or the entire world in solving difficult challenges — from moving low earth orbit space flight into the private sector, or to "automagically" recommending the perfect movie.[1] Other examples of Network innovation include creating *secondary markets* to connect with alternative consumers, or building *franchises* to license proprietary company thinking, capabilities, and content to paying partners.

1 These are references respectively to the Ansari X-Prize, developed to recognize new spaceship designs, and Netflix's challenge to developers to come up with an algorithm to improve its movie recommendation engine.

Network innovations are not about internal or IT networks; we use the term here to signify external relationships, partnerships, consortia, and affiliations.

❓

How to spot potential Network innovations:

Does the company work with other firms or surprising collaborators to develop new offerings that drive a shift from business as usual?

Has the company formed any unusual partnerships — for example, with firms that seem unrelated to its current business, or with competitors?

Conversely, does the company enable the offerings of other players by lending them its channels, processes, brand, or other unique assets?

Does the company collaborate with its suppliers and/or customers to develop, test, or market new products?

NETWORK INNOVATION STORIES

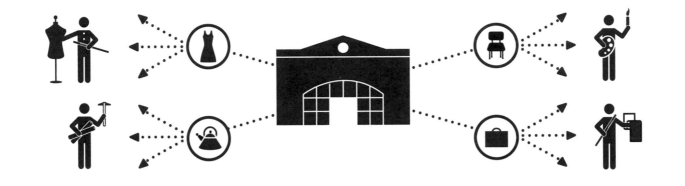

TARGET

The first Target store opened in Roseville, Minnesota, in 1962. It was a part of a new discount retail strategy from the Dayton Company, a regional department store. As the company's first president, Douglas Dayton, explained, Target was designed to "combine the best of the fashion world with the best of the discount world, a quality store with quality merchandise at discount prices." From the beginning, the stores were intended to be fun and welcoming for the whole family, with easy-to-shop displays.

In 1999, Target partnered with architect Michael Graves, who created an exclusive line of kitchen appliances for the store. Since then, the company has worked with more than 75 product designers and more than a dozen world-renowned fashion designers to create items that are only available at Target, burnishing the reputation and reach of both parties.

Later, Target expanded its network innovation to include partnerships with other retailers, such as Liberty of London, building pop-up shops that are only open for a short period of time. It's a deliberate strategy to create buzz, attention, and sales—and it's one that has had an impact on the bottom line. The company reported that a five-year collaboration with designer Isaac Mizrahi generated $300 million a year in profits, while a line of handbags designed by Anya Hindmarch sold out online within two minutes. These Network innovations have helped Target not only survive but thrive—despite intense competition from other big box retailers.

GLAXOSMITHKLINE

GSK developed "co-innovation" relationships, taking R&D challenges in a broad range of domains and opening them up for others to help solve. In 2011, it joined WIPO Re:Search, a collaboration of private and public sector organizations that uses open innovation to develop new treatments for neglected tropical diseases such as dengue and rabies.

NATURA

In 2012, the Brazilian cosmetics giant, Natura, had an internal R&D team of some 250 employees—modest for a company with $3.4 billion in sales. But Natura punches above its weight through a sophisticated network of relationships with 25 universities worldwide. Researchers contribute to an array of challenges in everything from skin science to sustainable technology. By 2008, 50% of the company's product pipeline had come from its open innovation program.

UPS AND TOSHIBA

The two companies struck an agreement that saw UPS technicians from the company's logistics arm, UPS Supply Chain Solutions, repair customers' broken Toshiba laptops at the parcel service's shipping hubs. This complementary partnership cut down on service time for Toshiba, and provided UPS with a new revenue stream.

HOWARD JOHNSON'S

A pioneer of modern restaurant franchising, Howard Johnson had opened 150 franchises by 1941. His system called for independent operators to pay to license Johnson's brand, food, supplies, and building design. This fostered rapid growth of the restaurant chain—costing far less in time and money than if he had tried to do it all himself.

CHAPTER 5
STRUCTURE
HOW YOU ORGANIZE AND ALIGN YOUR TALENT AND ASSETS

Structure innovations are focused on organizing company assets—hard, human, or intangible—in unique ways that create value. They can include everything from superior talent management systems to ingenious configurations of heavy capital equipment. An enterprise's fixed costs and corporate functions can also be improved through Structure innovations, including departments such as Human Resources, R&D, and IT. Ideally, such innovations also help attract talent to the organization by creating supremely productive working environments or fostering a level of performance that competitors can't match.

Good examples of Structure innovations include building *incentive systems* to encourage employees to work toward a particular goal, *standardizing assets* to reduce operating costs and complexity, or even creating a *corporate university* to provide sophisticated, continuous training. Structure innovations can be particularly difficult for competitors to copy, because they typically entail significant organizational changes and/or capital investments—and so they often provide a foundation for success over many years.

Be careful not to confuse Structure innovations for Process innovations. These two types are often closely related, but Structure innovations refer to the nature of your talent and assets and how they are organized. If you find yourself thinking about how the assets are actually being used in practice, you're probably thinking of a Process innovation.

❓

How to spot potential Structure innovations:

Does the company have a unique or unusual organizational structure?

Is the company known for attracting top talent in a particular field or function (for example, marketing or materials science)?

Does the company use hard assets in ways that are very different from competitors — for example, unusual standardization or diversity of machines or other equipment?

STRUCTURE INNOVATION STORIES

WHOLE FOODS MARKET

Teams are everything at Whole Foods; the company is well known for its radical decentralization of management. Each store is composed of self-directed teams that manage departments with unusual autonomy—making decisions about what products to stock and how to display them. Importantly, each team also makes decisions about who to hire; joining a team requires two thirds of its current members' approval. Each store is measured as an independent line on the Profit & Loss statement, and each team within the store has very clear performance targets.

Describing Whole Foods's structure as a "high trust organization," CEO John Mackey wrote in 2010 that "organizing into small interlocking teams helps ensure that trust will flow in all directions within the organization—upwards, downwards, within the team, and across teams."

That trust extends to the information Whole Foods shares across its teams and stores—including detailed information about each department and product sales and profitability. The transparency has been so radical that at one point the company's employees were all designated "insiders" by the SEC. But the information also fuels performance; teams use the data to learn what works company-wide, while peer reviews are used to benchmark employees, teams, and stores. This fosters a network where teams constantly try to outperform one another. So unlike at many retailers, decentralized innovations are amplified quickly instead of achingly slowly (if at all).

Mackey cofounded the company in Austin, Texas, in 1980 with a staff of 19 people. As of 2012, Whole Foods employed more than 65,000 people working in more than 310 stores in the United States, Canada, and the United Kingdom. The company reports that it made over $10 billion in 2011.

W. L. GORE

Since the company's founding in 1958, W. L. Gore has used a "flat lattice" organizational model. Internal teams are deliberately kept small to encourage input and innovation from all, and activities are managed by "commitments" rather than dictates. Every employee becomes a shareholder after one year.

SOUTHWEST AIRLINES

Until the purchase of AirTran in 2011, Southwest flew only one kind of aircraft — the Boeing 737. In doing so, it reduced service costs, streamlined operations, and allowed teams to execute fast turnarounds at airport gates. Since airlines can only make money when planes are in the air carrying passengers someplace, all of these characteristics are critical to Southwest's low-cost strategy.

TRINITY HEALTH

Hospitals and clinics within the Trinity Health system use standardized and highly integrated IT infrastructure. This means that practitioners have access to a common view of patient data. These systems also serve as the foundation for other programs, including data-driven initiatives to improve quality of care, and telemedicine to serve patients in rural clinics.

FABINDIA

A fabric, clothing, and home goods retailer in India, Fabindia pioneered the "Community Owned Companies" model, meaning that local artisans owned and ran the companies that supplied arts and handicrafts to Fabindia.

CHAPTER 6

PROCESS

HOW YOU USE SIGNATURE OR SUPERIOR METHODS TO DO YOUR WORK

Process innovations involve the activities and operations that produce an enterprise's primary offerings. Innovating here requires a dramatic change from "business as usual" that enables the company to use unique capabilities, function efficiently, adapt quickly, and build market–leading margins. Process innovations often form the core competency of an enterprise, and may include patented or proprietary approaches that yield advantage for years or even decades. Ideally, they are the "special sauce" you use that competitors simply can't replicate.

"Lean production," whereby managers reduce waste and cost throughout a system, is one famous example of a Process innovation. Other examples include *process standardization*, which uses common procedures to reduce cost and complexity, and *predictive analytics*, which model past performance data to predict future outcomes — helping companies to design, price, and guarantee their offerings accordingly.

A Process innovation must include a methodology or capability that is substantially different from and superior to industry norms. For example, once lean production has become standardized, as it has in many industries, it can no longer be considered an innovation — unless your signature way of using it delivers unmatched efficiency and cost advantage.

❓

How to spot potential Process innovations:

What is the company uniquely skilled at doing or delivering across products, services, and platforms?

Are the company's variable costs or working capital substantially lower than at competitors or when compared with industry norms?

Does the company own a cluster of patents around a particular technology, methodology, or process?

PROCESS INNOVATION STORIES

ZARA

The first Zara store opened in downtown A Coruña, Spain, in 1975. Now run by the holding company Inditex, the apparel and accessories retailer reimagined the fashion supply chain. As Miguel Helft wrote, it sped up the process of a piece of clothing moving from sketchpad to shop floor: "in just three weeks, the clothes will hang in stores from Barcelona to Berlin to Beirut."[1] Its stores, meanwhile, are sited in high-end locations in major shopping areas, to connect easily with its intended base of fashion-forward clientele: In 2011, Zara paid $324 million to buy space on Fifth Avenue in New York.[2]

As Suzy Hansen detailed in a long look at the company for *The New York Times Magazine*,[2] the company uses an integrated and efficient production system of design, production, logistics, and distribution, which drives short turnaround times and allows store managers to keep stock at a minimum. Its designers can quickly review production issues and respond to changing fashion trends. Meanwhile, suppliers and distributors are carefully located around the world to promote efficiency, while Zara's internal logistics system is set up so that the time between when orders are received at distribution centers and when merchandise is actually delivered to stores is as short as possible.

Employees process a non-stop flow of information from stores that conveys shoppers' desires and demands to Zara's 200-person creative team. As Hansen put it, "managers field calls from China or Chile to learn what's selling, then they meet with the designers and decide whether there's a trend." New styles arrive in stores twice weekly. This sees Zara using its supply chain to its advantage, as it maximizes inventory turns and allows the company to respond to emerging trends briskly.

1 "Fashion Fast Forward," by Miguel Helft, *Business 2.0*, May, 2002: http://tentyp.es/XGKPsM.
2 "How Zara Grew into the World's Largest Fashion Retailer," by Suzy Hansen, *The New York Times Magazine*, November 9, 2012: http://tentyp.es/12bPkkU.

HINDUSTAN UNILEVER

Products traditionally sold in large bottles or multi-use packs were disaggregated and sold as small, single-use sachets. This catered to the large portion of the Indian population without the means or the inclination to purchase goods in larger quantities.

ZIPCAR

The "FastFleet" system not only did away with lot attendants and enabled drivers to access cars automatically, it also allowed Zipcar to track how its cars were being used. That meant management at the car-sharing company could balance inventory and quickly identify issues with any of the vehicles.

TOYOTA

The car maker's famous "lean" production system reduced waste and excess, driving astonishing efficiency and continual product and process improvements throughout the company.

IKEA

IKEA developed flat-pack furniture with no variation by region or country. Its products included the same hardware and instructions regardless of where they were purchased, thus helping to streamline the company's internal production processes.

CHAPTER 7

PRODUCT PERFORMANCE

HOW YOU DEVELOP DISTINGUISHING FEATURES AND FUNCTIONALITY

Product Performance innovations address the value, features, and quality of a company's offering. This type of innovation involves both entirely new products as well as updates and line extensions that add substantial value. Too often, people mistake Product Performance for the sum of innovation. It's certainly important, but it's always worth remembering that it is only one of the Ten Types of Innovation, and it's often the easiest for competitors to copy. Think about any product or feature war you've witnessed — whether torque and toughness in trucks, toothbrushes that are easier to hold and use, even with baby strollers. Too quickly, it all devolves into an expensive mad dash to parity. Product Performance innovations that deliver long-term competitive advantage are the exception rather than the rule.

Still, Product Performance innovations can delight customers and drive growth. Common examples of this type of innovation include: *simplification* to make it easy to use an offering; *sustainability* to provide offerings that do no harm to the environment; or *customization* to tailor a product to an individual's specifications.

Even though "Service" is a separate type, service companies can and should also innovate using the Product Performance type of innovation. Do this by considering how to change the features and functionality of the service — delivering quality that competitors can't match, completing assignments with unmatched speed, offering unique options and flexibility, or offering other forms of performance.

❓

How to spot potential Product Performance innovations:

Does the company produce a notably superior offering that dominates market share or earns a substantial premium?

Conversely, are the company's products notably simpler and easier to use than those of competitors?

Do the company's products possess unique features and functionality that captivate customers?

Are the products uniquely styled or focused on particular niches and audiences in ways that others can't match?

PRODUCT PERFORMANCE INNOVATION STORIES

OXO GOOD GRIPS

The inspiration for OXO Good Grips came after Sam Farber watched his arthritic wife Betsey struggle to peel some apples. The retired housewares industry entrepreneur decided he could do better. Working with New York City–based design company Smart Design, and focusing on principles of "universal design," Farber launched the OXO Good Grips line of user-friendly tools in April 1990.

The utensils were priced at a premium. The potato peeler, for instance, was five times as expensive as the typical metal version. But the products proved so popular that their appeal transcended the intended audience of the infirm or movement-impaired and instead attracted a much larger audience of people who simply cared about home cooking and wanted to do it well.

Now owned by Helen of Troy, the company currently has more than 850 products on the market, with OXO Good Grips products created for nearly every room of the house. Designs include a salad spinner that can be used with one hand, liquid measuring cups that can be read from above, and a kettle whose lid opens automatically when tipped to pour. Through a licensing agreement, there is now even an OXO Good Grips surgical syringe.

DYSON

The Dual Cyclone technology featured in Dyson's first vacuum took 15 years—and over 5,000 prototypes— to launch. It included an innovative transparent, bag-free design that showed people exactly how much dirt was being sucked up off their floor. Within 22 months, it had become the best-selling vacuum in the UK.

MARS

With My M&M's, people are able to add their own messages, logos, or images to specific color M&M candies— personalizing the product and opening up new uses for the classic chocolates.

INTUIT

The popular TurboTax software eliminates manual calculations and formats results automatically so that American taxpayers can easily print or electronically submit their tax returns.

CORNING

Corning® Gorilla® Glass, a tough, thin, and scratch-resistant form of glass, was developed specifically for smartphones, tablets, PCs, and TVs. In 2012, it was used by 33 major brands in over a billion devices worldwide.

CHAPTER 8
PRODUCT SYSTEM
HOW YOU CREATE COMPLEMENTARY PRODUCTS AND SERVICES

Product System innovations are rooted in how individual products and services connect or bundle together to create a robust and scalable system. This is fostered through interoperability, modularity, integration, and other ways of creating valuable connections between otherwise distinct and disparate offerings. Product System innovations help you build ecosystems that captivate and delight customers and defend against competitors.

Product bundling, or taking several related products and selling them in a single package, is a common example of a Product System innovation. In the twenty-first century, technology companies in particular have used this type of innovation to build *platforms* that spur others to develop products and services for them— including app stores, developer kits, and APIs. Other Product System innovations include *extensions* to existing products, *product and service combinations*, and *complementary offerings*—which individually work just fine on their own, but are far better together (even ones as humble as peanut butter and jelly).

Product System innovations can include offerings
that you don't own or produce. In fact, it's often more
rewarding (and a lot more fun) to find ways for others
to create products and services that add value to yours.

❷

How to spot potential Product System innovations:

Does the company make multiple products that connect with one another in unique ways?

Are other players creating products that interface with the company's offerings — or even depend on them to function?

Does the company offer distinct products and services that can also be integrated or purchased as packages?

PRODUCT SYSTEM INNOVATION STORIES

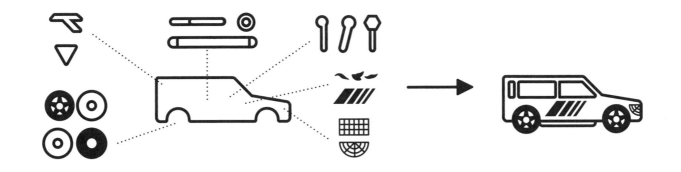

SCION

Scion greets its drivers with a proud slogan: "Scion—built by passion, not by committee." It's a reference to the fact that owners can pretty much design exactly the car they want to drive. This Toyota sub-brand was created to appeal to younger drivers, and the company has developed a sophisticated system that allows them to personalize their vehicles. Customers pick one of the five Scion cars as a base and then choose from a suite of add-ons and accessories, including offerings not only from Toyota, but also from accessory makers such as Alpine Audio. A separate website is dedicated to aftermarket parts such as neon lights, superchargers, carbon fiber B-pillars, and hundreds of other accessories—so that customers can continue to customize their rides long after they've driven off the dealer lot.

Scion has been able to offer its customizable cars and aftermarket parts as an integrated system that's more of a lifestyle than just a vehicle. Additional offerings include: Scion-curated music, art, and videos; digital apps; Scion-sponsored racing events; and many other extensions of the Scion experience.

MICROSOFT

Initially, the programs that went into MS Office were offered as individual products. Now bundled together, the integrated system became a productivity suite widely used by businesses worldwide.

MOZILLA

The non-profit organization rose to prominence with Firefox, a web browser built on an open-source platform allowing independent developers to make hundreds of discrete plug-ins. In 2012, more than 450 million people around the world used Firefox.

OSCAR MAYER

"Lunchables" are packs of crackers, meats, cheeses, and desserts also sold separately by Oscar Mayer. This makes school lunches easy for parents to pack, and fun for kids to eat.

ELFA

Swedish designer Arne Lydmar started Elfa in 1948 to offer a smart storage solution. Based on three central components (a drawer system, a shelving system, and sliding doors) the potential for customization of the furniture is virtually limitless.

CHAPTER 9

SERVICE

HOW YOU SUPPORT AND AMPLIFY THE VALUE OF YOUR OFFERINGS

Service innovations ensure and enhance the utility, performance, and apparent value of an offering. They make a product easier to try, use, and enjoy; they reveal features and functionality customers might otherwise overlook; and they fix problems and smooth rough patches in the customer journey. Done well, they elevate even bland and average products into compelling experiences that customers come back for again and again.

Common examples of Service innovations include *product use enhancements*, *maintenance plans*, *customer support*, *information and education*, *warranties*, and *guarantees.* While human beings are still often at the heart here, this type of innovation is increasingly delivered through electronic interfaces, remote communications, automated technologies, and other surprisingly impersonal means. Service can be the most striking and prominent part of the customer experience, or an invisible safety net that customers sense but never see.

If your primary offering is itself a service, its features and functionality will be classified as Product Performance (despite the word "product"). Service innovations comprise the additional support and enhancements you provide around your core offerings.

❷

How to spot potential Service innovations:

Do customers rave about their interactions with the company — particularly those instances where things went wrong and the company somehow made everything right?

Has the company implemented websites, help lines, or other methods that highlight additional product features or applications or that make it easier to use its services?

Does the company provide any interesting guarantees, warranties, or other forms of assurance around its offerings?

Are there robust communities that celebrate the services, help customers connect with like-minded users, or otherwise enhance their experience?

SERVICE INNOVATION STORIES

ZAPPOS

Established in 1999, Zappos has set a new benchmark for customer support and service in online retail. At Zappos, *Deliver 'WOW' through service* is the first of the company's 10 core values.

Zappos' customer service reps are empowered to do just about anything they need to do to ensure users have a good experience. This includes sending shoppers flowers or spending hours on the phone to ensure they find exactly the right products. When Zappos finds itself out of stock of a needed item, its reps will famously order the product from a competitor and ship it overnight to ensure it arrives on time.

Amazon thought this tremendous Service appeal was worth $1.1 billion when it acquired Zappos in 2009. The company now generates annual gross sales of over $1 billion annually, and showcases millions of products from over a thousand clothing and shoe brands, ranging from everyday wear to high fashion luxury apparel.

The success of the company led to a spinoff consultancy, Zappos Insights, which offers to help other companies to install its methods and customer-centric culture.[1]

1 This is a great example of a Profit Model innovation for an online retailer.

HYUNDAI

Launched in the middle of the severe recession in 2009, the "Assurance" program guaranteed that customers who bought or leased a new Hyundai vehicle could walk away from both the car and its payments if they lost their job during the first year of ownership.

MEN'S WEARHOUSE

The men's apparel company promised free lifetime pressing of any purchased suit, tuxedo, sport coat, or slacks at any of its locations in the United States. This was added value that was perfect for business travelers (and those who hate ironing).

7-ELEVEN

The convenience store chain offered a wide range of supplementary services in its shops in Japan. It let customers pay personal bills for credit cards and mobile phones, provided postal services, and even gave customers space to drop off or receive packages.

SYSCO

With over $43 billion in annual revenues, Sysco is one of the largest food distributors in North America. To elevate its value in the relatively commoditized industry, executives created Business Reviews, a free consulting service helping clients to design menus or plan back-of-the-house logistics.

CHAPTER 10

CHANNEL

HOW YOU DELIVER YOUR OFFERINGS TO CUSTOMERS AND USERS

Channel innovations encompass all the ways that you connect your company's offerings with your customers and users. While e-commerce has emerged as a dominant force in recent years, traditional channels such as physical stores are still important — particularly when it comes to creating immersive experiences. Skilled innovators in this type often find multiple but complementary ways to bring their products and services to customers. Their goal is to ensure that users can buy what they want, when and how they want it, with minimal friction and cost and maximum delight.

Channel innovations are particularly sensitive to industry context and customer habits. *Flagship stores* can be an extremely valuable Channel innovation, creating signature venues that showcase a firm's brand and offerings, while *pop-up stores* may be useful for a short, sharp splash at the holidays. In contrast, *selling directly* through e-channels or other means can reduce overhead costs, maximizing margins and cost advantage. Or you might pursue *indirect distribution* or *multi-level marketing,* either of which recruits others to shoulder the burden of promoting and/or delivering an offering to the end customer.

You may see an overlap between Channel and Network innovations. This type is about how you deliver the offering and the touchpoint of the exchange, not about whom you work with to get an offering to market.

❓

How to spot potential Channel innovations:

Does the company deliver its offerings to customers and users in ways that challenge or confound what is usual within the industry?

Does the company use different channels in complementary ways — for example, showcasing products in retail outlets but delivering them through direct or virtual channels?

Do customers tell others about their memorable interactions with the firm?

Do other players — including partners, customers, and even competitors — help sell or deliver the company's offerings?

CHANNEL INNOVATION STORIES

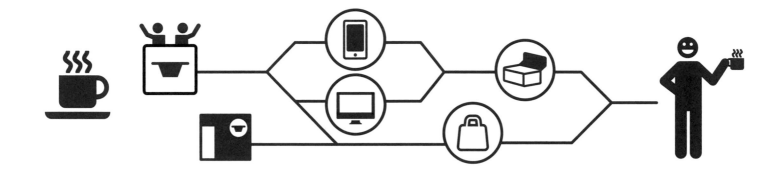

NESPRESSO

Nespresso was founded in Switzerland as a brand for coffee aficionados. Its iconic capsule technology locked customers into the system from the get-go (a Product Performance and Product System innovation). Nespresso uses and integrates an admirable array of channels to make sure its customers can get those capsules as easily as possible. The firm has over 270 unique retail stores and coffee shops of its own worldwide, it operates kiosks within partner stores such as Macy's and Bloomingdale's, and it also features a direct, online Nespresso Club that offers an efficient ordering channel for new coffee (including email alerts to remind customers that they'll soon run out of product).

Since 1996, Nespresso has also provided business-to-business solutions, partnering with hotels such as The Ritz-Carlton and Hyatt Hotels & Resorts, 650 star-rated chefs, and airlines including British Airways, Lufthansa, and Qantas Airways. The Nespresso Chef Academy offers leading chefs a chance to participate in classes and an opportunity to study every aspect of coffee. There is also the Nespresso Coffee Sommelier Program for professional sommeliers who want to learn about harmonizing coffee with foods and wine. These channels drive additional capsule sales and create even more opportunities for the company to introduce its unique coffee technology to new customers.

NIKE

NIKETOWN stores were primarily designed to provide an immersive, impressive experience to shoppers. Stores often include treadmills so that runners can put shoes through their paces. Employees are hired for their athleticism—one recent hire in the Chicago store had played professional basketball.

M-PESA

The 2007 joint venture between mobile phone giant Vodafone and Safaricom allowed Kenyan residents to deposit, send, and withdraw money using their cell phones and simple SMS messaging. By the end of September 2012, the service had more than 16 million active users and 70 million agents across eight countries throughout Africa.

AMAZON

The on-demand Whispernet service on the Kindle is a closed wireless network that is free for customers. This allows users to purchase and download an e-book—ready to read in less than 60 seconds.

XIAMETER

Specialty chemicals giant Dow Corning launched a web-based sales channel in 2002. Its mandate was to provide customers with a new way to buy silicone. Cost-conscious buyers without the need for technical support or advice were able to select from thousands of product options, choose the pricing levels right for them, and lock in price and volume commitments, in a simple but effective, no-frills model that ran alongside the mother company.

CHAPTER 11

BRAND

HOW YOU REPRESENT YOUR OFFERINGS AND BUSINESS

Brand innovations help to ensure that customers and users recognize, remember, and prefer your offerings to those of competitors or substitutes. Great ones distill a "promise" that attracts buyers and conveys a distinct identity. They are typically the result of carefully crafted strategies that are implemented across many touchpoints between your company and your customers, including communications, advertising, service interactions, channel environments, and employee and business partner conduct. Brand innovations can transform commodities into prized products, and confer meaning, intent, and value to your offerings and your enterprise.

Brand innovations include *extensions* that offer a new product or service under the umbrella of an existing brand. Alternatively, they might make a company stand for a *big idea* or a *set of values*, expressing those beliefs transparently and consistently. In business-to-business contexts, Brand innovations aren't limited to the final manufacturer or the consumer-facing producer of a product; *branding your components* and making customers aware of their value can build both preference and bargaining power.

Brand innovation is not simply a successful campaign or marketing strategy, and it's more complex than simply creating a new brand. It requires designing and expressing brand in ways that are both distinct from the competition and relevant to customers.

❓

How to spot potential Brand innovations:

Does the company have an unusually distinct or vivid identity, particularly compared to its rivals?

Do the company's customers and users see themselves as part of a distinct community or movement centered around the brand?

Is the company's brand used by other business partners — including suppliers, customers, or even competitors?

Has the company extended a brand to an unusually diverse array of businesses, or used its brand to foster integration and connectivity across offerings?

BRAND INNOVATION STORIES

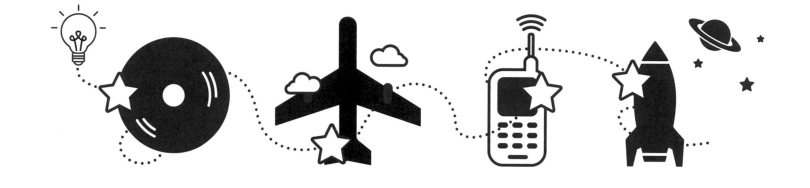

VIRGIN

Conceived in 1970 as a mail order business selling cheap records, Richard Branson opened the first Virgin Record Shop on Oxford Street in London in 1971. The following year he opened the first residential recording studio—and the rest is music history. Branson became indelibly involved in the music business, releasing Mike Oldfield's Tubular Bells on the Virgin Music record label in 1973 and notoriously signing the Sex Pistols in 1977.

These days, Virgin describes itself as a leading "international investment group." It now includes branded companies such as Virgin Atlantic Airways and Virgin Active, and employs approximately 50,000 people in 34 countries. Global branded revenue in

2011 was approximately $21 billion. Companies are autonomous, with each one enjoying the global power of the Virgin brand. This also means that less successful ventures, such as Virgin Cola, do not destroy the mother company.

The Virgin portfolio stretches across a dizzyingly diverse array of sectors, including mobile telephony, transportation, financial services, media, and fitness. In general, the leaders of the firm look for arenas that are important but a little tired and dull— assuming they can inject a much-needed dose of fun. One high profile initiative in recent years is Virgin Galactic, Branson's concerted effort to create commercial space travel.

TRADER JOE'S

The supermarket chain carries few national brands; instead, it creates "destination" private labels by cutting out the middleman and going direct to suppliers to find unique food products, beverages, and housewares.

INTEL

The "Intel Inside" brand elevated the branding of the company's processors, one of the most important components in a computer — increasing the perceived value of any product showing the brand over non-marked alternatives.

AMERICAN HEART ASSOCIATION

The Heart Check Mark certification is bestowed on those food products that meet specific nutrition profiles. (Manufacturers must pay to receive this stamp of approval.)

METHOD

These eco-friendly home care products avoid harmful chemicals and are pretty enough to leave on display in your home. Meanwhile, the company's campaigns invite customers to join its "People Against Dirty" community.

CHAPTER 12

CUSTOMER ENGAGEMENT
HOW YOU FOSTER COMPELLING INTERACTIONS

Customer Engagement innovations are all about understanding the deep-seated aspirations of customers and users, and using those insights to develop meaningful connections between them and your company. Great Customer Engagement innovations provide broad avenues for exploration, and help people find ways to make parts of their lives more memorable, fulfilling, delightful — even magical.

Increasingly, we see these innovations taking place in the *social media* space, as many companies move away from "broadcast" communications toward delivering more organic, authentic, and mutual interactions. We also see companies using technology to deliver *graceful simplicity* in incredibly complex areas, making life easier for customers and becoming *trusted partners* in the process. However, as ever, technology is only a tool. Even simple gestures like elegant and intuitive *packaging* can extend and elevate the experience customers have with a company — long after the point of purchase.

Customer Engagement innovation is often embedded in some of the other types (notably Brand or Service) and can be difficult to spot. That's okay. Focus on the point of interaction with consumers and on how to connect and delight them.

❷

How to spot potential Customer Engagement innovations:

Does the company take something arcane, difficult, or complex and make it easy for users to accomplish or master?

Do the offerings confer a unique identity, status, or sense of recognition to users?

Do the company's offerings take on an identity and life of their own?

Do customers talk about how a product or service has become a part of their lives?

CUSTOMER ENGAGEMENT INNOVATION STORIES

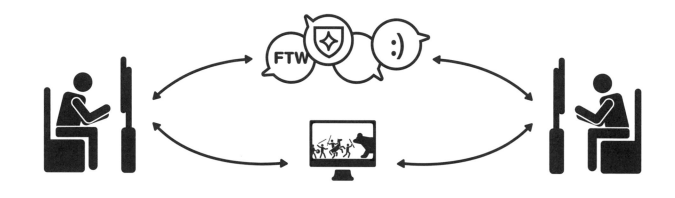

BLIZZARD ENTERTAINMENT

Along with Blizzard's other successful, massively multiplayer online role-playing games, World of Warcraft (WoW) is designed to challenge millions of players even as it engages them deeply. Much of the game's content is designed to encourage collaboration between players, who team up in virtual groups of real people to vanquish wily and dangerous enemies, all to advance through progressive stages of the game.

From the beginning, Blizzard's founders have emphasized the importance of focusing on engaging players in powerful and compelling ways. "Everything we do at Blizzard Entertainment is based on the success of the gaming experiences we provide our players," reads the company's mission statement. The game includes a wealth of ways in which players can connect and communicate with one another, from its heavily trafficked online forums to sophisticated in-game voice chat capabilities.

By following this simple philosophy, the company has enjoyed billions of dollars of success. World of Warcraft has more than 11 million subscribers worldwide, while its online home for gamers, Battle.net, hosts millions of gamers every day. The fourth expansion, World of Warcraft: Mists of Pandaria, was released in September 2012 and sold 2.7 million copies in its first week on sale.

Note: Players aren't obliged to play together, but the games have been specifically designed so that some of the most sought-after prizes are only accessible to those who have teamed up with others. Guilds take matters of recruitment incredibly seriously, and players organize according to skills, accomplishments, and playing styles. Guilds even develop their own logos and playing strategies, and top teams design complex dashboards to codify, mine, and learn from the tens of thousands of new ideas and advances that roll out constantly.

MINT.COM

The online financial management system makes the complex seem simple by auto-updating information from a user's personal accounts, tagging and categorizing purchases, identifying savings opportunities, and automatically creating budgets.

FAB

Leading design experts curate the objects offered for sale on this website — creating a unique, design-driven point of view and forging a sense of trust from customers that this is the go-to venue for the next cool thing.

FOURSQUARE

"Mayorships" are granted to users who most regularly "check into" specific locations using this geo-based service. The ensuing battle for status and recognition has led to heated competition among consumers — and the venues vying for their patronage.

APPLE

The computer giant first shows off its new hardware and software to developers and affiliates at its World Wide Developers Conference (WWDC). The conference allows Apple's partners to play with — and provide feedback on — the company's new technologies. In 2012, tickets for the WWDC (which cost $1,599 apiece) sold out in less than two hours.

PART TWO: IN SUMMARY
MEASURE UP

When using the Ten Types, remember these two important ideas:

1. DON'T SET THE APERTURE TOO WIDE

Trying to use the Ten Types to analyze an entire organization will only drive you crazy. Instead, focus on a particular platform within the business. For instance, don't try to dissect the whole of Google; you'll glean far more insight by focusing on Search or Gmail. (Of course, in some cases, like Zipcar or Netflix, the business is the platform and therefore the only unit available to analyze. Don't panic. That's fine, too.)

2. KEEP THE BAR APPROPRIATELY HIGH FOR CREDITING INNOVATIONS

Given that the framework essentially covers the whole spectrum of business, it can be tempting to give yourself credit just because you're doing *something* within an innovation type. Don't. Carefully analyze what you're doing and don't mistake activity for innovation. Be realistic, set the bar high, and remember: true differentiation doesn't come easily. On the other hand, remember that innovations don't have to be new to the entire world—only to a particular market.

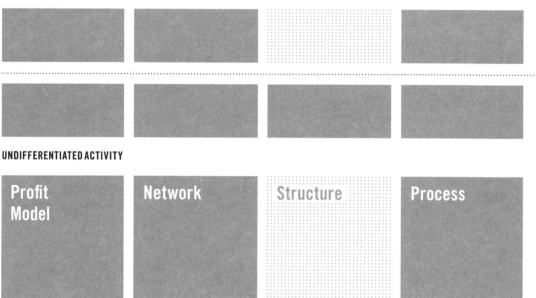

DIFFERENTIATED ACTIVITY

UNDIFFERENTIATED ACTIVITY

Profit Model   Network   Structure   Process

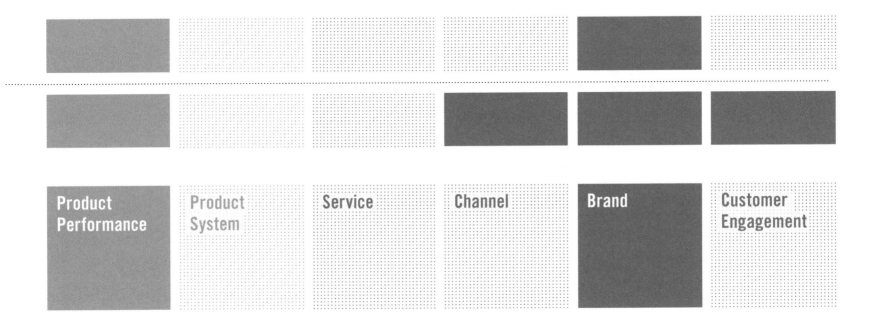

Product
Performance

Product
System

Service

Channel

Brand

Customer
Engagement

MORE IS MIGHTIER

MIX AND MATCH INNOVATION TYPES FOR GREATER IMPACT

Using more types of innovation produces more sophisticated and surprising results—and does so in ways competitors can't easily spot or copy.

CHAPTER 13
GO BEYOND PRODUCTS
HOW TO AVOID BEING EASILY COPIED

Stand in front of a grocery store's cereal aisle and you may be confronted with more than 130 different boxes of flakes, Os, pops, or puffed forms of grain slathered with varying amounts of sugar. Move to the detergents and you will see a wall of powders, liquids, bleaches, softeners, stain removers, and more, stretching on for twenty feet. Move to oral care and you may encounter 42 different variants of Crest toothpaste alone. Then just try to pick out a toothbrush. Sheesh.

Yet if you were to go into virtually any of the world's largest firms that make the items sold in that grocery store today, you would find that most of what they are cooking up are yet more such product variants and line extensions. *"Surely, we will sell more if we make one in mango flavor, no? What if we make the potato chips with pink Hawaiian sea salt?"* Changes like these are easy in big firms — they don't require factories to be retooled — so they're common.

There's only one problem: as an innovation strategy, it's nearly useless.

WHY PRODUCT PERFORMANCE ISN'T ENOUGH

There's nothing wrong with product performance innovation *per se*. In fact, depending on industry or context, such innovation may be necessary to cut through the noise of existing offerings. When a PC first gets designed with special chips for managing graphics, or includes a nice little biometric feature that starts it up securely with just your fingerprint, users value these advances. But if that's all you use, this steady progression of new functions and features is insufficient for continued success and differentiation. Today, nearly every category is hyper-contested. Also, suppliers can only succeed if they can sell their little specialty ingredient or functional doohickey to all the market players in an ecosystem, not just one. That means any unique effect is swiftly eroded.

Remember that a firm's overall performance inexorably erodes through the phenomenon known as the *cost of complexity*. Pickup truck wars illustrate this trend.[1] For several decades, the key to marketing a pickup truck has been to assert that yours is more macho than everyone else's. Toughness and torque are keys, with horsepower and towing power detailed in *basso profundo* voiceover. To dramatize just how tough these trucks are, we see ads showing them being thrown off cliffs, driven through fiery tunnels, and molested by robots in underground bunkers. It's certainly a relief to know that these fine vehicles will survive such ordeals, but thankfully such situations seldom arise in real life. When all the trucks are mighty macho, innovation that helps the truck driver or owner do something else is what matters.

Today, almost any design can be knocked off in record time, whether you work in textiles or technology. Launch any new gadget and an engineering deconstruction will quickly appear online showing the components used, with clear speculations about the suppliers and costs of each one.[2] Twenty thousand products were introduced at the 2013 International Consumer Electronics Show, including dozens of new ultrabooks, OLED TVs, next-generation smartphones, and 3D printers. There is always room for thoughtful designs in the world, but who'd like to make a bet on how many of these will be successful in the marketplace? It's safe to say that a large percentage of them will enjoy only a short and troubled life.

Apple represents the apotheosis of gadget-lust. Still, with reliable regularity, it adds to its arsenal of beautifully designed technology objects, causing the technorati to swoon on cue. Yet Apple's products are just the tip of an innovation spear that has been carefully designed from start to finish. Even before he became CEO, Tim

1 Another example comes from larger grocery or drug store chains, which will charge "slot fees" to enter any item into their computing systems and place it on the shelf. Add a wintergreen flavor to your toothpaste, put it in three sizes and that's three new slot fees you have to pay to get a store to carry it. Multiply this by a couple of dozen chains all using these practices, and you quickly discover you are swimming upstream when trying to go to market with several hundred new line extensions a year.

2 iFixit is just one of many websites that does this routinely for Apple devices.

The Plagiarius Award is a black gnome with a gold nose, to signify "illicit earnings from product imitation."

Cook had won praise for the way in which he drove efficiencies through every part of Apple's supply chain. For example, many analysts believe the company has a substantial cost advantage on flash memory due to its supply chain management. The platform of iTunes and the App store has allowed it to generate enormous value from an ecosystem of developers and record labels keen to connect with Apple's audience. That makes any of the devices that connect to that ecosystem much more valuable and appealing. 25 billion songs had been downloaded by February 2013, an indication of a lucrative business model by anyone's standards.

So, while Apple designs beautiful products, the point is that there is much more to its success than "mere" product performance or industrial design.

It's not that product performance is unimportant. Rather, challenge your team to add other types of innovation to achieve a bigger and more sustainable competitive advantage.

Aktion Plagiarius is a small organization based in Solingen, Germany, that informs the public about the negative impact of fakes and plagiarisms on not only the economy but also on small companies and individual designers. Each year, it holds a competition to name and shame some of the most outrageous plagiarists. The winners are plentiful and often audacious. A knock-off of James Dyson's "Air Multiplier" fan, created by a company in China, won an award in 2012. It has the iconic O-ring of the British inventor's design, only with a more bulbous base and inelegant controls.

Sometimes it's more than a matter of pride or money at stake. Medical equipment has been expertly copied on the outside; but who's to say what quality of engineering has gone into the functionality of the equipment itself? In the 2008 awards, the copy of a faucet originally designed by Dornbracht was found to contain 200% more lead than allowed by German law.

Even now, many leading innovators are known for the performance and features of their products—yet a closer look at their efforts reveals many other types of innovation at play.

1 "Starbucks has always been vocal about its desire to be this third place for its customer," wrote Alice G. Walton in "Starbucks' Power Over Us Is Bigger Than Coffee: It's Personal," *Forbes*, May 29, 2012: http://tentyp.es/X5pcB6.

MICROSOFT > PC

Part of the reason that Bill Gates and his partners were able to build Microsoft was their early understanding of the power of licensing. The practice led to the development of systems like MS Office, an integrated software platform that has endured in various incarnations since August 1989.

AMAZON > BOOKS

The Seattle "e-tail" giant may have begun its business by selling books, but it quickly diversified to try and fulfill its mission statement: "To be Earth's most customer-centric company where people can find and discover anything they want to buy online." In 2012, the company worked with over 2 million third-party sellers.

STARBUCKS > COFFEE

Starbucks may have huge scale (by July 2012 it was operating 17,651 stores in 60 countries) but as Alice G. Walton noted in *Forbes*, from the beginning it was intended to be much more than just another coffee shop.[1] By offering a "third place" between home and work, the company built a community of regular consumers.

VIRGIN > MEDIA

Richard Branson's Virgin has diversified considerably since its early days as an independent record label. The Virgin Group now includes branded companies worldwide, in sectors from mobile phones to transportation, media to music.

*Next we'll share some select innovations —
deconstructing each one to show the specific types at work.*

FORD
INVENTS AN INDUSTRY

The Model T was the star product for the fledgling Ford Motor Company back at the beginning of the twentieth century. It made Ford the Apple of its day, and Henry Ford the equivalent of Steve Jobs. History books make a big deal of the simplicity of the car's design and the moving assembly line. And these were important, not least because they helped make it possible for workers to have a hope of buying the car that they were building—thus helping to build the American middle class.

What the history books too often ignore is that there were 87 other car companies in existence at the time. Were it not for his use of multiple types of innovation, Henry Ford would almost certainly not have gotten his company to survive. In fact, he only really saw success when he introduced a radical innovation idea: instead of selling cars directly to customers, he sold them to dealers, creating a new business model and a better pattern of cash flow. Dealers helped spur demand and engagement at a local level—and they used their credit and cash to buy the cars wholesale, lowering Ford's capital requirements and risks.

The first Model T was introduced in 1908. Within a year, 10,000 sales brought in more than $9 million.

Profit Model

Wanting to make a high-quality, low-cost vehicle, Ford made the $850 Model T the most reliable cheap automobile. Meanwhile, Henry Ford demanded 50% payment upfront, unlike other manufacturers at the time.

Network

Henry Ford aimed to control his entire supply chain—a strategy that would later be called vertical integration. In 1927, he invested in rubber plantations in South America that would make enough tires for 2 million cars, while he set up the River Rouge steel factory immediately adjacent to his assembly line in Detroit.

Structure

In 1914, Ford introduced the $5 workday, paying twice the minimum wage to all workers over the age of 22. He also reduced the working day from nine to eight hours. This not only reduced employee turnover, but also meant workers could afford to buy the products they built.

Process

Ford introduced the moving assembly line in 1913; the time to build a Model T dropped from 12 hours and eight minutes to 93 minutes. By 1923, 2 million cars were rolling off the line annually.

Detail of a photograph showing the Ford assembly line in Oklahoma City, 1913.

Detail of a photograph showing a Ford dealership in 1931.

Detail of a photograph showing applicants crowded outside a Ford plant in 1914, after the $5 workday was announced.

Product Performance

Product System

Service

Channel

Brand

Customer Engagement

The Model T was designed to be a no-frills car that anyone with a basic tool set could repair; more than half of the engine parts cost 10 cents or less and were available at regular hardware stores. This meant users could cheaply maintain the vehicle themselves.

Reflecting Ford's farm upbringing, modification kits were sold to help owners transform their cars into utility vehicles—tractors, sawmills, even snowmobiles. Farmers could attach a device to provide power for sawing wood, pressing cider, or pumping water.

Ford built a network of local, independent dealers to make the Model T available in nearly every city in North America. These franchises not only publicized the car but also created local motor clubs, spreading the popularity of the vehicle and generating sales.

In its day, Ford was synonymous with "American know-how." Henry Ford also founded a Motion Picture Department in 1914; many of the films promoted the company's own vehicles. In the mid 1920s, over 2 million people watched the movies every month.

GOOGLE

INVENTS A NEW MARKETING SYSTEM

Larry Page, CEO of Google, once described the "perfect search engine" as something that "understands exactly what you mean and gives you back exactly what you want." Attaining this has been the goal since Page and Sergey Brin launched the company in 1998. Initially just another search engine in a crowded market, Google established itself as a popular choice, in the main due to the accuracy of results over its immense index of web pages.

Google determines which sites on the web offer content of value and elevates these higher in its search results. It essentially remains a self-sustaining business: "As the web gets bigger, this approach actually improves, as each new site is another point of information and another vote to be counted," reads its mission statement. Yet it wasn't until 2000 that Google figured out a way to build a billion-dollar business. It was then that it introduced its integral advertising program for creating online campaigns connected to search terms; AdWords has been the money-generating backbone of Google ever since.

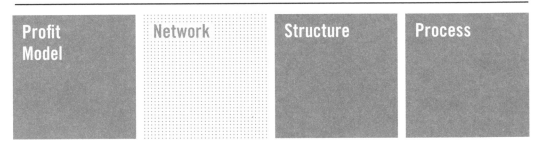

Profit Model	Network	Structure	Process
Known as "do-it-yourself ads," AdWords began as simple text advertisements that users could buy via a bidding process. Google implemented a "pay-per-click" model, which meant it only collected a fee when a user clicked on an ad. Advertising accounted for 96% of Google's $37.9 billion in revenues in 2011.		Google has worked hard to attract and incentivize great scientists and engineers. It also offers healthy, substantial, and free meals and services within its facilities to keep its people functioning effectively around the clock. Employees can take up to 20% of their time to work on a new concept or project.	Company founders Larry Page and Sergey Brin developed the "PageRank" link analysis algorithm while they were students at Stanford University. The algorithm ranked web pages according to the number of links connecting to them.

Below: AdWords are pithy text ads shown at the top and side of search results pages. This offered users a simple, clean experience of web search, while providing an effective system for advertisers.

Left: Google Doodles on the search engine's home page call attention to historical dates, events, and holidays with wit and whimsy, and drive visitors to return frequently— if only to see the latest installment. From top to bottom, the doodles shown here commemorate Monet's birthday, the World Cup, the discovery of DNA's double-helix, and Thanksgiving. Increasingly, the doodles are customized for locales and countries around the world in which Google operates.

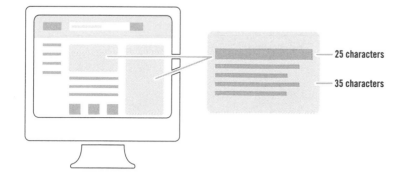

25 characters

35 characters

Product Performance

Beyond PageRank, Google helped those who were searching by stipulating that ads could only contain 25 characters in a headline and 35 characters in a description. This enormously simplified the results for consumers—and the impact for advertisers.

Product System

In 2003, Google launched AdSense as an additional form of advertising. Now, publishers of any size could earn money from targeted Google ads displayed on their own websites.

Service

Google provides integrated advertising services to help major customers communicate effectively with their target audiences. Staff also work directly with clients to help them buy Adwords that will generate the most sales.

Channel

More recently, Google has shifted to include location-specific information and mobile devices in its search results. This radical rethink of search led to acquisitions of firms such as Zagat and Motorola Mobility to make for both smarter searches (showing local restaurants) and better devices (various Android smartphones).

Brand

Google's home page has been spare and clean since day one. But the company has proven willing to be playful—especially with its logo, which through the Google Doodles program underscores the whimsical personality of the company.

Customer Engagement

MICROSOFT
INVENTS INTEGRATED OFFICE TOOLS

"As the majority of hobbyists must be aware, most of you steal your software. Hardware must be paid for, but software is something to share. Who cares if the people who worked on it get paid?" So wrote an impassioned Bill Gates in 1976. Then the general partner of the new technology start-up Micro-Soft (sic), Gates wasn't prepared to let the matter drop, and the letter shows the genesis of the strategy that has helped sustain the company in ensuing years: charging for licenses of software solutions.

Years later, Microsoft developed a system to combine its products. Introduced in August 1989, MS Office integrated popular applications Word, Excel, and PowerPoint, has been installed on millions of desktops and is the chosen business software of many professionals.

Profit Model	Network	Structure	Process

By bundling together popular applications, Microsoft offered cheaper prices than if the consumer bought the programs separately.

Microsoft's User Research Studios collect daily data from those customers who opt in. This helps them to identify errors or problems that are commonplace—and fix them, a low cost pathway to continuous improvement.

Product Performance

Product System

Service

Channel

Brand

Customer Engagement

Microsoft Office was introduced as a suite of desktop applications containing Word, Excel, and PowerPoint for both the Windows and Macintosh operating systems.

In the 1990s, Microsoft made changes to address the rise of the Internet. As such, Office was designed to be web-compatible, and include the ability to incorporate automated upgrades and third party add-ins.

MCDONALD'S
INVENTS A CONVENIENT FOOD SYSTEM

Ray Kroc first met Dick and Mac McDonald when he visited the brothers' San Bernardino restaurant to sell them some food mixers. Impressed with the efficiency of the pared-down burger joint and excited by the idea of launching it as a nationwide franchise, Kroc launched the first McDonald's in Des Plaines, Illinois, in April 1955. The 100th restaurant opened in Fond du Lac, Wisconsin, in 1959.

Kroc developed McDonald's as a system whereby franchisees and suppliers were partners, not lackeys. The company's motto: "In business for yourself, but not by yourself." Even today, McDonald's buys and builds all of its properties and leases restaurants to individuals who guarantee they will be involved in day-to-day operations. In this way, it aims to maintain the personal commitment of its workers to the success of each location. By the end of 2010, 80% of the company's 33,500 restaurants were franchises, with only a handful being operated directly by McDonald's.

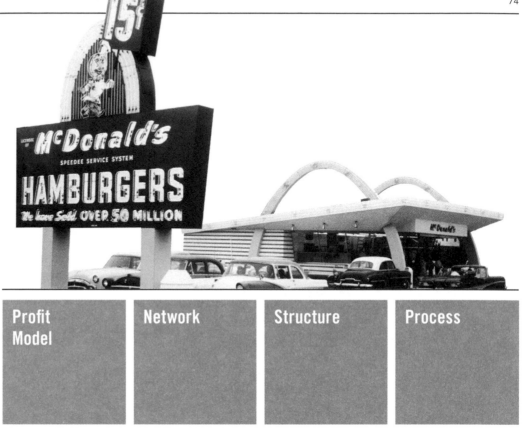

Profit Model

McDonald's buys the land and provides the building for a restaurant, with the franchisee paying monthly base rent or a percentage of monthly sales as rent. Franchisees also pay a monthly fee based upon sales performance.

Network

McDonald's relies on a global partnership with Coca-Cola for beverages. Its independent distribution network has huge firms such as Martin-Brower and Golden State Foods that deliver daily everything a particular restaurant might need—from tables to a single ketchup packet.

Structure

In 1961, McDonald's opened Hamburger University to teach restaurant operations procedures. Since then, more than 80,000 restaurant managers, mid-managers, and owner/operators have graduated from the facility.

Process

Franchisees are encouraged to develop and launch new food items, which will be offered in other restaurants if they prove popular. Franchisee Herb Peterson came up with the Egg McMuffin in 1971, helping McDonald's to launch a breakfast business that now represents 15% of the company's sales.

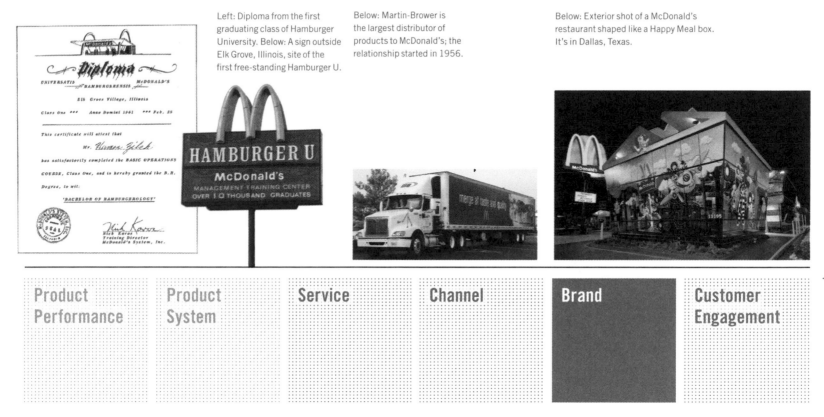

Left: Diploma from the first graduating class of Hamburger University. Below: A sign outside Elk Grove, Illinois, site of the first free-standing Hamburger U.

Below: Martin-Brower is the largest distributor of products to McDonald's; the relationship started in 1956.

Below: Exterior shot of a McDonald's restaurant shaped like a Happy Meal box. It's in Dallas, Texas.

Product Performance

Product System

Service

Channel

Brand

Customer Engagement

Branding was an integral part of the McDonald's restaurants right from the get-go. From the distinctive designs of the buildings themselves, to the Golden Arches, to characters such as Ronald and the Hamburglar, the chain has consistently used brand attributes to be family-friendly.

LEXUS
INVENTS A NEW
LUXURY CAR EXPERIENCE

"Can we create a luxury car to challenge the very best?" That was the question posed by Toyota chairman Eiji Toyoda at a secret board meeting at the company's headquarters in 1983. "Yes," came the answer from his team. Six years and half a billion dollars later, the Lexus luxury brand arrived, originally offering two models, the LS 400 and the ES 250.

To stand out in the crowded market, the new luxury division aimed to differentiate itself via the customer experience. "Lexus will do it right from the start," reads the so-called Lexus Covenant, signed as a commitment of faith by all of the car's dealers. "Lexus will have the finest dealer network in the industry. Lexus will treat each customer as we would a guest in our home." As such, the company launched with a campaign to personalize service. Its relentless focus has paid off: by 1991, the brand was the best-selling import in the United States, outselling both Mercedes and BMW. Meanwhile, it was the top-selling luxury brand vehicle in the US in the decade from 2000 until 2010.

Profit Model   **Network**   Structure   Process

Out of thousands of parties interested in owning a Lexus franchise, the company selected only 121 dealers for the car's first year of business; even by 2012, only 231 dealers were certified in the United States. That helps Toyota to support its dealers properly, generating profits for all.

Left: The Elite of Lexus trophy, a special award given to dealers who excel at sales, service, and overall owner support.

Below: OpenRoad Lexus' cafe in Richmond, BC, features satellite TV and wireless internet to go along with its cappuccino bar.

Below: Guests at the Jim Hudson Lexus dealership in South Carolina can use dedicated spaces in the showroom as their home and office away from home.

Product Performance	Product System	Service	Channel	Brand	Customer Engagement

The quietness of the engine was highlighted as a performance factor. This was famously the focus of a 1990 advertisement showing a pyramid of champagne glasses balanced on the hood of a Lexus while the engine revved at full throttle.

Understanding that getting a car serviced was a source of frustration for owners, Lexus appointed "diagnostic specialists" to explain what was going on with a customer's vehicle. The loaner car provided was a Lexus, not a compact, then the serviced auto would be cleaned before being returned to the owner.

Lexus dealerships regularly feature cappuccino bars, boutiques, and media centers to hold to the basic tenet laid out at the car company's launch, that it would "treat each customer as we would a guest in our home."

CHAPTER 14
STRENGTH IN NUMBERS
INNOVATIONS USING A COMBINATION
OF TYPES GENERATE BETTER RETURNS

As children, we like our music simple. *Happy Birthday to You. Twinkle Twinkle Little Star. Row, Row, Row Your Boat.* One note at a time, steady cadence, melody is everything.

Thus it is with **simple innovation**. These use one or two types of innovation and every company needs to pursue them. Failure to consistently, relentlessly improve the known is one of the surest routes to failure. Unfortunately, too many firms do *only* simple innovation. In today's contested markets, simple innovations alone are never enough for long-term success. They can build a lead on competitors, but they don't create the firms, brands, or platforms that thrill us.

As we get older, the music we like gets more sophisticated too. At some point we learn to love chords, harmonies, complex rhythms, syncopation, themes, and variations. Similarly, when a market grows up and gets complicated, it demands more **sophisticated innovation**, which uses many types of innovation combined elegantly and orchestrated with care. Under the covers, inside your firm, these

require working across internal boundaries and silos—challenges that bring additional complexity. You will cut through this with multi-disciplinary teams to bring in the necessary talent and knowledge, and with systems in place to tell everyone how they can tackle tough challenges with curiosity, confidence, and courage.

Naturally, sophisticated innovations are more difficult to pull off, not least because they have longer development horizons than simple innovations. But consider the flip side: once you launch them, they are likely both to delight customers and confound competitors. Often you will be able to succeed with them for years before challengers can catch up. Almost all of the enterprises that we celebrate as leading innovators routinely use multiple types of innovation—and handily outperform the average firms that innovate more naïvely. Let's take a closer look.

SIX PRINCIPLES FOR USING THE TEN TYPES EFFECTIVELY

1

UNDERSTAND ALL TEN TYPES
Virtually all projects can improve just by knowing and deeply understanding the value and subtleties of each of the types.

2

DE-EMPHASIZE RELIANCE ON PRODUCTS AND TECHNOLOGY
These are the easiest capabilities for competitors to copy.

3

THINK ABOUT CATEGORIES AS WELL AS TYPES
Consciously try to imagine new ways to configure assets, build platforms, and foster fresh experiences.

4

USE THE TYPES THAT MATTER MOST
Use diagnostics to understand which types you and others in your industry tend to overlook.

5

UNDERSTAND WHAT YOUR USERS REALLY NEED
User research can help you know what is relevant to customers and what surprises other types might help to deliver.

6

USE ENOUGH OF THE TYPES TO MAKE A SPLASH
Using five or more types, integrated with care, is nearly always enough to reinvent a category and become newsworthy.

INNOVATOR ANALYSIS BY THE NUMBERS

In 2011, we performed detailed Ten Types analyses on two groups of companies. The first featured "average innovators," which we contrasted with a second group comprising "top innovators."[1] For each company, we took a particular product or service[2] and analyzed it according to the Ten Types framework, assessing all the types of innovation that had gone into producing or delivering it.

We then aggregated those individual analyses to determine the average number of types used by each group.

First, let's take a look at the average innovators. As you can see in the chart below, these companies tend to use a low number of types, with a majority gravitating toward producing simple innovations.

NUMBER OF TYPES USED BY AVERAGE INNOVATORS

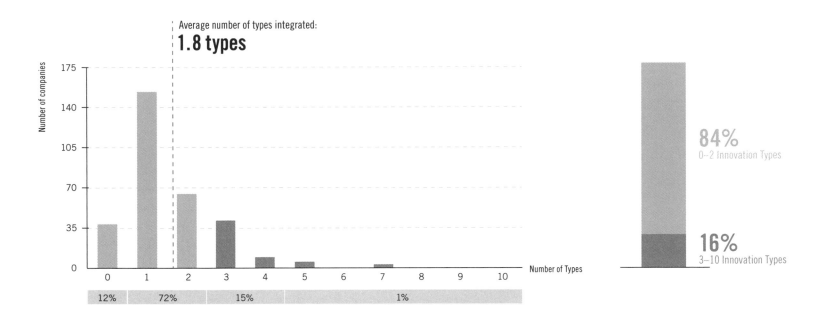

Average number of types integrated:

1.8 types

Number of companies

175

140

105

70

35

0

0   1   2   3   4   5   6   7   8   9   10   Number of Types

| 12% | 72% | 15% | 1% |

84% 0–2 Innovation Types

16% 3–10 Innovation Types

Compare this with the data we got from the top innovators, those companies that have repeatedly launched successful offerings. These firms, it turns out, integrate *twice* as many types of innovation as the average innovators. In doing this, they create more robust and more easily defensible offerings.

1 "Average innovators" featured companies announcing innovations in 2009–2011, compiled via scans of journals and social media resources. "Top innovators" were defined by lists of the world's most innovative companies, compiled by *BusinessWeek*, *Fast Company*, *Forbes*, and *Technology Review.*

2 It is a mistake to ask how many types of innovation are used by a company like, say, Apple. The analysis must be more granular to be useful. Analyze key offerings thoroughly enough and you can generalize to show how many types live at the heart of a winning platform.

NUMBER OF TYPES USED BY TOP INNOVATORS

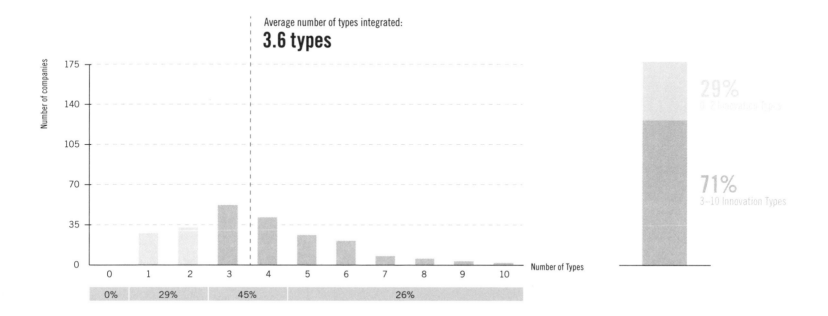

Average number of types integrated:

3.6 types

Significantly, the top innovators outperform the S&P 500.

Integrating more types of innovation can help deliver superior financial returns.

TOP INNOVATOR PERFORMANCE BY THE NUMBERS

This chart takes a more detailed look at the top innovators, public companies using one or two, three or four, and five or more types. We charted their performance over five years, benchmarked against the S&P 500.

Obviously, it is impossible to credit innovation alone for the performance premium of these firms. Still, it is reasonable to argue that innovation does contribute to the value of a firm, including the future expectations that investors value.

Having analyzed and used the Ten Types for more than 15 years, we can now confidently generalize: you must look beyond products in order to innovate repeatedly and reliably. By combining multiple types of innovation, you will be more assured of bigger and more sustainable success.

Here's a way for you to practice, using a game we call "Spot the Innovation." Try to identify which of the types are evident in the following company offerings, culled from diverse geographies and industries. Then turn over the page to see how we break down each one.

SPOT THE INNOVATION
GINGER HOTELS

Please Help Yourselves

Ginger Hotels, a subsidiary of the Indian Hotels Company Limited, is a chain of hotels focusing on the roughly 34 million Indians traveling each day who do not want to pay for high end hotel luxury. Ginger was developed as a "Smart Basics" concept with the late strategy consultant C.K. Prahalad,[3] and was designed specifically to offer a very different kind of service to business travelers on a budget. This includes web booking and a "live rates" online service that allows customers to check for the best rates available that day.

Ginger Hotels are aimed at business travelers who care more about affordable prices and fundamental comforts rather than luxuries. As Kaushik Mukerjee reported, Ginger properties are built on a much smaller footprint than many hotels in the category, geared towards a low operating cost per room.[4] Meanwhile, items that really matter to hotel guests are included, but unnecessary services are not. "Vending machines, check-in kiosks, ATMs, wi-fi connectivity, etc. helped lower service costs while offering good value to the customers," wrote Mukerjee. Additional amenities such as laundry and food are outsourced to partners such as Jyothy Fabricare and Café Coffee Day, "which further enhances the price-performance ratio," he continued. Automated payment mechanisms and check-in via the web or a "Central Reservation System" reduce the number of staff needed onsite; those who are there are trained to ensure they can represent the brand effectively.

3 See Prahalad's pioneering book, *The Fortune at the Bottom of the Pyramid*, still seminal reading for those looking to understand more about this topic.

4 Kaushik Mukerjee's "Innovation Holds the Key" was published in *Indian Management*, September 2009: http://tentyp.es/Tas6qB.

HOW DID YOU DO?
GINGER HOTELS

By innovating in both the Configuration and Experience categories, Ginger appealed to a demographic previously ignored by much of the hotel industry. Did you spot all the types at work?

Profit Model | **Network** | **Structure** | Process | **Product Performance** | Product System | **Service** | Channel | **Brand** | Customer Engagement

CONFIGURATION — OFFERING — EXPERIENCE

NETWORK

Ginger Hotels's partnership with Café Coffee Day allowed the chain to run its outlets on the hotel premises. The hotels also kept delivery menus from a local restaurant; guests could call to have this food delivered.

STRUCTURE

As Kaushik Mukerjee reported (see the link on the previous page), whereas in regular business hotels the room to manpower ratio is 1:3, for Ginger that figure is 1:0.36. It managed with this skeletal staff by outsourcing services such as facility management, laundry, maintenance, and food and drink services.

PRODUCT PERFORMANCE

Subscribing to a philosophy of "Smart Basics," Ginger followed the advice of "Bottom of the Pyramid" strategist C.K. Prahalad to focus on creating a hotel especially for price-conscious customers.

SERVICE

Self-service facilities such as vending machines and check-in kiosks encouraged customers to look after themselves.

BRAND

The brand was designed to represent simplicity, consistent with staying at a nice place that was also reasonably priced.

SPOT THE INNOVATION
DELL

A small number of brilliant moves in the mid 1990s made Dell a darling of the personal computer industry and a hero of the business community at large. Specifically, Dell revolutionized the PC world's business model by dramatically reducing its own inventories and collecting money before a consumer's PC was assembled or shipped.

To make its business model effective, Dell targeted the long-term corporate accounts of customers with predictable purchasing patterns and low service costs. It developed customer-specific Intranet websites and targeted its latest products at second-time buyers who required less technical support than new customers, and who paid by credit card. This channel required considerably less supervision than a bricks-and-mortar store.

A weekly "Lead-Time Meeting" allowed senior executives to interpret demand and supply and ensure there would be no unsold inventory. Meanwhile, sales staff were able to see dynamically which computer components and configurations were available at any time, and were empowered by a new internal mantra: "Sell what you have."

By selling online and assembling PCs only after they were ordered, Dell dramatically shortened its "cash conversion cycle," extending the gap between when a customer paid for products and when Dell paid its suppliers. The initiative paid off: In fiscal year 1994, the company's revenues were $2.8 billion; by fiscal year 1998, that figure was $12.3 billion.

HOW DID YOU DO?
DELL

Dell innovated extensively within the Configuration category of the framework, pairing that with some fresh thinking within both Channel and Service. Here's our analysis of the types at work within Dell. Did you get them all?

Profit Model	Network	Structure	Process	Product Performance	Product System	Service	Channel	Brand	Customer Engagement

CONFIGURATION · OFFERING · EXPERIENCE

PROFIT MODEL

Dell's short "cash conversion cycle" meant that it collected cash from consumers (and earned interest on this money) before having to pay suppliers. This fresh idea dramatically lowered its working capital needs and changed the dynamics of the personal computer industry.

NETWORK

Dell concentrated its partner base into fewer than 100 suppliers that accounted for 80% of purchases. The most important factors in supplier selection were quality, service, and flexibility.

PROCESS

Dell matched supply and demand on a daily, weekly, and monthly basis. Meanwhile, every PC was built to spec, which also helped the company to avoid being stuck with unsold inventory.

SERVICE

24/7 telephone ordering and technical support were used at Dell before most other industry players thought to offer them. Many of its most important services were highly tailored for key corporate accounts—so that big firms could hire a new employee and get Dell to send over the necessary technology.

CHANNEL

By selling its computers online rather than in stores, Dell freed up cash and cut out middlemen. Dell also developed customer-specific Intranet websites to help corporate clients.

SPOT THE INNOVATION
FEDEX

Frederick W. Smith founded FedEx after noting the inefficiencies of the routes used by most air freight shippers, particularly for time-sensitive shipments. Wanting to resolve the problem, he started the company in 1971. On April 17, 1973, the company's first night of continuous operation, 14 aircraft took off from Memphis International Airport, delivering 186 packages overnight to 25 cities across the United States. The company did not show a profit until July 1975, but it did become the premier carrier of high-priority goods: businesses and some customers were willing to pay premium prices for guaranteed deliveries.

Since then, FedEx has become synonymous with the speedy delivery of packages. The company's investments in process and service include its creation of a centralized computer system known as COSMOS, "Customer Operations Service Master Online System," which monitors every phase of a parcel's delivery cycle and means that customers can track their packages at every moment.

FedEx smartly targeted business customers looking for reliability. Clients could take advantage of the company's cargo aircraft fleet (the largest in the world) to ensure their parcels arrived where they needed to be on time and in good shape. It has also developed different services for both employees (who use hand-held scanners to capture detailed package information) and customers (who can track the progress of their parcels online). More recently, the company developed SenseAware, a service allowing people to track information such as temperature, location, and exposure to light in near real-time.

HOW DID YOU DO?
FEDEX

FedEx innovated across the framework, incorporating multiple types of innovation throughout its business. In this way, the package delivery service has been able to harness technology in ways that expedite its service and improve the quality of its offering for customers.

Profit Model	Network	Structure	Process	Product Performance	Product System	Service	Channel	Brand	Customer Engagement

CONFIGURATION · OFFERING · EXPERIENCE

PROFIT MODEL
FedEx founder and CEO Fred Smith identified a demand for the efficient delivery of time-sensitive shipments—betting that customers would be willing to pay a premium for the service.

PROCESS
FedEx pioneered the first automated customer service in 1978, and continues to streamline its "just in time" global business. Handheld scanners became standard in 1986; an online shipping management system was introduced in 1994.

PRODUCT PERFORMANCE
FedEx learned which customer actions led to failed or delayed deliveries. It translated this data into an emphasis on simplicity, especially in forms, packaging, and online interfaces—to make it as easy as possible for customers to use the service.

SERVICE
FedEx created a best-in-class tracking service to allow senders to monitor a package that "absolutely, positively has to be there overnight!"[4] The SenseAware system, meanwhile, pairs a multi-sensor device with a web-based application allowing customers to monitor their shipments in near real-time.

CHANNEL
Early in 2004, FedEx bought Kinkos, Inc. This expansion gave FedEx many more outlets where customers could drop in to prepare, pack, and ship their parcels.

4 FedEx chose to invest heavily in this signature capability after executives realized that call centers were routinely besieged by customers wanting to know where their parcel was. The majority of the time, the delivery had been made—but the parcel was in limbo somewhere within the receiving company's mail room or hallways. By helping customers figure this out themselves, FedEx saved hundreds of millions of dollars each year that it otherwise would have had to spend on expanding the call centers.

SPOT THE INNOVATION
LEGO

Ole Kirk Kristiansen founded the LEGO Group in 1932, naming his company via the contraction of two Danish words, "leg" and "godt," which mean "play well." The iconic plastic bricks were patented in 1958. Today, there are approximately 4,200 different LEGO elements available in 58 colors, with more than 9,000 possible combinations. In 2011, more than 36 billion elements were made.

But the LEGO brand is no longer just about bricks. Some 4 billion so-called "minifigures" have been produced over the years. And, in order to compete with new competition from technological products such as iPads and video games, executives jumped on the licensing bandwagon, signing up popular franchises such as *Indiana Jones* and *The Lord of the Rings*. The company does not break out the specifics of its sales figures, but its chief executive declared in

2011 that sales of licence-based product lines such as *Star Wars* and *Harry Potter* had been "considerably above expectations."

The company has also expanded its own offerings into more upscale LEGO sets aimed at adults — including elaborate versions of iconic Frank Lloyd Wright buildings such as Fallingwater or the Guggenheim museum in New York City. And it got in on the technology game itself with the release of robotics assembly kits sold under a new brand called LEGO MINDSTORMS, the result of a long collaboration with engineers at the MIT Media Lab. The LEGO Group also began to release video games and DVDs, some of which became bestsellers. The bets seem to have paid off. In 2011, the LEGO Group's revenues increased by 17% to 18,731 million Danish Kroner ($3.13 billion).

HOW DID YOU DO?
LEGO

Note how the LEGO Group is focusing on building a platform with its own product. Working with the likes of major movie studios, executives have been imaginative in thinking about ways to expand the business for kids and big kids alike.

Profit Model	Network	Structure	Process	Product Performance	Product System	Service	Channel	Brand	Customer Engagement

CONFIGURATION · · · · · OFFERING · · · · · EXPERIENCE

NETWORK

The LEGO Group created licensing agreements with major motion picture companies. This allowed it to create toy sets of iconic characters from franchises such as *Star Wars* and *The Lord of the Rings*.

PRODUCT SYSTEM

The LEGO blocks sold today can still clip into the original plastic blocks first patented and released in 1958, the sign of a uniquely enduring product system. The company also produced a special line of highly prized robotics assembly kits sold under the LEGO MINDSTORMS brand.

CHANNEL

The LEGO Group's online store offers expensive LEGO sets such as a $300 version of the Death Star from *Star Wars* or a LEGO version of Villa Savoye, designed by Le Corbusier. Major retailers such as Toys"R"Us and Target carry the core line of LEGO construction toys, while certain exclusive items are offered only through the company's dedicated retail stores and other direct-to-consumer channels.

CUSTOMER ENGAGEMENT

LEGOLAND Billund opened in 1968 and quickly became Denmark's most popular tourist attraction outside of Copenhagen. The sixth park was opened in Malaysia in 2012. The parks are now owned and operated by Merlin Entertainments Group, under license from the LEGO Group.

SPOT THE INNOVATION
METHOD

Founded in San Francisco in 2000, Method was the brainchild of two roommates-turned-entrepreneurs. Branding expert Eric Ryan teamed up with former climate scientist Adam Lowry to create a non-toxic line of natural home care products. The various offerings are now sold in more than 40,000 retailers worldwide, including Target, Whole Foods, and Kroger. In 2012, the company was bought by European eco-pioneer Ecover to form what was described as "the world's largest green cleaning company."

With a strong emphasis on sustainability and environmental sensitivity, the vast majority of Method's cleaning bottles are made from 100% post-consumer recycled plastic while the company itself is a "Cradle to Cradle" endorsed company; more than 60 of its products are certified with the C2C stamp of environmentally

friendly approval. Internally, Method practices what it preaches: it offsets its carbon emissions, works within a LEED-certified sustainable office, and it does not test its products on animals.

Method has also innovated its brand, building a company that stands for much more than just tedious cleaning. As well as being eco-friendly, packaging has been designed to be both colorful and countertop-friendly, while the company not only has a wide following on leading home decor and design blogs, but also hosts its own community site, known as "People Against Dirty."

HOW DID YOU DO?
METHOD

Method is building from the right side of the Ten Types framework, executing customer engagement and brand innovations to create a whimsical company that is nonetheless deadly serious about its products. Here's our breakdown of the types of innovation at play.

Profit Model	Network	Structure	Process	Product Performance	Product System	Service	Channel	Brand	Customer Engagement

CONFIGURATION		OFFERING		EXPERIENCE	

STRUCTURE

Method outsourced production to more than 50 separate subcontractors to develop a nimble and flexible manufacturing process.

PROCESS

In a process the company calls "greensourcing," Method worked with suppliers and manufacturers to track the environmental impact of making its products. It also identified best practices to improve the water, energy, and material efficiency of its manufacturing processes.

PRODUCT PERFORMANCE

Method's product not only kills germs and grime, it was developed to avoid using toxic chemicals or destructive production practices. The company adhered to "the precautionary principle," meaning that if there was a chance that an ingredient wasn't safe, it didn't use it.

BRAND

With its readily identifiable, bright, and colorful packaging (originally created by industrial designer Karim Rashid), Method built a big following in home décor and design blogs and its bottles have prompted instant on-shelf recognition.

CUSTOMER ENGAGEMENT

The company's "People Against Dirty" community offered all the usual customer perks, deals, and early looks at new products. But it also widened the brand's appeal by inviting anyone who is interested in making the planet a cleaner place to join its gang. The tactic is perfectly in line with the rest of the company's brand promise, and extended its reach to potential customers.

THINK BIGGER. BE BOLDER.

Companies rely on simple core innovations to continuously improve their offerings. The challenge is to complement those developments with bolder, transformational innovations that open up new markets and provide new growth opportunities.

Always look for the next larger frame to place around both your business and a particular innovation challenge. Examine broader patterns and shifts in your industry, across current and potential customers and users, and in society more broadly to design an innovation that anticipates change and competitive responses.

In building and launching your innovation concepts, think about the minimum number of types of innovation you'll need at launch to make a splash. It's okay to add additional types over time if you can't do everything at once. Focus on the moves you can make first to see early success. Ask yourself which types you will need to use to accomplish those, and then figure out how you'll grow and expand the innovation.

PART THREE: IN SUMMARY
WORK ACROSS

Remember these two smart ways of using the Ten
Types to ensure that you're getting the most from
the framework.

1. GREAT INNOVATIONS GO BEYOND PRODUCTS

Innovation focused on the center of the framework
is useful, but it's not enough to build lasting success.
New products are fairly easy to copy, which allows
competitors to catch up quickly. That's much harder
when you use other types of innovation—for
example, those from within the "Configuration" or
"Experience" categories.

**2. INTEGRATE MULTIPLE TYPES TO CREATE THE
STRONGEST INNOVATIONS.**

It is possible to produce useful innovations using
only one or two types. But in our experience,
innovations that combine more types are not only
more defensible, they also tend to generate better
returns. Thinking about how you might add two
or three types to the ones you are already using will
open up new possibilities and strengthen your
innovation concept.

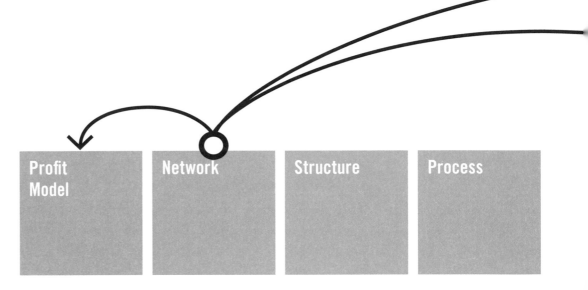

Profit Model   Network   Structure   Process

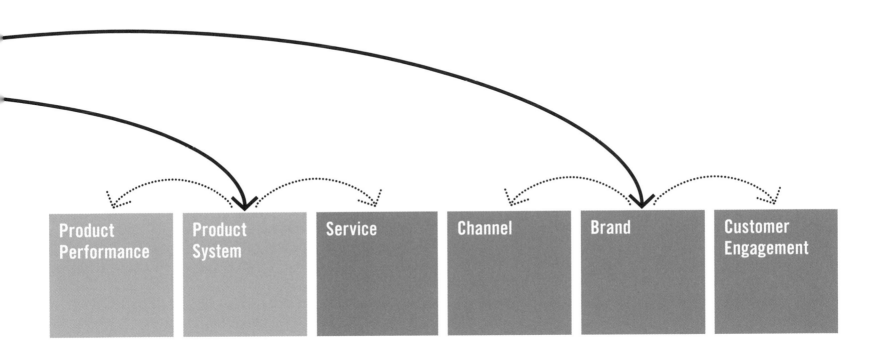

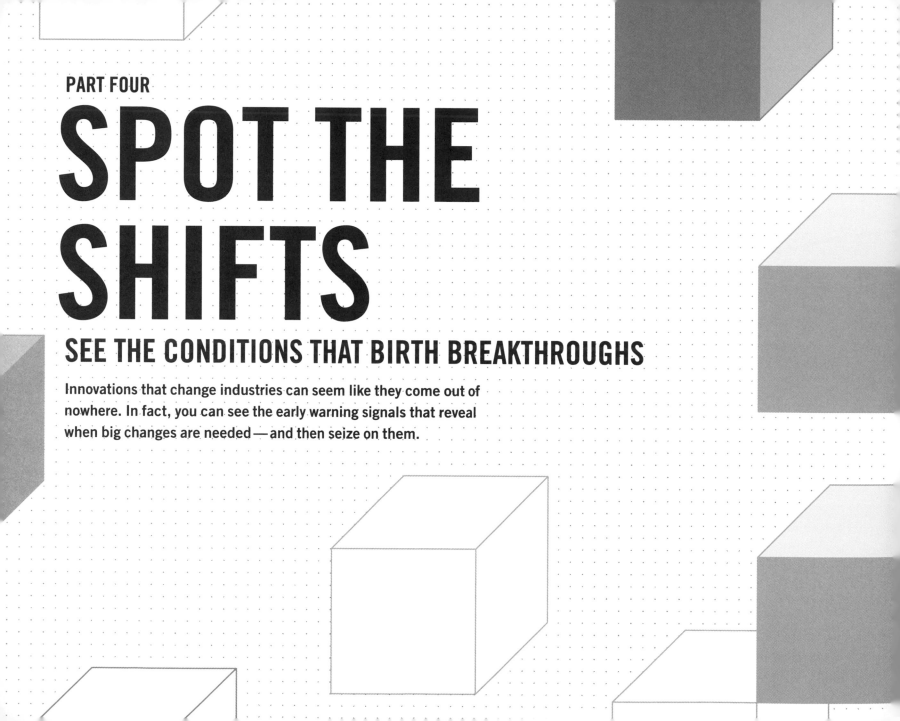

SPOT THE SHIFTS

SEE THE CONDITIONS THAT BIRTH BREAKTHROUGHS

Innovations that change industries can seem like they come out of nowhere. In fact, you can see the early warning signals that reveal when big changes are needed — and then seize on them.

CHAPTER 15
MIND THE GAP
UNCOVER YOUR BLIND SPOTS

Innovation efforts mostly fail. Even when development teams do well, most firms can still find ways to screw up the execution. Despite high hopes and best efforts, projects often just can't get off the ground. When that happens, everyone involved is typically embarrassed — so they work hard to scrub any mention of the effort from their resumés.

Treating innovation as a discipline demands that you do the opposite. When a project fails, treat it forensically: "Why didn't it work? Did any part of it succeed? What should we do differently next time?" And when you see success? Don't assume that it is entirely due to your personal brilliance. Chances are, outside factors were at work there, too.

Also remember that how you succeeded in the past influences the way you approach the future. By putting past projects under a spotlight, it is possible to understand your innovation patterns. Being conscious about what you do and how you do it is a key step toward mastering innovation as a discipline.

Here are some helpful guidelines for using the Ten Types of Innovation diagnostically to make sure your organization is not missing out on potential opportunities.

NOT EVERYTHING IS INNOVATION

The Ten Types cover the arc of business, so it's likely that you'll be doing *something* in many of them. But remember: "Something" is not necessarily innovation; it might be an incremental improvement; it might simply be your everyday business. Be precise, and rate all activity according to the following scale: No activity; "me-too" activity; and differentiating activity. Only the latter counts for our purposes.

ANALYSES SHOULD HAPPEN AT THE PLATFORM LEVEL

Analyze discrete, integrated programs. Trying to assess a corporation as a whole is meaningless and unhelpful. So, instead of trying to figure out Apple's entire approach to innovation, think about iTunes. Instead of looking at all of Google, focus on Google Search or Google Docs. You will learn more by taking apart the Mini Cooper strategy than you possibly could by examining all of BMW Group.

THINK IN TERMS OF YOUR INDUSTRY

Peg your analysis to the competitive landscape. You need to understand your place in it, and remember that innovation isn't simply about what you're doing differently. (What if you've been lagging behind the market movers for years? Congratulations on catching up, but that won't see you build any meaningful advantage.) This is about what will create genuine new value.

ANALYSES MUST BE LEVEL

Try not to use different timeframes in your analysis. An innovation you introduced years ago likely doesn't count anymore, especially if the rest of the industry has since caught up or blown past it. Naturally, an exception should be made if the old innovation continues to provide genuine differentiation or competitive advantage, but this is rare.

LEARN FROM THE PAST

We've applied the Ten Types to scores of different situations and industries. Typically, users get a moment of discovery early on where they see how useful it can be to explain either successes or failures. By using the Ten Types to examine what went right or wrong, you can reveal the gap between what you do now and what you must do in the future. Leaders usually discover that the Ten Types can directly help with individual innovation initiatives, and the framework can even reframe or influence their entire approach to business.

Think about a recent innovation project. Where might you usefully have added types of innovation?

What do the patterns of your innovation successes look like? What do the patterns of your innovation failures look like?

Which types of innovation do you regularly use in your organization? How might you introduce some of the others?

Here's an illustrative analysis in which a company took a hard look at 12 of its different product lines. Projects were judged according to whether or not they had returned their cost of investment, and then organized so that executives could look at the patterns. By being honest and precise about where they had been successful (and less than successful), they were able to see clearly where they had been focusing their attention. Note that it's perfectly possible to do well even when using only a few types; you're more likely to succeed by combining types from different categories.

INTERNAL TEN TYPES ANALYSIS

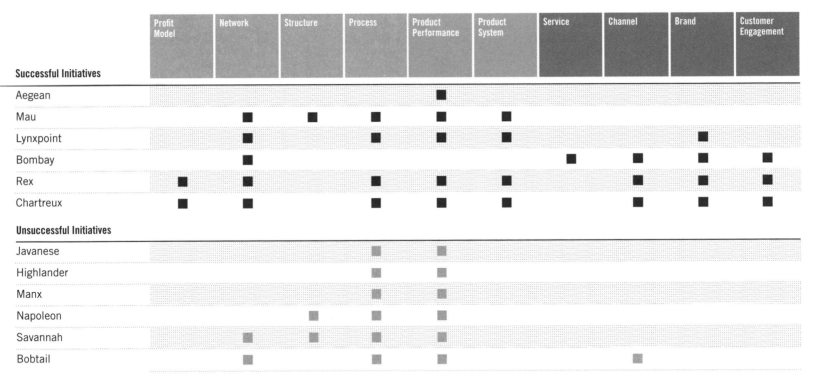

	Profit Model	Network	Structure	Process	Product Performance	Product System	Service	Channel	Brand	Customer Engagement
Successful Initiatives										
Aegean					■					
Mau		■	■	■	■	■				
Lynxpoint		■		■	■	■			■	
Bombay		■					■	■	■	■
Rex	■	■		■	■	■		■	■	■
Chartreux	■	■		■	■	■		■	■	■
Unsuccessful Initiatives										
Javanese				■	■					
Highlander				■	■					
Manx				■	■					
Napoleon			■	■	■					
Savannah		■	■	■	■					
Bobtail		■		■	■			■		

Offerings incorporating multiple types across the framework were reliably more successful. Unsuccessful initiatives used types that were clustered towards the center of the framework. While the company could give itself credit for trying ambitious combinations of types, it didn't distribute them broadly. While the Ten Types is no guarantee of success, experience shows us that a wide-ranging distribution of types of innovation is a smart bet.

CHAPTER 16
CHALLENGE CONVENTION
SEE WHERE YOUR COMPETITORS ARE FOCUSING —
AND THEN MAKE DIFFERENT CHOICES

"Neither Redbox or Netflix are even on the radar screen in terms of competition." —Jim Keyes, CEO, Blockbuster, 2008

No one can be expected to get everything right all of the time. And it's not fair to pick on people who make a prediction. After all, predictions often miss the mark, or at least get the details wrong. And most predictions can be proven incomplete if you test them far enough into the future. But the number of doozies spouted in the name of either innovation or insight is pretty astounding. In 2011, a mere three years after this quote from Blockbuster's CEO, the bankrupt company was sold to DISH Network for around $320 million.

Here's the thing. Blockbuster didn't think it was missing the bigger picture.[1] On the contrary, in the same interview, the CEO outlined a bold strategy for success, including a pivot toward becoming more of a mass media retailer. But he was still trying to figure out how to get folks into his stores when, in fact, those same folks were increasingly refusing to get off the couch to buy *anything*. Blockbuster missed a critical moment that upstart competitors saw and were more committed to seizing.

Industries are plagued with pervasive and unarticulated beliefs about how things are done. Over time, good practices can harden into ossified layers of behaviors that are done by rote. Too often, what might be best for actual customers is overlooked in the zeal to manage familiar behaviors. In time, that provides a great opportunity for an innovator to come along and serve customers in a new and better way. A critical skill in effective innovation is to identify, then systematically challenge, these orthodoxies.

Conventional wisdom argues that disruptive innovation tends to come from those not weighed down by what went before. A fresh eye and a clear head can certainly help when it comes to identifying an opportunity that has been repeatedly overlooked by others. If you're an incumbent, you can either expect inevitable disruption — or you can reframe your view of your field, and understand deeply the associated patterns of innovation. Use your intimate knowledge of your industry to your advantage; pick the trends and patterns you want to foster, and which ones you must respond to urgently. Look for opportunities to innovate differently from competitors and new entrants alike; to zig while others are zagging. This is how leaders shape the future of their fields — riding waves and making waves of their own.

Over the next few pages, take a look at one of our favorite ways of assessing — and visualizing — the amounts of innovation occurring within a particular industry.

1 "DVDs are a melting glacier," Keyes added in the interview with the *Motley Fool*'s Rick Aristotle Munarriz. "Yes, it's melting, but it's a slow melt." http://tentyp.es/135t08i.

THE IMPORTANCE OF INDUSTRY INNOVATION ANALYSIS

Classic analytic techniques—like SWOT or Five Forces—can help to create a broad picture of an existing industry, company, or sector. They can spotlight potential new areas of investment and outline the current boundaries of an industry. Finding these edges is a critical starting place for innovation: that's where the valuable new stuff typically lurks.

While nearly everyone knows how to do the classics, few people know you can analyze innovation patterns with equal rigor. Specifically, you can assess and visualize where others are spending resources—so that you can make more informed choices about where you'll place your bets. Then you may double down on an existing pattern, or perhaps find an opportunity to innovate in a new direction.

The dimensions of any industry innovation analysis are easy to name, but exploring and deciphering them takes careful study and hard work. You need to understand what is important to customers; get a sense of what is possible today and in the near future, and assess the economics—both for mainstream and fringe players. Then work to understand how these dimensions are changing over time, at what pace, and how other players are responding. When you tease apart the innovation patterns with this depth you get a bead on what's next.

Use the Ten Types as a diagnostic filter to frame your analysis. As you'll see next, detailed data analytics can reveal the volume and patterns of industry investment across the Ten Types over time—to become a source of sharp insights.

HOW TO CONDUCT AN INDUSTRY INNOVATION ANALYSIS

1

DEFINE YOUR BOUNDARIES
Be clear about which industries or categories you want to include in your analysis (and which ones are out of scope). Be sure to include any interesting firms that are already serving your customers in new ways—even if they don't fit the traditional definition of a player in your industry.

2

BE PRECISE ABOUT WHAT YOU MEAN BY "INNOVATION"
The terms you use to search will influence your results, so be crystal clear about how you are defining innovation. Use the names of the Ten Types (and related terms—like "partners" in addition to "network") to ensure you capture a broad frame of innovation.

3

SCAN MULTIPLE SOURCES
Pull together a diverse list of resources. Journals, magazines, periodicals, academic papers, analyst reports, and social media scrapers are all useful inputs. Be sure to cast your net far and wide to minimize blind spots. For instance, unpublished masters theses from global graduate schools are surprisingly useful.

4

VISUALIZE AND ASSESS THE RESULTS
Once you've run the analysis, you will have a big haul of information. There are different ways to treat it; one of the best is through visualization, which will make the dynamics you are trying to spot both easier to see and more revealing. We often show patterns using topographic maps (see over) or heat maps. The point is to see where innovation investment is clustered—and to identify *areas of omission* worth exploring.

5

IDENTIFY KEY FORCES OF CHANGE
With this analysis in hand, also bear in mind the broad drivers of change currently influencing society as a whole or your customers in particular. What technological factors apply? As sociologists like to say, "demography is destiny," so how is your customer base likely to shift? Considering these dynamics will help you to understand how your industry might change in both the near and long term.

6

STAND IN THE FUTURE
Take a snapshot of the most recent year of your analysis to reveal areas of potential opportunity within your industry. Where are people focusing currently? Which areas are being overlooked altogether? This helps inform where you should invest now to remain relevant, and helps you to identify future innovation themes that might allow you to change the game entirely.

INDUSTRY INNOVATION ANALYSIS
PERSONAL COMMUNICATION AND MEDIA DEVICES
1994–2004

Great innovation analytics are *visual*. They show changes over time in the cumulative, independent, uncoordinated actions of hundreds of companies, products, and services. We call these *Innovation Landscapes*, and invariably they reveal deep insights into existing innovation patterns.

This Innovation Landscape surveys 11 years of data from the mobile communications industry, capturing it at an intriguing point in its evolution. Cell phones, pagers, and PDAs were becoming mainstream by 1994, and companies were rushing to develop technology to cater to the surging demand. Initially, most of these were devices with a single utility, though more sophisticated and multi-functional handsets began to emerge as the decade wore on.

Design became a factor during this period, as products evolved from being bulky and black to lightweight and stylish. Usage evolved too, as handsets became less of an emergency-use-only item and more of a status symbol. The development of camera phones and portable gaming devices attracted a younger audience, driving greater demand and foreshadowing a time when even young children would be device-savvy.

The competitive landscape was crowded, with players such as Motorola vying against global competitors such as Nokia and Research in Motion. Technology start-ups such as Palm also looked to get in on the action, and new developments such as Ericsson's Bluetooth launched. Peripheral technology players were also clearly interested in the market, though they were still formulating a winning strategy.

1. NETWORK
Throughout the decade, personal devices became more integrated into consumers' daily and business lives. Manufacturers and content and service providers therefore had to figure out how to meet the new user needs. The steady activity here reflects new partnerships forged in efforts to stand out in the market.

2. PRODUCT PERFORMANCE
Released in 1996, Motorola's StarTac line of mobile phones was the cutting-edge of its time. But European manufacturers led by Nokia introduced digital models that would usurp Motorola's analog position in less than two years. Upstart companies such as Palm were just making a splash. As usual, much of the innovation activity in this industry took place within Product Performance.

3. PRODUCT SYSTEM
In 2003, manufacturers finally began to appreciate the value of owning the platform on which other companies might build their businesses. It was still early days, but the beginnings of new systems would flourish from here on out.

4. CUSTOMER ENGAGEMENT
Though still the mainstay of road warriors, phones began to appeal to a more general audience too, as consumers started using devices to connect with their social networks and to get daily bursts of "infotainment." This was an important trend on the upswing as 2005 rolled around.

HOW TO READ THIS GRAPH

This image shows innovation activity broken down according to the Ten Types and charted on a topographic map. Time marches forward along the left side, so that the dotted edge always reveals the innovation patterns of the most recent year. Peaks represent spaces in which innovators are crowding; valleys signal spaces with minimal investment.

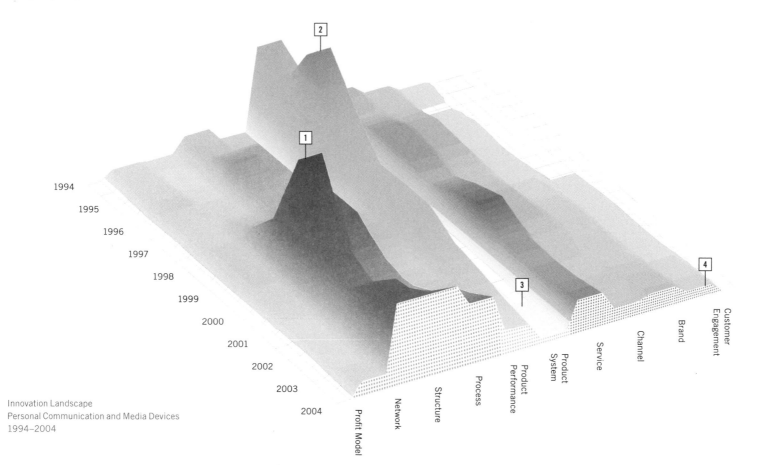

Innovation Landscape
Personal Communication and Media Devices
1994–2004

PERSONAL COMMUNICATION AND MEDIA DEVICES
WHERE WERE THE OPPORTUNITIES AND BLIND SPOTS?

Here's a cross-section of the innovation-related activity in personal communication and media devices in 2004, with our analysis of what the patterns reveal. The first thing to pay attention to is the valleys, rather than the hills. They show where an entire industry is overlooking a chance to innovate. Whenever you see this, even a small effort might get a terrific return on investment.

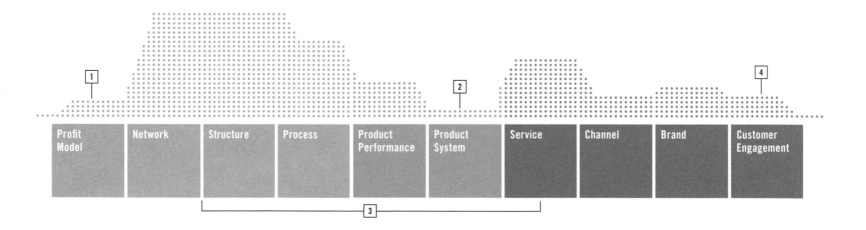

| Profit Model | Network | Structure | Process | Product Performance | Product System | Service | Channel | Brand | Customer Engagement |

1. UNDERINVESTMENT IN PROFIT MODEL INNOVATION

The profit model of the industry was low and flat, meaning that there was not much experimentation here. In simple terms, the industry had stabilized around providing phones "for free" as long as the customer signed a long-term contract.

2. OPPORTUNITIES FOR CROSS-INDUSTRY PLATFORMS

Platform plays are conspicuously absent. Even up to 2004, the digital content industry was relatively immature. A sophisticated platform that could integrate different types of media might create a genuinely game-changing new opportunity.

3. AREAS OF HYPER-COMPETITIVE FOCUS

The vast majority of industry investment in 2004 was centered on Network and Structure— essentially the war by multiple service providers to wire the world and make their own cellular network superior, and by manufacturers to create compatible devices and infrastructure technology. Separately, different service providers scrambled to create retail outlets—often through franchisees—to show off phones and provide a place for customers to sign contracts. None of this was particularly delightful, but it was the predominant basis of competition at that time.

4. NEED FOR CUSTOMER ENGAGEMENT INNOVATION

Brand and, particularly, Customer Engagement were still not a focus of innovation activity. This was almost surely because the firms calling the shots in the industry at the time were the service providers and they were far more focused on building infrastructure than on nurturing customer relationships. Typical of this time: the service providers insisted on including cameras in phones so that consumers would take and email more photos—thus using up more network bandwidth and incurring higher fees.

Hindsight is 20/20, of course, and all industries improve over time. But these insights, if attended to at the time, would have revealed that customers liked but didn't love their cell phones, and that the industry's dominant business and service model was creating sullen rather than loyal customers. Since then, some of those leading incumbents have stumbled badly and failed to adapt to a new environment in which platform ecosystems and customer–centered engagements are key. Indeed, the entire momentum has shifted away from the service providers to new smartphone device wars — with Apple's iOS and Google's Android way out front and Microsoft and Nokia scrambling to catch up.

INDUSTRY INNOVATION ANALYSIS
PHARMACEUTICALS
2000–2010

Back in 2000, things were simpler for pharma companies. Their business models had endured for years. Their innovation investments centered on Product Performance—discovering or synthesizing molecules that delivered proven clinical results. Their sales reps marketed to and dealt directly with physicians. Meanwhile, direct-to-consumer advertising was convincing TV viewers that insomnia, baldness, restless legs, or erectile dysfunction deserved urgent visits to those same doctors.

Things change. The blockbuster drug model became expensive and cumbersome as functional molecules without dangerous side effects were harder to find. Big disease states became hyper-contested as leading firms copied profitable medications, changing them just enough to sidestep patents.

Other technological advances enabled patients and physicians to share and analyze data online. Only 29% of physicians in the United States used electronic medical record systems in 2006; that

number zoomed to 50% by 2010. Technology provided tools to supplement or replace the data that had previously been carefully guarded by the pharma companies. With more information online, physicians became less willing to allow reps to hawk their wares in person. By 2010, only 27% of medical doctors considered leading biopharmaceutical companies to be a reliable source of information.

Meanwhile, rising costs of health care also shifted influence away from physicians and toward those who actually paid for the care. "Payers" were more likely to evaluate products in terms of economics, and that drove up the use of generic drugs. In fact, some of the most innovative pharma companies specifically helped to accelerate the shift to more affordable generic drugs as patents ran out, country by country. By 2010, 78% of prescriptions written in the US were for generic drugs—a tough shift for big pharma, where the biggest firms were addicted to staggering profits derived from patented molecules.

1. NETWORK

Many new partnerships, taking many different forms, emerged throughout this period. Pfizer teamed up with Boehringer Ingelheim to create an information resource for those suffering from chronic obstructive pulmonary disease. In the Netherlands, Amgen partnered with Medizorg Services to offer a support program for patients taking particular medications. And many pharma companies invested in bio-pharma start-ups, in effect to buy "options" on future innovations they hoped would be huge winners.

2. PRODUCT PERFORMANCE

This was a mainstay of most pharma companies' innovation strategy for years, with much attention paid to the development of functional molecules that could be marketed as blockbuster drugs. But as many subtly different molecules became available for the same diseases, executives needed to figure out how to produce effective drugs far more cheaply. That saw them shift their attention to Process innovation to see how they could be more effective and efficient.

3. CHANNEL

Notice the fairly constant innovation investment within Channel. That reflects the industry shift from its earlier model of relying on in-person communication between rep and physician to build alternative channels that would provide a digital interface for the physician (or medical student) and even patients themselves. One of many such examples is Bayer's *MS-Gateway*, a global portal for multiple sclerosis patients and caregivers.

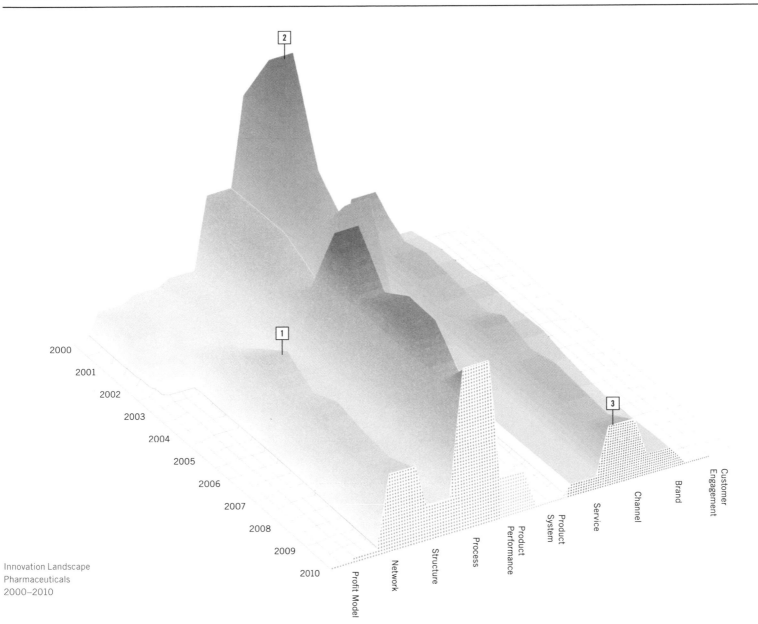

Innovation Landscape
Pharmaceuticals
2000–2010

PHARMACEUTICALS
WHERE WERE THE OPPORTUNITIES AND BLIND SPOTS?

Take a look at the cross-section of innovation-related activity in the pharmaceuticals industry in the year 2010. Pay attention to both the valleys and the hills. Those suggest where opportunities may exist — or an investment area it might be wiser to avoid.

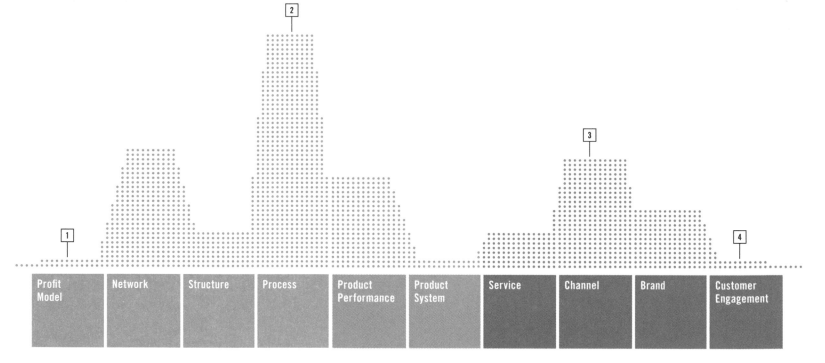

Profit Model · Network · Structure · Process · Product Performance · Product System · Service · Channel · Brand · Customer Engagement

1. OBVIOUS OPPORTUNITIES FOR PROFIT MODEL INNOVATION

The lack of innovation in Profit Model clearly provided a big opportunity for those looking to design new ways of approaching health care. In 2010, one of the main questions centered on how to move from a "fee for service" model to "fee for value," meaning that people had realized it would be smart to pay doctors for outcomes rather than the number of tests ordered.

2. AS PRODUCT PERFORMANCE DECLINES, PROCESS INCREASES

Cost pressures and a higher burden of proof for launching medications in crowded therapeutic areas meant that pharma companies shifted away from Product Performance development toward building new Process innovations, all in the name of finding cheaper and faster ways to make new drugs.

3. BUILDING NEW VIRTUAL CHANNELS

"Detailing" is industry terminology for when a pharma rep calls on a doctor. New advances in technology meant that by 2010, many of the major players were considering building new ways to cope with these demands online or virtually — using a process known as "e-detailing." Similarly, "e-prescribing" meant doctors could send prescriptions electronically to a pharmacist.

4. MOVING BEYOND SHARE OF VOICE TO GENUINE ENGAGEMENT

In the old days, pharma companies didn't have to worry about providing a great customer experience. Instead, they simply had to focus on telling physicians about the performance of drugs and their associated risks and warnings. As sources of health care information became abundant, these firms could have shifted toward designing a better and more engaging experience in sharing such information.

This snapshot of pharmaceutical innovation clearly shows that the historical model of blockbuster drugs derived from basic research and clinical trials was over. Pharma companies were casting around to find new answers, including a focus on Process innovation to identify new ways to develop new compounds. What most firms missed at the time was the chance to deliver a better experience for physician customers. Given changes in regulation and decreased access, a focus there might have provided critical advantage. This was a nascent trend in 2010, but there was room for experimentation. Likewise, as companies realized that it was hard to compete with generics, they began to play around with ideas of innovating around care itself — an appealing idea to payers, insurers, and patients alike.

REFRAMING YOUR INDUSTRY

❓

The Finnish architect and designer Eliel Saarinen said, "Always design a thing by considering it in its next larger context—a chair in a room, a room in a house, a house in an environment, an environment in a city plan." Considering the broader context of your industry helps you see opportunities your competitors will miss; it helps you understand how your products and services fit into customers' lives—and how you might play a broader or simply better role for them. Always look further afield than your competitors to see what ideas you might borrow from entirely different contexts and usefully employ in your own business. Bring all of this together with honest analysis of how you innovate internally, and there'll be a reasonable chance that your innovation efforts will be big, bold, and newsworthy.

Peeking at one industry through the window of another can be powerful. The key is to figure out how to innovate in a way that will surprise and confound competitors while delighting your customers. Here are some useful questions to ask:

What's changing?
Who's driving innovation in your industry? Are you constantly playing catch-up? Do you feel like you always have to react to new introductions from other companies? How might you be able to change that dynamic and force others to play by your rules for a change?

Where are the gaps?
Where are the wide-open spaces where no one is experimenting? Which types of innovation are your competitors overlooking—and how might you use them to your advantage? What areas have you typically ignored? How might you change that?

How can we challenge the status quo?
Industries are beset with beliefs about "the way things work." You may not be able to change these overnight—but being conscious of them is a great first step toward doing things differently.

How might we learn from others?
Look across industries for inspiration. How might you make other companies' models work for you? Coopting ideas from other spaces—and applying them in a new and interesting way can quickly turbo boost your innovation activity and transform your own industry.

Where are our own gaps?
Get a clear sense of which types of innovation you're using regularly and productively. Then understand the ones you're not using as often. How might incorporating new types into your repertoire change the way you play?

Left: Henry Ford West Bloomfield Hospital atrium.
Below: The demonstration kitchen in action.

Imagine you are in a hospital. What are the images that come to mind? Beeping equipment, perhaps? Squeaky floors and cold metal beds? One thing you probably wouldn't think of is a hotel. But hospital executives at the 191-bed Henry Ford West Bloomfield Hospital in Michigan looked for inspiration by hiring a former Ritz-Carlton VP as its CEO, to help the hospital borrow ideas from one industry to shake things up in its own.

For instance, they took a page from the hotel industry playbook and placed a premium on service, offering healthy food to patients and their visitors. A demonstration kitchen helped patients to learn about nutrition or how to manage conditions with specific dietary needs, such as diabetes. An in-hospital greenhouse, staffed by a resident farmer, delivered organic produce to the kitchen.

In 2011, the hospital generated millions of dollars from hosting and catering functions for companies and community groups.[1]

Executives also borrowed some Process and Structure innovation ideas from the hotel business: Operating rooms were redesigned to be identical to one another. Such modularity helps cleaning staff be efficient in hotels; in a hospital it diminishes the chance that surgical staff might make a serious error. Lighting in the operating room was also optimized; what soothes a hotel customer can aid recovery in a patient. All materials used within interiors were designed to be easy-to-clean and sanitary, critical in both industries.

1   See "Why it's Logical to go Radical," by Bill Taylor, Management Innovation Exchange, February 27, 2011: http://tentyp.es/VSJGNi.

CHAPTER 17
PATTERN RECOGNITION
SEE HOW INDUSTRIES AND MARKETS SHIFT—AND LEARN FROM THOSE WHO SAW THE SIGNS AND ACTED ON THEM

Two kinds of change impinge on innovation. Mostly what we see is the relentless evolution within industries that demands and drives continuous improvement. Changes in microchips make more functionality easy and affordable in our gadgets. Our cars, appliances, and smartphones steadily get more features and capabilities; our detergents make the whites whiter; our service industries become more responsive and customer-centric. Simply put, stuff gets better as market researchers discover what people need, and engineers and designers work their magic. Think of this as **improving the known**. It never stops.[1]

Ah, but now and then industries change fundamentally. This is harder to spot, much more ambiguous, and vastly more valuable to get right. Often it takes a special form of courage to tackle this kind of change—though good methods can de-risk the challenges and help lift the fog when you are trying to peer through it to imagine alternative futures. We term this **inventing the new**, and our central assertion is that this especially valuable, and historically rare, form of innovation is becoming easier to execute more reliably.

Next, we will deconstruct some firms, fields, and moments where leaders in tough competitive situations were able to squint at them to see different possibilities. With today's greater connectivity, better access to capabilities and capital, and shifting geopolitical and demographic norms, such disruptions are now frequent and hit many industries. So you need to detect and address such patterns, for both offensive and defensive reasons.

We have selected a diverse set of stories to assess and detail here. Without exception, they integrated multiple types of innovation to create a sophisticated offering that was distinctively different from the choices of their competitors at the time.

1   This is what Clayton Christensen termed "sustaining innovation" in his seminal 1997 book *The Innovator's Dilemma*. His essential point was that well-run firms, responding to their most demanding customers, tend to hyper-improve the known and systematically under-attend to the emerging needs of other customers — especially those who require less sophisticated functionality.

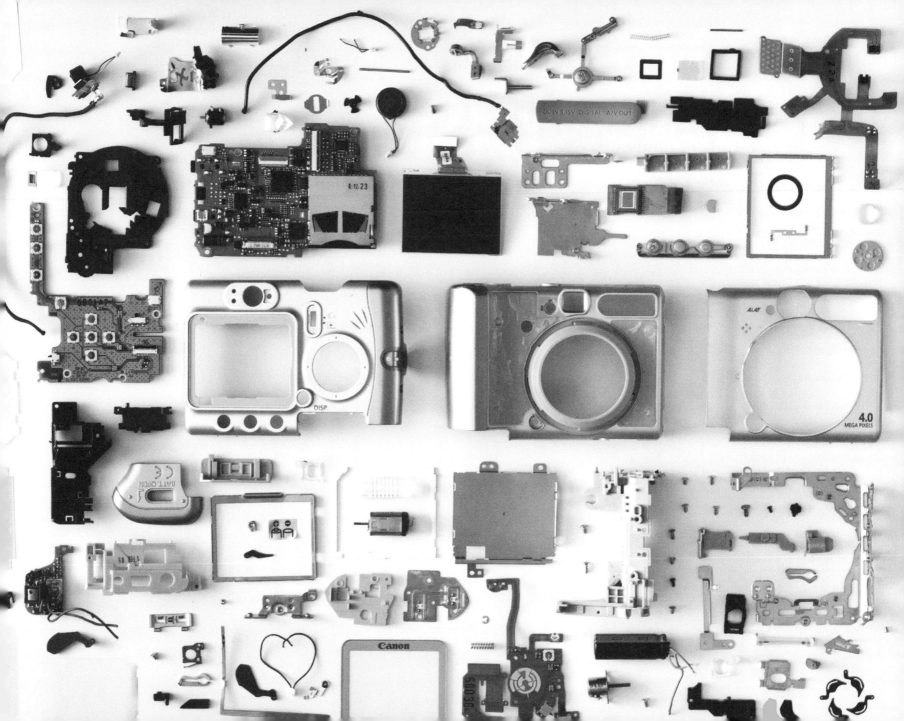

PROCTER & GAMBLE
ADDRESSES THE KEY CONCERNS OF NEW PARENTS

Disposable diapers weren't common in China in the 1990s. Many mothers still adopted traditional customs, including the use of "kaidangkus" — open-crotch pants so their little ones could simply relieve themselves anywhere, anytime. Conventional wisdom in China at the time also had moms believing that disposable diapers might actually be bad for baby. Meanwhile, these alternatives were still more expensive than reusable cloth diapers. So while some companies thought introducing cheaper versions of successful Western products to global markets was a sure bet, it turned out to be a bad one in China.[2]

When companies realized that their would-be customers weren't buying, they responded in fascinatingly different ways. For instance, at least one approach was to focus on Product Performance innovation. Executives at one multinational conducted extensive field research to figure out how the diapers were working in the real world. They challenged design engineers to create a leak-proof product. Focusing on the high-end of the market, its diapers were still relatively expensive, and its marketing strategy aimed to make the product appeal to the most affluent parents in society. It was a bold approach, and yet this focus on design failed to pay off.

With its Pampers product line, Procter & Gamble took a different tack. As Mya Frazier reported for CBS's *Moneywatch*, its team also went out into the field, visiting some 6,800 homes in eight cities throughout China. But they focused less on how the product worked and more on trying to figure out how to make a happy family. Insights from this process helped the team to reframe the problem and to bring in types of innovation from the edges of the Ten Types framework.

For instance, as Frazier's report showed, the team identified a real advantage to using disposable diapers: P&G research showed that babies fell asleep more quickly when wearing Pampers than wearing those made from cloth — and they slept for longer, too. The team moved the discussion away from the product's performance claims to address the broader benefits of using the product — one that happened to speak to a key concern of new parents.

To add credibility to their claims, they collaborated with the Sleep Research Center within the Beijing Children's Hospital to develop a program to monitor babies' sleeping patterns.[3] Later, in an example of Network innovation, they leveraged that research to reassure concerned parents that disposable diapers were both safe and

2 "How P&G Brought the Diaper Revolution to China," by Mya Frazier for CBS *Moneywatch*, January 7, 2010: http://tentyp.es/R6eM4a.

3 Details of P&G's research and marketing initiatives are included in Sheila Shayon's article, "Bottoms Up: Pampers Takes on China," *Brandchannel*, April 28, 2010: http://tentyp.es/SJVCSR.

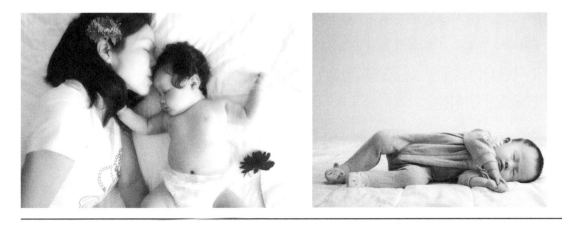

Porter Novelli has interesting insights on the construction of the Golden Sleep crowdsourced marketing campaign: http://tentyp.es/UuKnkM.

Details of this profit model strategy — and its impact — are included in Liu Jie's piece for *China Daily*: "Household paper giants clean up act": http://tentyp.es/QZkOll.

For further stats on the market, see *Euromonitor*'s August 2012 report: "Nappies/Diapers/Pants in China," http://tentyp.es/Rb9GVc.

healthy and the extra sleep would allow their babies to develop better. The campaign, launched in 2008, was known as "Golden Sleep" and also included some crowdsourcing, as they encouraged new mothers to upload photographs of their sleeping babies to a dedicated website.[4] A photomontage of 105,793 of the images was constructed in a retail partner's store in Shanghai; the campaign attracted more than 100,000 new members to the Pampers club.

"

P&G research showed that babies fell asleep more quickly when wearing Pampers diapers as opposed to those made from cloth — and they slept for longer, too. The team addressed the broader benefits of their product — one that spoke to a key concern of new parents.

P&G also innovated the Profit Model, pricing Pampers at three levels to appeal to parents of all incomes and allow them to trade up through the range as their financial situation improved.[5] In essence,

the team looked to understand the issues at play within the Chinese marketplace, and adapted its strategy and innovation to suit.

The use of different types of innovation paid off. By 2008, the China National Household Paper Industry Association estimated that P&G had won 31.3% of China's diaper market with its Pampers brand.[6]

AMERICAN GIRL

CONNECTS HISTORY WITH A NEW GENERATION OF GIRLS (AND THEIR MOTHERS)

For Christmas in 1985, Pleasant T. Rowland wanted to buy dolls for her two beloved nieces. To her horror, she discovered that the two popular choices of the day were Barbie Dolls, Mattel's juggernaut toy line (which she thought sent the wrong message), or Cabbage Patch Dolls (which she thought were unforgivably ugly).

Rowland wanted to come up with a new way to engage and connect with a generation of young girls. She thought back to a moment a few months earlier when she had accompanied her husband to a conference in Virginia. While he was in his meeting, she found herself touring the historical district, visiting the church that George Washington used to frequent and reveling in learning about colonial Williamsburg. Her idea: to create a version of her experience and apply it to toys. Where the makers of Barbie were celebrating girls being either a teen queen or a mom, Rowland decided to create American Girl dolls, each one situated in a specific historical context, with a richly detailed back story.

Her first fictional heroines included Kirsten Larson, a pioneer girl from 1854, Samantha Parkington, who lived in 1904, and Molly McIntire, a girl living through World War Two. Each one of them was developed with intricate storylines to provide "girl-sized" insights

into fundamental moments in America's history. Six stories were written for each doll, so the owner would know how her doll would have lived in her day.

Notice what she was doing. Where others were selling *dolls*, Rowland was selling *experiences* and seeding each with vivid, interesting stories. Her dolls were meticulously made and in a smart Profit Model move, had a premium price tag to show for it: each was (and still is) 10 times more expensive than a Barbie doll.

Each character was surrounded by a Product System innovation composed of many accessories for the dolls that fit the historic back story, and designed to help a girl engage in imaginative play. Books described the characters while clothes were available for each doll — along with matching versions of those outfits sized up for the doll owners. Years on, American Girl even produced girl-approved movies and "My American Girl" allowed girls to design their own doll, choosing factors such as hair and eye color.

Unable to break into the closed world of toy marketing (sales all happen at toy fairs held annually in major global cities), Rowland had only one available route to market: selling her dolls directly to

parents. Having blown all the money she had to produce the dolls and their stories, she printed catalogs, and sent them by mail to homes in time for Christmas in 1986. Then she and her few employees huddled in a cold warehouse in Madison, Wisconsin, to see if the phone might ring.[7] It did. Off the hook. In its first three months of business, American Girl sold $1.7 million worth of product.

Later, Rowland added Channel innovations, including stand-alone showcase stores designed to deepen and extend the idea that the firm was devoted to promoting healthy imaginations. So the stores had places for girls to learn how to cook or create and decorate objects to take home. The emphasis was on fun, which must be why they have become a cherished destination for families.

Always at American Girl, Customer Engagement was key. Even now, girls can bring their doll into the store for a hairstyle or for a cup of tea (no soda; this is to be a truly grown-up experience). Dolls, sitting in hook-on seats, dine next to the girls. There's even a doll hospital for precious toys that have been involved in some heinous accident (a crayon-on-face daubing, for instance, or a home-made-hairstyle-gone-wrong). These experiences proved so popular that American Girl also tried a Network innovation, partnering with hotels to offer

a special package in which the dolls are treated to turndown service for their own teeny tiny beds. All of this is done in the name of creating a magical experience for girls and their parents—and it certainly provided a new model for approaching the toy industry.

Rowland's ability to look beyond where industry incumbents were competing, along with her savvy combination of the different types of innovation, helped her generate longer-term success. Since 1986, over 21 million American Girl dolls have been sold, alongside 139 million American Girl books. In 2012, the company boasted the largest consumer toy catalog in the United States, while its dedicated magazine has a circulation of over 450,000 (and receives more than 5,000 pieces of reader mail every issue).[8]

NIKE

BUILDS AN ATHLETIC EMPIRE THAT GOES WAY BEYOND HIGH-PERFORMANCE SHOES

From its very beginning, when Bill Bowerman was making a new kind of track shoe at home by curing rubber in his wife's waffle iron, Nike believed fervently in high performance *gear*. In the first stage of its existence, it mostly focused on investing in Product Performance engineering and design. The big shift Nike helped to precipitate during its early years was the notion that any serious athlete needed lots of special equipment for each sport—especially lots of different shoes.

Of course, it occurred to Nike cofounder Phil Knight that star athletes mattered too. In 1985, the company recruited NBA rookie Michael Jordan to comment upon, adopt, and use a new signature shoe. From this start, Nike learned that the marketing—and aggressive sponsorship—of the very best athletes in each sport mattered almost as much as the gear itself. Smart monitoring of apparently peripheral sports paid off when the athletes snapped up titles and sparked devotion in fans everywhere.

Bold campaigns like the "Just Do It" ads began in 1988. All of this helped to solidify Nike's position as a major sporting world player, able to shape the destiny of sports and their stars. By the end of the decade the company boasted revenues of $2 billion.

In November 1990, Nike unleashed a Channel innovation in the form of Niketown. These flagship stores provided "retail as theatre"—and a controlled way for the company to showcase products and to convince consumers that this was more than just your average shoe seller. It also signaled a shift from the company's previous focus on product to now including Brand innovations.

But think for a moment. Does it make sense for a shoe company to sell shoes from expensive stores on the world's costliest retail streets in cities such as New York, London, Paris, Chicago, and Beijing? Niketowns cost many millions of dollars to design and build, and they were humdingers, as stores go, even fancier than the Apple stores that came along over 10 years later, in May of 2001. To be fair, the stores were also wildly popular, with customers packed in from open to close seven days a week.[9] But it's clear even from a quick back-of-the-envelope calculation that you simply cannot sell enough pairs of even the most expensive shoes to make the investment in such an emporium pay off in conventional terms.

The brilliance here is that Nike didn't expect to do so. The executives indirectly paid for the showcases out of their advertising budgets, calculating that this marketing would do as much for their brand as

9 Some years ago we worked with Chicago's Museum of Science and Industry— an impressive, sprawling museum that takes up the space of more than four city blocks and houses an actual coal mine, a captured World War Two German U-boat, and many other astonishments. We were shocked and disappointed to learn from its leaders that the Niketown on Michigan Avenue outdrew the museum for visitors nearly every day of the year.

Far left: Niketown flagship stores use the company's products and sponsorships to serve as a focal point of brand and messaging. Here, the New York City Niketown showed its support for the 2010 US world cup team.

Left: The Nike+ product system harnesses various technologies to forge a connection with a worldwide community of runners.

any ad campaign ever could. Then there's the other purpose of the stores, beyond delighting consumers: the after-hours private industry events held to show other retailers how they might market Nike shoes and gear more effectively. Nike has hosted the buyers of, say, Foot Locker, inviting them to schmooze with sports stars and designers. This is all done in the name of ensuring two things: that the category as a whole gets sophisticated marketing programs, and that when a competitor's product is shown next to a Nike shoe on the wall of a conventional retailer, a consumer may be willing to pay a buck or two more because he likes the Nike brand.

Nike certainly didn't have a lock on the sporting market; while it fought back a strong campaign from Reebok, others such as Adidas, Puma, and Fila gave the Beaverton, Oregon–based firm a decent run for its money by producing lots of variants of well designed shoes, all including clever performance features and claims. Rivals also copied the focus on marketing; after 1993, Adidas increased its ad spending from 6% to 12.5% of sales and by the end of 1998 it was the number one athletic footwear brand in Europe.

The millennium, too, brought different challenges, as Nike and all of the other players were forced to adapt to the pressures of an ever more global marketplace. That's the thing with innovation: it's never done. Nike will have to manage the shifting allegiances of its fashion-forward audience as long as it continues to thrive. It will need to figure out new ways to deal with the fragmentation of traditional media as a means to promote a product.

Hence the introduction of products such as Nike+, a Network innovation with Apple leading to a Product System to harness technology and connect with a worldwide community of runners. In Channel, meanwhile, Nike continues to push new frontiers, as witnessed by its Nike Sportswear retail stores, where consumers can work with the company's designers to customize footwear, and more recently, its dedicated "Brand Experience" outposts.

It's this constant motion forward that counts, and for the time being at least, the company's outlook remains strong: in 2011, Nike's fiscal 2015 revenue target was a range of $28-30 billion.

As president and CEO Mark Parker put it that same year: "At Nike, Inc. we run a complete offense, and it's based on a core commitment to innovation. That's how we stay opportunistic, serve the athlete, reward our shareholders, and continue to lead our industry."

PART FOUR: IN SUMMARY
SHIFT YOUR FOCUS

Study the landscape in three directions. This will help you to understand the broader shifts and cultural changes shaping your world — and allow you to get ahead of the pack and innovate where your competitors least expect it.

1. LOOK WITHIN
Understand where you or your enterprise has tended to focus efforts historically. This will highlight potentially stale patterns and methods of innovating — and help you challenge or change them.

2. LOOK AROUND YOU
Examine what others are doing within your industry to get a clear picture of your competitive environment — and then consider how you might innovate differently.

3. LOOK INTO THE DISTANCE
Also examine what others are doing outside of your industry — particularly those who are solving a challenge that's analogous to yours. Learning from others can provide new ways to think about what you do and how you do it.

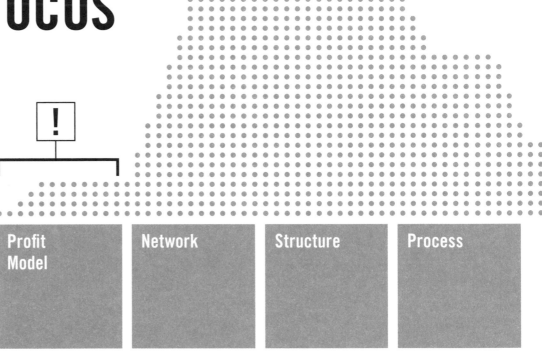

Profit Model   Network   Structure   Process

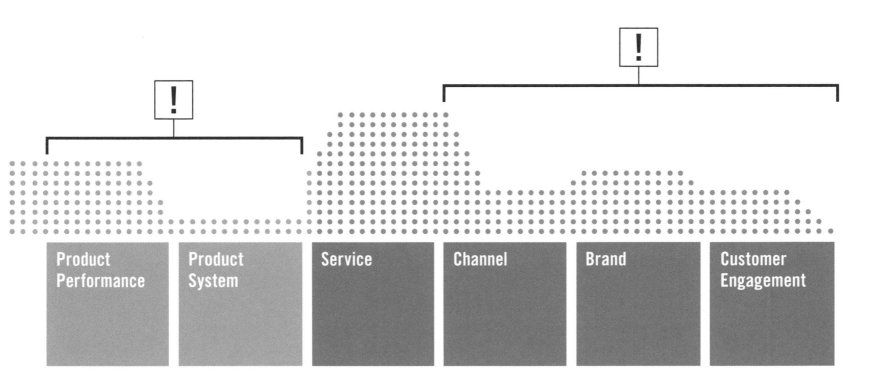

PART FIVE

LEADING INNOVATION

USE BETTER PLANS TO BUILD BREAKTHROUGHS

Sophisticated innovations share similar components at their core.
By deconstructing and distilling the work of successful innovations,
the building blocks for new concepts emerge.

CHAPTER 18

DECLARE INTENT

BY BEING CLEAR ABOUT WHERE AND HOW YOU WILL INNOVATE, YOU MASSIVELY INCREASE YOUR ODDS OF SUCCESS

To lead innovation, you need to see how others are innovating and spot how you could shift the status quo. Then assess how much sophistication will be needed to drive that shift. Put simply: *"Where and how should we innovate? How much innovation do we need?"*

To do this well, draft an "Innovation Intent." This is a concise articulation of your initiative's goal. Its wording can be imprecise, but not random. The underlying idea is to remove the recklessness of a fuzzy declaration like, "Give me breakthrough ideas that make me go 'wow!'" Instead, help your collaborators know where to begin and what will constitute victory.

A classic Innovation Intent came from President John F. Kennedy in his address to Congress on May 25th 1961: *"First, I believe that this nation should commit itself to achieving the goal, before this decade is out, of landing a man on the moon and returning him safely to the earth."*[1] In one pithy sentence, JFK declared an ambition and had an unambiguous goal embedded right in it (to get the astronaut back successfully before 1970 dawned). President Kennedy did not know *how* this might be done. Instead he laid out a challenge, set a time frame to get it done, then he worked to install and trust the talent to deliver it. This is how breakthroughs happen—not through serendipity or unbridled creativity, but by creating a vivid goal and challenging a team to make it real.

In considering your intent, remember that using more types of innovation will typically make your initiative more defensible and likely to yield higher returns. But note the flipside. More types take more effort to integrate. They often require larger teams and more coordination as you cut across silos. All of this will demand more complex development processes—so there will be more ways to fail.

Scientists embrace a principle known as Occam's razor. This suggests that when formulating a hypothesis, start with one that requires the fewest assumptions—and make it more complex only when necessary. This principle of parsimony should also guide your innovation work: take on the minimum amount of complexity needed. If you're looking to transform an industry, you may need to integrate five types; if you're looking to reinvigorate an existing product, then fewer will likely be needed.[2]

Part Four of this book demonstrates that it's easier to succeed when you innovate differently from others. This chapter will help you choose that course and set sail.

1 Even NASA deemed this goal "unthinkable" at the time of JFK's speech, since the US had only a few manned space flights under its belt prior to the President's challenge.

2 There is no such thing as the "right" number of types; the answer depends on your unique context. If there is a universal law, it's this: always plan ahead and be prepared to add a few more types within a few years of your innovation's launch. After all, no offering is ever so great that competitors simply shrug their shoulders and declare: "You win, we lose. We'll give up now and go find some other line of work..."

Consider these two fundamental questions when crafting your Innovation Intent:

Question 1: How can we innovate differently?

Assess where everyone else in an industry is focusing—and use this to identify some specific types you can focus on initially to be distinctively different and shift the field.

Question 2: How ambitious do we need to be?

Determine how many types you should use at first to get noticed and achieve your goals—and note others you might add in later stages.

SET DIRECTION:
THE THREE
INNOVATION SHIFTS

When you squint at who's doing what in your field, the net innovation actions of all companies are almost always focused on one or more of three distinct centers of gravity: ***business model, platform,*** or ***customer experience.***

Understanding the center of gravity in a market will clarify what you and your competitors are doing now—so that you can either consciously double down, or choose a different course. To figure this out, ask yourself two simple questions:

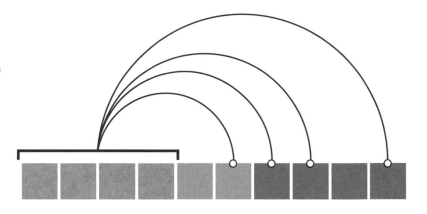

❓

---

1. **What is the current driving force of innovation activity in your industry?**

   In most cases it will be focused on the offerings—whatever is being done to make a better mousetrap. Within industries such as entertainment and hospitality, it will probably be on experience elements, while within industries such as financial services, real estate, and airlines the focus will often be more on configuring capabilities, assets, and networks. No matter what you and your competitors do now, ask: *"what might we do differently?"* If others are focusing on products and services, could you unveil a new profit model? Or might you create a new platform if the rest are creating great customer experiences?

2. **What are the critical types of innovation at work?**

   If you removed any of the types, would the offering or business fall apart? Zipcar has seven types of innovation at play—but remove its FastFleet Process and its metered use Profit Model and it becomes just a regular old rental car company. That's why we see Zipcar as primarily a business model shift.

BUSINESS MODEL SHIFT

This kind of innovation focuses first on configuring assets, capabilities, and other elements of the value chain to serve customers and make money differently. For example, even firms that mostly sell hardware, like GE and Johnson Controls, are discovering that the real value comes from using pay-for-performance models that find ways to guarantee that customers use their products effectively. Create this shift by focusing initially on the left side of the framework (the types include Profit Model, Network, Structure, and Process). Then move across to the right to add the supplemental types you need to make the business model hum.

Zipcar reimagined how it might tackle the rental car industry by creating a networked fleet of cars and developing a new way for customers to reserve and pay for the rides. The result: drivers pay by the hour for cars conveniently parked in nearby neighborhoods.

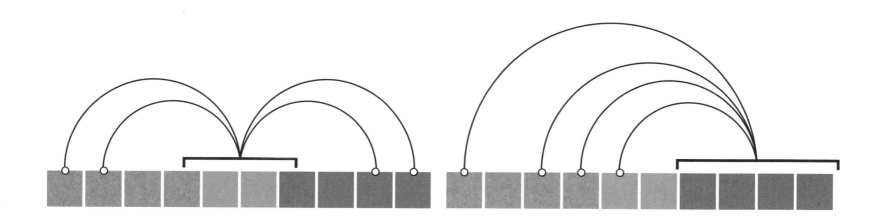

PLATFORM SHIFT

All too often industries are centered around products that have added features and functions over time, but little else. Platform-driven innovation instead focuses on reinventing, recombining, or finding fresh connections across capabilities and offerings to create new value for customers. Develop one by focusing first on the center of the framework (Process, Product Performance, Product System, and Service). Integrate these types to create a solid foundation, then move toward both ends of the framework to add others you need to make your platform work.

Amazon built a strong e-commerce platform selling books to consumers. It has since leveraged its own infrastructure, experience, and data to drive wave after wave of innovation from this foundation — from providing web services for other enterprises to catalyzing the e-book industry.

CUSTOMER EXPERIENCE SHIFT

This kind of innovation initially connects, serves, and engages customers in distinctive ways, influencing their interactions with your enterprise and offerings. Focus first on types on the right side of the framework (Channel, Service, Brand, and Customer Engagement). Then move across to the left to add other types you need to make the experience work. Note: standards of customer experience have changed radically in recent decades; once customers get a taste of Zappos-level service, they tend to expect it — regardless of category or industry.

Starbucks created a global franchise by taking the principles of European coffee shops and applying them at scale. The goal: to provide retail environments that gave customers consistent service and product wherever they were in the world.

HOW TO CHOOSE THE RIGHT SHIFT

Examine the current center of gravity in the market or industry. Observe the way that current participants play, how that either fulfills or disappoints customers, and imagine how you could deliver a new promise. The heart of innovation is understanding when a broad shift is called for, and driving it forward with courage and conviction.

These issues are highly contextual and worthy of deep examination. It typically takes us at least a month of intense work to crack them — which makes solving them for you on a few pages virtually impossible. Still, these principles can suggest the right questions to ask to jump-start your analysis and help you hone your instincts.

❓

WHEN SHOULD YOU SHIFT TOWARD A NEW BUSINESS MODEL?

Great business models radically alter where value is created and how it is amplified. This shift is most successful when there are fewer opportunities to win by creating better offerings or experiences, and more opportunities by changing how you create and deliver them. Focusing on a new business model can succeed in any context, but we've seen it create particular value in asset-intensive industries such as automobiles and heavy manufacturing, in highly regulated industries such as health care and aerospace, in business-to-business contexts, and in commodities. But the paradoxical nature of digital economies — where unit costs drift toward zero even as the network value grows — also fosters exciting opportunities to use this shift in these contexts.

INDICATIONS FOR FOCUSING ON A NEW BUSINESS MODEL:

External

- Elements of the value you (or your competitors) provide are significantly under- or over-priced.[3]
- There is a significant group of customers that would love to use the primary offerings in a market, but can't afford them or rationalize their expense.
- There are few variations or experiments in processes, organizational structures, supply chains, and so on in an existing market — and also few collaborations between players.

Internal

- You see ways to change a market's generally accepted profit model in ways that will benefit its customers (and you).
- You see ways to structure your assets and/or do your work in surprising ways that will change the fundamental economics of a market.
- You understand your business system and offerings so well that you can offer reliability, flexibility, or guarantees that competitors won't be able to match.

3 A useful tool for understanding the value your offerings create for customers versus the prices charged is Economic Value Estimation, or EVE. Tom Nagle, John Hogan, and Joe Zale pioneered the approach and discuss it extensively in their book, *The Strategy and Tactics of Pricing* (the fifth edition of which was published by Prentice Hall, 2010).

?

WHEN SHOULD YOU SHIFT TOWARD A NEW PLATFORM?

Great platforms make it easy for customers to do hard things. Platform-driven innovations are most productive when customers struggle to do challenging tasks, and when you see fresh opportunities to help them by connecting previously disparate communities, capabilities, or offerings. The hyper-networked nature of digital technology has fostered many different platforms, from e-commerce solutions to social networks, but this approach can be harnessed by any industry. Consider focusing here first when you see a set of customers that is clearly finding it difficult to piece things together, and needs ways to reduce complexity, friction, or cognitive burden—especially if the solution involves orchestrating many firms together into a seamless network.

INDICATIONS FOR FOCUSING ON A NEW PLATFORM:

External

- Customers can't get the solutions they need without exerting considerable skill or effort to pull all of the pieces together (for instance, you see customers "hacking" products, or existing offerings are too complicated for many of them).
- There is a community or group with shared interests or needs but no central hub or forum that brings them together.
- There is broad demand for a particular set of capabilities or assets in a market, but it is too complex for customers or other players to develop.

Internal

- You see ways to extend, diversify, or expand your current offerings, or connect them in surprising ways.
- You see ways to take your signature assets or capabilities and enable customers and other players to access them.
- You see ways to co-opt your customers, competitors, and/or other players and put them to work for you.

?

WHEN SHOULD YOU SHIFT TOWARD A NEW CUSTOMER EXPERIENCE?

Great experiences are essential whenever a category has grown over-contested, stale, or too complicated. This shift is a good bet in contexts where you can build enduring relationships with customers, when they are hungry for better (or simply fresher) interactions, and particularly when the normal industry experience is a drag. This shift can prove vital when dealing with a highly networked customer base, where news of one good (or bad) experience can spread like wildfire. Still, Customer Experience–driven innovation can succeed in any industry—even in staid business-to-business contexts or government services, where becoming the easiest firm to work with can even overcome competitive gaps in price or quality.

INDICATIONS FOR FOCUSING ON A NEW CUSTOMER EXPERIENCE:

External

- Customers routinely complain about their buying or service experiences—or worse, they actually expect them to stink.
- There is a significant group of customers that ignores a market because its touchpoints lack personalization, wit, elegance, or other humanizing attributes.
- Most players focus on capturing customers by creating punitive switching barriers such as long contracts with termination penalties or technology lock-in such as proprietary and closed interfaces.

Internal

- You see ways to deliver a different buying experience to customers; one that is far more compelling, simple, or seamless than current market norms.
- You see ways to engage customers differently—appealing to their values, sense of self, and their connections with other customers and users.
- More broadly, you already excel at delivering customer experiences in one market and believe you can transplant that excellence to another context.

THE THREE LEVELS OF INNOVATION AMBITION

CHANGE THE KNOWN

FEWER TYPES

1

Think about any new idea across a spectrum of three different levels of ambition. Do you want to *change the known*, *change the boundaries*, or *change the game entirely?*[4]

CORE INNOVATION: CHANGE THE KNOWN

Inside any known category there are always ways to deliver new quality, utility, or delight to customers; doing so usually demands changing only one or two types of innovation. Established firms routinely develop improvements to keep their products fresh and competitive, a process designers describe as "*Find a problem and fix it!*" These core innovations can confer real advantage—though usually not for long, as competitors will typically copy or respond to them swiftly. This is why it's unusual for new market entrants to succeed with core innovations; they don't make enough difference and are quickly countered by incumbents. Focus here if you're already established in an industry or category and want to shake things up a bit—or to push yourself to experiment with one or two types that you and others don't generally use. This is most effective if you're already the category leader.

4 For a good study on managing a portfolio of initiatives across ambition levels, see "Managing Your Innovation Portfolio" by our colleagues, Geoff Tuff and Bansi Nagji, in the May 2012 issue of *Harvard Business Review*.

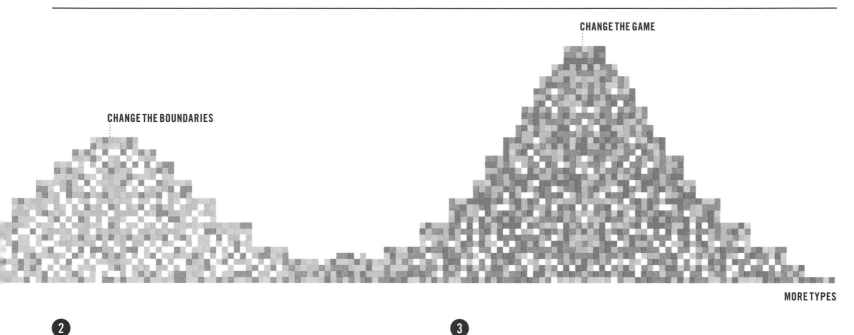

CHANGE THE GAME

CHANGE THE BOUNDARIES

MORE TYPES

2

ADJACENT INNOVATION: CHANGE THE BOUNDARIES

Interesting things start to happen when you *reframe* an offering compared to everyone else — usually by tackling a bigger challenge and delivering more comprehensive solutions for customers. This level of ambition usually brings new customers to a market and changes what all participants can expect from it. Adjacent innovation is bolder than core innovation, and so it typically demands three or four innovation types. Firms that successfully deliver such innovations often change the way they work — adapting their existing capabilities or developing entirely new ones. Naturally this makes adjacent innovations riskier than core innovations, but this also makes them tougher to copy. Adjacent innovations can generate years of advantage and force other players to respond to the new expectations you are setting. One reliable way to achieve this level of ambition is to broaden your promise compared to others — for example, the way Method designed household cleaners to address consumers' concerns about aesthetics and the environment, not just cleaning effectiveness.

3

TRANSFORMATIONAL INNOVATION: CHANGE THE GAME

On rare occasions you may choose to challenge and change everything. Expect this ambition to radically alter your entire industry structure. It will demand five or more types of innovation, orchestrated with care, to produce entire new businesses (as opposed to only new offerings). Transformational innovations erase the boundaries between once-distinct markets and irrevocably change what is expected from competitors and consumers alike. As the name suggests, these innovations change the rules for all involved — and this doesn't occur often. Yet every firm should have at least one or two transformational innovations lined up, and actively imagine them as either offensive or defensive options. The riskiest form of innovation, this will demand the deepest thought and the most commitment. Conversely, it will generate the highest return.

HOW TO CHOOSE THE RIGHT LEVEL OF AMBITION

Pay attention to what's happening now. For any given industry there is already a background rate of change. Is the rhythm slow and predictable, or crisp and sometimes abrupt? How much change do customers expect and what can they absorb? Are you moving fast enough to stay relevant to them? Consider competitors: do you need to accelerate the rate of change to throw them off balance?

Much like choosing the right shift, context is everything when it comes to setting ambition. The basic principle: when you make a novel and unpredictable shift, you can initially get by with a lower level of ambition, and you may only need to use a few (surprising) types of innovation. Here are some broad principles to help you get started.

❓

WHEN SHOULD YOU CHANGE THE KNOWN AND PURSUE CORE INNOVATION?

Every firm must steadily change the known. It drives organic growth and helps you keep pace with competitors, or set a pace for them. For complex industries, doing this with exquisite discipline may be the heart of a great innovation strategy — for example, as Toyota did for years with its Toyota Production System, which is designed to produce at least a million advances a year in making cars and trucks. If you're an entrepreneur or trying to enter a new market, core innovation is unlikely to help you secure a beachhead; either look to a higher level of ambition, or be ready to add additional types to your initial foray quickly.

INDICATIONS FOR CORE INNOVATION:

External

- You already have strong offerings in the market that are driving good growth, and you can continue to build on their strength and source of advantage.
- Most of your competitors are focusing on Product Performance–driven innovation, and you see an opportunity to use other types.
- A market is suffering from a general lack of innovation — but also has high barriers to new entrants (such as capital requirements or regulatory complexity) that limit the threat of disruption.

Internal

- You need to generate money quickly — and can accept a relatively modest return from an initiative.
- Your firm has assets or capabilities already in place that you can use to drive additional advantage in your current markets.
- The appetite for risk in your organization is currently low, and/or you are ill-equipped to take on more innovation complexity (for instance, there is a dominant focus on execution or rigid siloes in place between functions or units).

❓

WHEN SHOULD YOU CHANGE THE BOUNDARIES AND PURSUE ADJACENT INNOVATION?

Adjacent innovation is key in two situations: when you need to drive new growth from your current assets and capabilities, or when you need to change the dynamics in your current markets. Watch for an opportunity to apply an existing capability to a new market (for instance, using medical imaging technology for airport security). Or notice when there's a way to serve customers in an expansive way (say, by adding service offerings to your existing product lines). Trying to make a splash and really get noticed? This is likely the lowest level of ambition that will help you to do so.

INDICATIONS FOR ADJACENT INNOVATION:

External

- Your existing offerings are generating less growth; they face increased competitive pressure, or you see ways to use them to attract new customers.
- Most of your competitors are using types beyond Product Performance with some care and consistency, but they rarely integrate more than one or two types.
- A market is growing stale—either it is no longer generating the returns you need, or you see a chance to shift the way you do business and change the tablestakes for competitors.

Internal

- You need an initiative to generate significantly more growth than more modest innovation efforts—and you can give it reasonable time to generate returns.
- Your firm has assets and capabilities that can be applied in new ways to create new advantage—either by repurposing them or investing in them to add flexibility, utility, or new complements.
- Your organization is willing to take on more risk and consider opportunities that will take it into new realms or require it to play differently in its current markets.

❓

WHEN SHOULD YOU CHANGE THE GAME AND PURSUE TRANSFORMATIONAL INNOVATION?

Every firm should practice imagining innovations that will change everything. This is simply good discipline and, like scenario-based planning, will help you imagine new options that can shift customer expectations and competitor actions. Move from merely imagining them to launching them when you see an opportunity to create an entirely new market or to play guerrilla warfare and throw much more powerful firms off balance. Transformational innovators disrupt markets because they play by entirely different rules and use entirely different capabilities and assets from the norm. The flipside matters too: transformational innovation carries the greatest risk and demands the most commitment to succeed.

INDICATIONS FOR TRANSFORMATIONAL INNOVATION:

External

- You need to increase the growth driven by your current offerings dramatically— and realize you need to fundamentally change them to deliver that growth.
- Competitors are taking increasingly bold actions that demand response—or you see a way to alter the structure of a market fundamentally (for instance, by redefining its customers or the assets and capabilities needed to serve them).
- A market is stagnant, barriers to entry are plummeting, and its boundaries are blurring and eroding—increasing the threat of disruption.

Internal

- You have enough time available to allow this initiative to mature and generate outsize returns—and you need to generate radical new growth.
- You are prepared to rethink and reconfigure the assets and capabilities you have today, as well as invest in developing or acquiring completely new ones.
- Your organization is willing to take on substantial risk and consider entirely new options and opportunities that reframe both who you serve and how you serve them.

```
forName(String name, boolean        modifiers)) {                    return new EnclosingMethodIn    }              return name;          ma.length(); i++) {
initialize,                       Class caller = Reflection.        fo(enclosingInfo);             }                                add(ma.get(i));
loader)
    throw
    if (l
      Se
getSecurit
    if
ClassLoade

GET _ CLASS

      }
    }
    retur
initialize
    }

    public T
      throw
IllegalAcc
    {
    if (S'
!= null) {
      ch
PUBLIC, Cl
getCallerC

    retur
    }

    private
      throw
IllegalAcc
    {
    if (c
null) {
      if

IllegalAcc

newInstanc
lang.Class'

    }
    tr

= getConst
DECLARED);

AccessCont

Privileged

run() {

c.setAcces
```

LEARNING FROM OBJECT-ORIENTED PROGRAMMING

Now and then industries change fundamentally. This doesn't occur often and is usually the result of some profound technological disruption. As an illustration, only a person born before 1970 will remember life prior to the impact of personal computers. For children born later, that time before the digital era seems quaint and vaguely ancient. One consequence of such epochal change: virtually all players are affected downstream in a massive cascade.

Consider some long wave innovation exemplars. Replace horses with autocars and you inadvertently invent auto dealers, service stations, drive-in movie theaters or restaurants, toll roads, and (over enough time) most of life in the suburbs. Create airplanes and you eventually get surprises like families that live far apart or overnight package delivery services. Develop medical imaging (x-rays, CT scans, MRI scans) and you invariably usher in new ways of diagnosing and treating patients. Design great shipping ports plus cargo ships and you create the basic engine of globalization. Seeing these long waves is hard but valuable, and the people who see such big shifts a little sooner or a little more clearly than others often become the pioneers of valuable new fields.

In the 1960s it started to become clear that the newfangled devices called computers might be important. Even in the earliest days of the digital revolution it was obvious that the limits to growth would come not just from processing speed but also from software development. This turned out to be prophetic. Invariably, the tasks that people want computers to tackle grow in complexity and sophistication, and the code needed to do the work gets bloated and nearly impossible to manage. Few people realize that today's high-end automobiles routinely have 10 to 12 times the computer processing power of a first generation IBM PC, and depend on millions of lines of code to operate. Developing such systems takes substantial time, money, and requires teams with specialized knowledge.

One of the few clichés about innovation that's actually true is the one that says necessity is the mother of invention. In the early days of the digital revolution, technology pioneer Alan Kay, working at the time on the ARPA project at the University of Utah, thought about the software challenge and helped to pioneer object-oriented programming (OOP). This revolutionary new approach had one key insight at its core: building a programming language around the idea

```
      } c                                              public java.net.URL           c.getName();                    }                          }
(NoSuchMethodException e) {       private native Object[]       getResource(String name) {         int index = baseName.                                    }
      throw new InstantiationEx   getEnclosingMethod0();          name = resolveName(name);     lastIndexOf('.');          void addAll(Method[] ma) {    if (newPos != method
ception(getName());                                               ClassLoader cl =                   if (index != -1) {       for (int i = 0; i < ma.length;  length) {
                                  private EnclosingMethodInfo     getClassLoader0();                 name = baseName.         i++) {                          methods = Arrays.
      }                           getEnclosingMethodInfo() {         if (cl==null) {            substring(0, index).replace('.', '/')      add(ma[i]);         copyOf(methods, newPos);
    Constructor<T> tmpConstructor  getEnclosingMethod0();         Object[] enclosingInfo =           // A system class.        +"/"+name;
= cachedConstructor;
```

Your Code Has Bugs

It might be difficult to imagine, but computers predated integrated circuits. In the earliest days of honking big, room-sized computers like the ENIAC, all the hard work was done by vacuum tubes arranged in massive arrays. They were warm. They glowed with light. They attracted moths. They led to the wonderful, perhaps apocryphal story of computer scientist Grace Hopper reporting an "actual case of bug" in the machine, coining a term now commonly used for software errors. Let's see if we can debug innovation.

5   Java is one of many modern languages that depend on and advance the original ideas of object-oriented programming. Today over 4 billion devices in active use depend on Java code. If you had to develop custom code for each of those types of machines the progress of modern life would slow to a crawl.

of *reusable modules.*[5] With OOP, objects are data, files, and other common computing elements, described distinctly. Then, other related objects can be swiftly created, identified, or managed by the system. Most tasks can be described as methods or subroutines and made efficient, repeatable, and easily managed without lots of buggy code that needs to be custom developed for every new task.

The modularity of object-oriented computing revolutionized the computer industry. Similar advances can now be at the center of a twenty-first century innovation revolution. Just as with OOP, this system democratizes the field, making it easier for the average team to innovate reliably and robustly, and dramatically lowering the cost and risk of bold innovation.

HERE'S WHAT WE HAVE DONE:

Using the Ten Types of Innovation analytically, we have specifically identified more than 100 generic innovation tactics—modular ways to achieve each type of innovation (these are our objects).

Next, we found ways to arrange these tactics in sophisticated combinations that are robust enough to build integrated innovations (these are our subroutines). Put together, these are plays in a breakthrough innovation playbook.

We'll use these plays to illustrate how innovation can be driven by using smart tactics in surprising combinations. We will deconstruct some archetypal examples showing how they work, and reveal how you can construct a similar breakthrough of your own. The list is illustrative, not exhaustive, but you may find that one or two of them will inspire your own work.

Our goal is basic but vital: *we are trying to make it easier to help teams reliably build bold breakthroughs*.

CHAPTER 19
INNOVATION TACTICS
A TOOLKIT THAT TURNS THE TEN TYPES
INTO BUILDING BLOCKS FOR INNOVATION

We discovered the Ten Types of Innovation by empirically analyzing great innovations to determine the properties they shared. Recently, we took on another piece of analysis to deepen this discovery. Our basic analytical question: *"which reliable, generic techniques exist for each of the Ten Types?"*

We call these Innovation Tactics. There are over 100 discrete ones[1] that we have analyzed and codified. Just as the Ten Types are not new, neither are these tactics. Many have existed for decades or even centuries, such as publications using subscriptions as their Profit Model. For each we have defined a sense of their uses and limitations. This gives them a pragmatism that stems from simple recombination, like atoms that make molecules, Lego building bricks that make whatever you want, or reusable objects that make robust digital programs. Take these discrete building blocks of innovation, then recombine them to create bold breakthroughs.

This is valuable precisely because it is not mere copying. When you combine multiple tactics in fresh ways, you produce new constructs—without taking on vast amounts of risk that the new idea can't be built. Most successful innovations are not brand new inventions, but rather they integrate many disparate and distributed known ideas into something that feels new and noteworthy. Netflix, for example, used a subscription model to upend the video rental industry. Zipcar used a bunch of smart tactics, no one of them unprecedented, to create an approach to renting cars that was altogether fresh.

We think these *combinations of tactics* are a big deal. As you discern the tactics and underlying structure that went into creating any particularly great innovation, you'll also start seeing themes that echo across many others. Themes and variations are nothing new, of course. They lie at the heart of what people love about music, poetry, and art. Now we are discovering that they may also live at the heart of newsworthy innovations. Individual tactics should give you the confidence to know that if you promise something that is hard to execute, there is a robust way of delivering it. Combinations of tactics—entire innovation plays—can give you the courage to transform any staid market boldly, with some sense of how to bring together all the pieces needed into some coherent new whole.

Think of this as orchestration rather than invention. Now let's see what it takes to make you a maestro…

1 When we first did this analysis we found 104 discrete tactics. A year later, as we write this, the number had grown to 112. New ones come along regularly but not swiftly. Rest assured we are pretty obsessive-compulsive about tracking them. So the collection is always current at tentypesofinnovation.com.

INNOVATION TACTICS

Here are all the Tactics we have defined to date, organized according to the Types. We are constantly on the lookout for new ones. If you can think of others we should feature, drop us a line at tentypes@doblin.com.

PROFIT MODEL

Ad-Supported
Provide content or services for free to one party while selling listeners, viewers, or "eyeballs" to another party.

Auction
Allow a market—and its users—to set the price for goods and services.

Bundled Pricing
Sell in a single transaction two or more items that could be sold as standalone offerings.

Cost Leadership
Keep variable costs low and sell high volumes at low prices.

Disaggregated Pricing
Allow customers to buy exactly—and only—what they want.

Financing
Capture revenue not from the direct sale of a product but from structured payment plans and after-sale interest.

Flexible Pricing
Vary prices for an offering based on demand.

Float
Receive payment prior to building the offering; earn interest on that money prior to delivering the goods.

Forced Scarcity
Limit the supply of offerings available, by quantity, time frame, or access, to drive up demand and/or prices.

Freemium
Offer basic services for free while charging a premium for advanced or special features.

Installed Base
Offer a "core" product for slim margins (or even a loss) to drive demand and loyalty; then realize profit on additional products and services.

Licensing
Grant permission to a group or individual to use your offering in a defined way for a specified payment.

Membership
Charge a time-based payment to allow access to locations, offerings, or services that non-members don't have.

Metered Use
Allow customers to pay only for what they use.

Microtransactions
Sell many items for as little as a dollar—or even only one cent—to drive impulse purchases.

Premium
Price at a higher margin than competitors, usually for a superior product, offering, experience, service, or brand.

Risk Sharing
Waive standard fees or costs if certain metrics aren't achieved, but receive outsize gains when they are.

Scaled Transactions
Maximize margins by pursuing high-volume, large-scale transactions when unit costs are relatively fixed.

Subscription
Create predictable cash flows by charging customers upfront (a one time or recurring fee) to have access to the product or service over time.

Switchboard
Connect multiple sellers with multiple buyers. The more buyers and sellers who join, the more valuable the switchboard becomes.

User-Defined
Invite customers to set the price they wish to pay.

NETWORK

Alliances
Share risks and revenues to jointly improve individual competitive advantage.

Collaboration
Partner with others for mutual benefit.

Complementary Partnering
Leverage assets by sharing them with companies that serve similar markets but offer different products and services.

Consolidation
Acquire multiple companies in the same market or complementary markets.

Coopetition
Join forces with someone who would normally be your competitor to achieve a common goal.

Franchising
License business principles, processes, and brand to paying partners.

Merger/Acquisition
Combine two or more entities to gain access to capabilities and assets.

Open Innovation
Obtain access to processes or patents from other companies to leverage, extend, and build on expertise, and/or do the same with internal IP and processes.

Secondary Markets
Connect waste streams, by-products, or other alternative offerings with those who want them.

Supply Chain Integration
Coordinate and integrate information and/or processes across a company or different parts of the value chain.

STRUCTURE

Asset Standardization
Reduce operating costs and increase connectivity and modularity by standardizing your assets.

Competency Center
Cluster resources, practices, and expertise into centers that support functions across the organization to increase efficiency and effectiveness.

Corporate University
Provide job-specific or company-specific training for managers.

Decentralized Management
Devolve decision-making governance closer to the people or business interfaces.

Incentive Systems
Offer rewards (financial or non-financial) to provide motivation for a particular course of action.

IT Integration
Integrate technology resources and applications.

Knowledge Management
Share relevant information internally to reduce redundancy and improve job performance.

Organizational Design
Make form follow function and align infrastructure with core qualities and business processes.

Outsourcing
Assign to a vendor responsibility for developing or maintaining a system.

PROCESS

Crowdsourcing
Outsource repetitive or challenging work to a large group of semi-organized individuals.

Flexible Manufacturing
Use a production system that can rapidly react to changes and still operate efficiently.

Intellectual Property
Use a proprietary process to commercialize ideas in ways that others cannot copy.

Lean Production
Reduce waste and cost in your manufacturing process and other operations.

Localization
Adapt an offering, process, or experience to target a specific culture or region.

Logistics Systems
Manage the flow of goods, information, and other resources between the point of origin and the point of use.

On-Demand Production
Produce items after an order has been received to avoid carrying costs of inventory.

Predictive Analytics
Model past performance data and predict future outcomes to design and price offerings accordingly.

Process Automation
Apply tools and infrastructure to manage routine activities in order to free up employees for other tasks.

Process Efficiency
Create or produce more while using less in terms of materials, energy consumption, or time.

Process Standardization
Use common products, procedures, and policies to reduce complexity, costs, and errors.

Strategic Design
Employ a purposeful approach that manifests itself consistently across offerings, brands, and experiences.

User-Generated
Put your users to work in creating and curating the content that powers your offerings.

PRODUCT PERFORMANCE

Added Functionality
Add new capabilities to an existing offering.

Conservation
Design your product so that end users can reduce their use of energy or materials.

Customization
Enable altering to suit individual requirements or specifications.

Ease of Use
Make your product simple, intuitive, and comfortable to use.

Engaging Functionality
Provide an unexpected or newsworthy feature that elevates the customer interaction from the ordinary.

Environmental Sensitivity
Create offerings that do no harm—or relatively less harm—to the environment.

Feature Aggregation
Combine a number of existing features from disparate sources into a single offering.

Focus
Design a product or service for a particular audience.

Performance Simplification
Omit superfluous details, features, and interactions to reduce complexity.

Safety
Increase the customer's level of confidence and security.

Styling
Impart a noteworthy style, fashion, or image to create a product that customers covet.

Superior Product
Develop an offering of exceptional design, quality, and/or experience.

PRODUCT SYSTEM

Complements
Sell additional related or peripheral products or services to a customer.

Extensions/Plug-ins
Allow additions from internal or third-party resources that add functionality.

Integrated Offering
Combine otherwise discrete components into a complete experience.

Modular Systems
Provide a set of individual components that can be used independently, but gain utility when combined.

Product Bundling
Put together several products for sale as one combined offering.

Product/Service Platforms
Develop systems that connect with other partner products and services to create a holistic offering.

SERVICE

Added Value
Include an additional service or function as part of the base price.

Concierge
Provide premium service by taking on tasks for which customers don't have time.

Guarantee
Remove customer risk of lost money or time from product failure or purchase error.

Lease or Loan
Let customers pay over time to lower their upfront costs.

Loyalty Programs
Provide benefits and/or discounts to frequent and high-value customers.

Personalized Service
Use the customer's own information to provide perfectly calibrated service.

Self-Service
Provide users with control over activities that would otherwise require an intermediary to complete.

Superior Service
Provide service(s) of higher quality, efficacy, or which offer(s) a better experience than any competitor.

Supplementary Service
Offer ancillary services that fit with your offering.

Total Experience Management
Provide thoughtful, holistic management of the consumer experience across an offering's lifecycle.

Try Before You Buy
Let customers test and experience an offering before investing in it.

User Communities/Support Systems
Provide a communal resource for product and service support, use, and extension.

CHANNEL

Context Specific
Offer timely access to offerings that are appropriate for a specific location, occasion, or situation.

Cross-Selling
Offer appealing additional products, services, or information that will enhance an experience in situations where customers are likely to want to buy them.

Diversification
Add and expand into new or different channels.

Experience Center
Create space that encourages your customers to interact with your offerings—but purchase them through a different (and often lower cost) channel.

Flagship Store
Create a retail outlet to showcase quintessential brand and product attributes.

Go Direct
Skip traditional retail channels and connect directly with customers.

Indirect Distribution
Use others as resellers who take responsibility for delivering an offering to the final user.

Multi-Level Marketing
Sell bulk or packaged goods to an affiliated but independent sales force that turns around and sells it for you.

Non-Traditional Channels
Employ novel and relevant avenues to reach and service customers.

On-Demand
Deliver goods in real-time whenever or wherever they are desired.

Pop-Up Presence
Create a noteworthy but temporary environment to showcase and/or sell offerings.

BRAND

Brand Extension
Offer a new product or service under the umbrella of an existing brand.

Brand Leverage
Allow others to use your brand name to lend them your credibility and extend your company's reach.

Certification
Develop a brand or mark that signifies and ensures certain desirable characteristics in third-party offerings.

Co-Branding
Combine brands to mutually reinforce key attributes or enhance the credibility of an offering.

Component Branding
Brand a discrete piece of the offering to make the whole appear more valuable.

Private Label
Provide goods made by others packaged under your company's brand.

Transparency
Let customers see into your operations and participate with your brand and offerings.

Values Alignment
Make your brand stand for a big idea or a set of values and express them consistently in all aspects of your company.

CUSTOMER ENGAGEMENT

Autonomy and Authority
Grant users the power to shape their own experience.

Community and Belonging
Facilitate visceral connections to make people feel they are part of a group or movement.

Curation
Create a distinct point of view to build a strong identity for yourself and give your followers exactly what they want.

Experience Automation
Remove the burden of repetitive tasks from users to simplify their lives and make new experiences seem magical.

Experience Enabling
Extend the realm of what's possible to offer a previously improbable experience.

Experience Simplification
Reduce complexity and focus on delivering specific experiences exceptionally well.

Mastery
Help customers to obtain great skill or deep knowledge of some activity or subject.

Personalization
Alter a standard offering to allow the projection of the customer's identity.

Status and Recognition
Offer cues that confer meaning, allowing users—and those who interact with them—to develop and nurture aspects of their identity.

Whimsy and Personality
Humanize your offering with small flourishes of on-brand, on-message ways of seeming alive.

HOW TO USE THE INNOVATION TACTICS

THREE WAYS OF ENGAGING WITH INNOVATION TACTICS

The tactics can be used to build an innovation concept from scratch, or to enrich and amplify an existing idea or business. Ask yourself these questions to clarify where you are today—and to spark ideas about where innovation might take you tomorrow.

What innovation shift are you pursuing?

Is the shift Business Model-driven, Platform-driven, or Customer Experience-driven? The answer will help you understand which tactics to focus on using first. If you're pursuing Business Model–driven innovation, focus on Configuration tactics first—new profit models, networks, structures, and processes—and then work your way over to the right of the framework. Conversely, if you're pursuing Customer Experience–driven innovation, focus on the Experience tactics first—new ways of engaging customers, new brands, channels, and service experiences—and then work your way to the left.

What is your initiative's ambition level?

Are you looking to change the known, the boundaries, or the entire game? Your ambition level will help you understand how many tactics you should consider using. If you're pursuing core innovation, one or two tactics—particularly if they are different from those used by competitors—may be sufficient. Conversely, if you're pursuing transformational innovation, you'll probably need at least five distinct tactics integrated with care.

1

ANCHOR AND EXTEND

Select an "innovation anchor" around which you will build your concept or business. This should lie at the core of the value you deliver to customers and how you beat competitors. It could be one of the Ten Types, or a specific tactic within a type. From there, consider which other types and tactics are required to make your concept work—and which additional ones could help support and amplify its impact.

2

ADD AND SUBSTITUTE

Define the tactics that you're already using in your current concept or business. Then poke around. First try adding tactics from other innovation Types that you aren't using today. Next, try substituting tactics—swapping out ones that you're already using and replacing them with those that might improve your operating economics or your customers' satisfaction. Be bold. Try many new possibilities.

3

ARRAY AT RANDOM

Pick three to six tactics randomly. Challenge yourself to imagine new businesses and offerings that would use them. This particular approach prompted us to craft a special version of the tactics as a deck of cards. It really can be fun to take a team, deal them a poker hand of innovation, and see what they do to build a business around the tactics they are dealt.[2]

2   People always ask us if they
    can get a set of cards. Ping
    us at tentypes@doblin.com
    and we'll try to help.

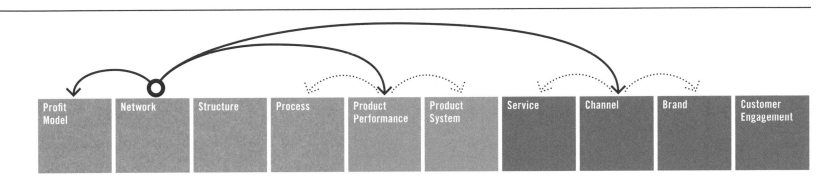

TACTICS IN USE: EXISTING OFFERING

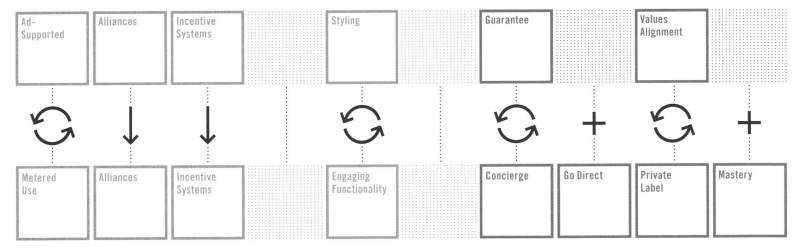

TACTICS IN USE: NEW OPTION

CHAPTER 20
USING THE INNOVATION PLAYBOOK

A SELECTION OF PLAYS (AND THE COMBINATION OF TACTICS YOU'LL NEED TO IMPLEMENT THEM)

Innovating with discipline demands a sense of what you're doing and why. Remember the two critical innovation questions: **"How ambitious do we need to be?"** and **"How can we innovate differently?"** Now you're ready to combine specific types and tactics to fuel your mission. While selecting a random array of them is one approach, it helps to examine similar solutions to the one you're trying to build.

Thinking this way is similar to what great professional teams and coaches do all the time. Athletes drill *plays* over and over—until they can execute each one flawlessly. Coaches read situations in the heat of the game—to select the right play at any given moment from a full team *playbook*.

CALLING THIS PLAY

COLLABORATIVE CONSUMPTION
Leverage connectivity to upend traditional forms of ownership and change the way customers relate to your goods and services.

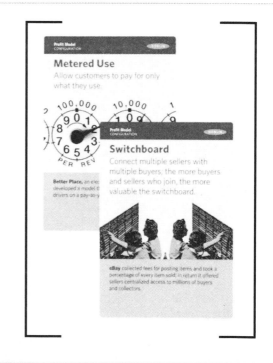

HAD RESULTS LIKE THIS:

❶
.... **ZIPCAR**
US-based car rental by the hour. Competitors also taking this approach include Autolib', Daimler's Car2Go, and BMW's DriveNow.

❷
.... **VÉLIB'**
Large-scale bike-sharing system based in Paris, France. Similar systems operate in locations such as Hangzhou, China, and Washington DC.

❸
AIRBNB
Peer-to-peer room and home rental service. Other firms using a similar formula include MetroFlats and VRBO.

❹
.... **CHEGG**
College textbook rental service in the US. RentTheRunway is a similar offering for fashion, while Japan-based ToyLib rents toys.

❺
.... **MOVIRTU**
Mobile phone-sharing plan for developing countries that allows large groups of individuals to share a single phone.

...and more.

Process Automation
Apply tools and infrastructure to manage routine activities in order to free up employees.

Zipcar developed its "Fast Fleet" system to track usage patterns, gather customer usage of vehicles, and alert fleet managers of car issues. The data is critical to keeping Zipcar's system balanced and functioning effectively.

Safety
Increase the customer confidence and secu...

Volvo's vehicles included pione... to keep passengers safer than t... in other vehicles.

Service
EXPERIENCE

User Communities/ Support Systems
Provide a communal resource for product/service support, use and extension.

Brand
EXPERIENCE

Values Alignment
Make your brand stand for a big idea or a set of values and express them consistently in all aspects of your company.

Method designed a countertop-worthy line of eco-friendly home care products that eschewed harmful chemicals, ugly design, and invited customers to join its "People Against Dirty" community.

PLAYS THAT BUILD A DEEP GAMEPLAN

These sophisticated innovations are distilled from many industries. By breaking them apart to see the core tactics at work, it is possible to see that the underlying combination can be easily adapted, evolved, and reused. Next, we deconstruct some classic examples of each play in action and show surprising configurations of the tactics at work. We clarify what shift and what level of ambition is being used each time. We don't detail every tactic that's involved. Instead, we focus on those that are at the heart of each play. Use these to help construct similar breakthroughs of your own.

Learning again from sports teams, we expect great firms will be skilled at choosing specific plays in different situations—varying them over time to build a winning overall gameplan. This constantly keeps competitors guessing and off balance.

BUSINESS MODEL-DRIVEN

OPEN INVITATION
Encourage other people to work with you, whether they're individual experts or strangers in the crowd.

Tactics at Work
[OPEN INNOVATION or CROWDSOURCING] + COMPETENCY CENTER

COLLABORATIVE CONSUMPTION
Leverage connectivity to upend traditional forms of ownership and change the way customers relate to your goods and services.

Tactics at Work
[METERED USE or SWITCHBOARD] + PROCESS AUTOMATION + [SAFETY or USER COMMUNITIES/SUPPORT SYSTEMS or VALUES ALIGNMENT]

FREE-BASED
Give away basic offerings for free to attract many users and then make money off of them in multiple ways.

Tactics at Work
FREEMIUM + ENGAGING FUNCTIONALITY + [MICROTRANSACTIONS or MEMBERSHIP or AD-SUPPORTED or SWITCHBOARD]

RADICAL OPTIMIZATION
Move beyond standard operational efficiencies to make it painful for other firms to compete with you.

Tactics at Work
IT INTEGRATION + PROCESS AUTOMATION + PROCESS STANDARDIZATION + GUARANTEE

PREDICTIVE BUSINESS
Mine data to model behaviors and breakdowns, allowing you to make promises, predict outcomes, and drive efficiencies for customers.

Tactics at Work
[RISK SHARING or METERED USE] + PREDICTIVE ANALYTICS + PRODUCT BUNDLING + GUARANTEE

PLATFORM-DRIVEN

FRANCHISE
Develop signature offerings and experiences that you—and others—use to develop ecosystems of extensions.

Tactics at Work
SUPERIOR PRODUCT + COMPLEMENTS + BRAND EXTENSION

EXCHANGE
Establish hubs of activity and commerce for any given resource, interest, market, or industry.

Tactics at Work
SWITCHBOARD + USER GENERATED + USER COMMUNITIES/SUPPORT SYSTEMS

COLLABORATIVE CREATION
Connect communities with canvases and toolkits that encourage them to create offerings for you.

Tactics at Work
CROWDSOURCING + PROCESS AUTOMATION + USER COMMUNITIES/SUPPORT SYSTEMS + [VALUES ALIGNMENT or STATUS AND RECOGNITION]

COMPETENCY-DRIVEN PLATFORM
Open up key assets and capabilities and let others use them to power their own businesses.

Tactics at Work
COMPLEMENTARY PARTNERING + INTELLECTUAL PROPERTY + SUPERIOR PRODUCT + DIVERSIFICATION

EXPERIENCE ECOSYSTEM
Build a seamless system of products, services, and extensions that interoperate and connect in consistently elegant and beguiling ways.

Tactics at Work
LICENSING + ALLIANCES + STRATEGIC DESIGN + PERFORMANCE SIMPLIFICATION + PRODUCT/SERVICE PLATFORMS + GO DIRECT

CUSTOMER EXPERIENCE-DRIVEN

STATUS-BASED
Use subtle or explicit cues to confer status to your customers—creating elite groups that engage rabidly with your products and services.

Tactics at Work
LOYALTY PROGRAMS + PERSONALIZATION + STATUS AND RECOGNITION

IMMERSION
Create environments that captivate and mesmerize customers, fostering new levels of engagement and commitment.

Tactics at Work
STRATEGIC DESIGN + FLAGSHIP STORE + EXPERIENCE ENABLING

CONNECTED COMMUNITY
Leverage the power of social ties to deepen experiences and encourage consumers to share common interests, activities, and the offerings that support them.

Tactics at Work
FOCUS + USER COMMUNITIES/SUPPORT SYSTEMS + VALUES ALIGNMENT + COMMUNITY AND BELONGING

VALUES-BASED
Make your products stand for something and foster a movement—focusing on a particular constituency, cause, or reason for existing.

Tactics at Work
FOCUS + TRANSPARENCY + VALUES ALIGNMENT + WHIMSY AND PERSONALITY

SIMPLIFICATION
Radically ease the complicated, nagging, or arcane for customers—allowing them to accomplish things they simply couldn't have done before.

Tactics at Work
EASE OF USE + ENGAGING FUNCTIONALITY + EXPERIENCE SIMPLIFICATION + WHIMSY AND PERSONALITY

INNOVATION PLAY
OPEN INVITATION

THE PLAY AT WORK
GLAXOSMITHKLINE CONSUMER HEALTHCARE

Shift:
BUSINESS MODEL

Ambition:
CHANGE THE KNOWN

Industry:
OVER-THE-COUNTER DRUGS AND COSMETICS

ENCOURAGE OTHER PEOPLE TO WORK WITH YOU, WHETHER THEY'RE INDIVIDUAL EXPERTS OR STRANGERS IN THE CROWD.

Open innovation methods and approaches have become prevalent over the last decade for a simple reason—*All of us are smarter than any of us.* We believe open innovation is fundamental to innovation effectiveness today. The Open Invitation play takes it a step further by hard-coding open innovation into how the enterprise does business on an ongoing basis.

GlaxoSmithKline's Consumer Healthcare executives understand they can't do everything on their own. As such, they have cultivated a number of outside partners with which the company's scientists work to collaborate on new ideas and share the risk of development. GSK has various systems and infrastructure that invite external scientists to collaborate with its global brands to develop new ideas and new products. A full 50% of its product pipeline is now open to influence from outside technology and capabilities.[1]

1 This figure was cited in an interview with then-director of open innovation at GSK Consumer Healthcare, Helene Rutledge: http://tentyp.es/QZSGOK.

2 Rutledge on the toothpaste as classic Open Innovation: "Technology was borrowed from an adjacent category where there is deep expertise, the product was developed using externally sourced experts, and the final product was successful beyond original expectations."

3 "P&G Asks: What's the Big Idea?" by Jena McGregor, *BusinessWeek*, May 4, 2007: http://tentyp.es/XcReMZ.

ANOTHER BUSINESS USING THE OPEN INVITATION PLAY
PROCTER & GAMBLE

"Once seen as insular, the consumer products giant is now famous for its open approach to innovation," wrote Jena McGregor in *BusinessWeek* in 2007.[3] She was writing about P&G's "Connect + Develop" program, which started as a growth initiative within the company and was still applied philosophy in 2013. It involves collaborations with outsiders to develop new offerings, such as working with a candlemaker to create Febreze Candles or developing the skin cream Olay Regenerist with a French cosmetics company (Open Innovation). P&G has groups of multi-disciplinary teams (Competency Center) and, as McGregor noted, also has a process for attracting, working with, and rewarding collaborators (Crowdsourcing).

Tactics:

Network		Structure		Process
OPEN INNOVATION	+	**COMPETENCY CENTER**	+	**CROWDSOURCING**
Obtain access to processes or patents from other companies to leverage, extend, and build on expertise and/or do the same with internal IP and processes.		*Cluster resources, practices, and expertise into centers that support functions across the organization to increase efficiency and effectiveness.*		*Outsource repetitive or challenging work to a large group of semi-organized individuals.*

GSK works with independent scientists and research firms to identify, access, and develop key technologies for use in its consumer healthcare products—for example, the foaming technology used in its Aquafresh Isoactive toothpaste, the result of a collaboration with four separate partners.[2]

GSK Consumer Healthcare has global, brand-focused innovation hubs, where innovation associates, R&D scientists, marketing experts, and sales staff are located in open-space work environments that facilitate open discussion and foster creativity. "If you're a packaging designer and you're sitting across from a clinician, you don't need to schedule a meeting to share ideas—which could take a month," explained Robert Wolf of GSK. "You just lean over and start talking. And these informal interactions spark creative energy."

GSK's open innovation portal, dubbed "Innovation at GSK," allows external parties to search for the company's technology and product needs, and offer ideas for collaboration. Projects are developed using a signature Innovation Pathway—a 24-month process of development that is guided by an open innovation manager and liaison team to shepherd the process.

INNOVATION PLAY
COLLABORATIVE CONSUMPTION

Shift:
BUSINESS MODEL

Ambition:
CHANGE THE BOUNDARIES

Industry:
RENTAL CARS

4 This was prompted by an early, painful, and public lesson for Airbnb when a person's apartment was trashed and robbed by a renter.

LEVERAGE CONNECTIVITY TO UPEND TRADITIONAL FORMS OF OWNERSHIP AND CHANGE THE WAY CUSTOMERS RELATE TO YOUR GOODS AND SERVICES.

The term "collaborative consumption" has been in use since the 1970s but has really risen to prominence in more recent years, having blossomed into a global movement to reduce waste and think about the greater and more common good. In an era of increasing scarcity, population density, and connectivity, we expect to see more and more enterprises use this particular play.

Founded by two friends who wondered aloud how they might bring the European idea of car-sharing to Cambridge, Massachusetts (and beyond), Zipcar has truly taken off since its beginnings in 2000. Indeed, the company confounded almost all of the norms of the traditional rental car industry. Its cars could be rented by the hour instead of only by the day. It didn't oversee either lots or attendants; instead, "Zipcars," as its rentals were known, were distributed in garages throughout cities, while a swipe of the "Zipcard" unlocked the vehicle. Instead of targeting traditional business renters, Zipcar was aimed at people who didn't need a car full-time (or who didn't want the hassle of owning one). Zipcar not only rethought how to offer rental cars—it fundamentally reimagined what that industry could be.

ANOTHER BUSINESS USING THE COLLABORATIVE CONSUMPTION PLAY
AIRBNB
Airbnb provided an alternative to hotels by connecting travelers with spare rooms (Switchboard). This helped hosts earn money and helped travelers find unique accommodations—all with a smaller ecological footprint than most hotel rooms. The site offered handy tools to help owners create listings and set parameters around who can rent the room (Process Automation). Airbnb served as a clearinghouse, withholding payment for 24 hours after travelers check in—so they had recourse if the room didn't live up to the ad. It also offered up to $1,000,000 in insurance to landlords to reduce the risk of welcoming strangers[4] (Safety). As of 2012, Airbnb offered more than 200,000 listings in 33,000 cities in 192 countries (User Communities/Support Systems).

Tactics:

Profit Model
METERED USE
Allow customers to pay only for what they use.

+

Process
PROCESS AUTOMATION
Apply tools and infrastructure to manage routine activities in order to free up employees for other tasks.

+

Product Performance
SAFETY
Increase the customer's level of confidence and security.

+

Zipcar members, or Zipsters, as the company likes to label them, are charged a small membership fee. Above that, drivers are only charged when they take out a car. This flexible metered use model allows customers to rent cars for as little as an hour at a time.

The core of Zipcar is its Fast Fleet system—a GPS and wireless data system that lets customers into the cars, tracks usage patterns, gathers data, and alerts internal fleet managers of any issues with cars. This system is vital in managing and tracking how the cars are used, which drives the profitability of a rental business with relatively expensive assets (such as cars).

Zipcar offers simplicity of use—integrating a driver's insurance, gas, and all other additional expenses into a single hourly rate. This reassures those renting a car that everything will be taken care of if there's an accident; also that the car will be in a good state when they pick it up. If a previous driver does leave a car in bad shape—either full of fast-food wrappers or empty on gas—there is also a telephone hotline for the community to report it.

Brand
VALUES ALIGNMENT
Make your brand stand for a big idea or a set of values and express them consistently in all aspects of your company.

The company's logo is green on purpose. Zipcar's brand signals values around responsibility and environmental benefits of shared car usage. As chairman and CEO Scott W. Griffith described in the company's 2011 annual report, "We are 'Wheels When You Want Them.' Our brand connotes simplicity, convenience, innovation, freedom, fun, sustainability, community and smart consumption."

INNOVATION PLAY
FREE-BASED

THE PLAY AT WORK
LINKEDIN

Shift:
BUSINESS MODEL

Ambition:
CHANGE THE KNOWN

Industry:
SOCIAL MEDIA

GIVE AWAY BASIC OFFERINGS FOR FREE TO ATTRACT MANY USERS AND THEN MAKE MONEY OFF OF THEM IN MULTIPLE WAYS.

What could be more innovative than making money by giving something away for free? Historically, this model has been largely confined to digital services, where the incremental cost of delivering a website, media, or other digital content trends toward zero even as the number of users grows. This helps enterprises that use this strategy to scale quickly and create multiple revenue streams, including premium offerings, advertising, and partner referrals.

Launched in May 2003, LinkedIn was an early online social network. Dedicated to helping professionals build their personal network, *Forbes* (and many others) reported that it had more than 200 million members by the beginning of 2013.[5] LinkedIn has some attributes of a very traditional free-based play—offering basic services for free while charging for premium services, and earning much of its revenue through hiring services, lead generation, and advertising.[6] This kind of diversification in revenue is important in making this type of play profitable.

5 "LinkedIn Tops 200 Million Members" by Tomio Geron, *Forbes*, January 9, 2013: http://tentyp.es/XaqZln.

6 For a closer look at LinkedIn's business model, see "LinkedIn Wants to Make More Money From Job Recruiters" by Quentin Hardy, *the New York Times*, October 18, 2011: http://tentyp.es/WZGphb.

7 Adam Clark Estes breaks down LinkedIn's profit model in "How LinkedIn Makes Money," *The Atlantic*, August 5, 2011: http://tentyp.es/159UmOn.

ANOTHER BUSINESS USING THE FREE-BASED PLAY
ZYNGA

San Francisco-based gaming company Zynga uses a similar set of tactics—many users play its compulsively addictive games for free (Engaging Functionality, Freemium), but a small portion buy in-game items that enhance play (Microtransactions). A limited amount of additional revenue is earned through advertising and partner referrals (Ad-supported). As of this writing, this business model is under pressure and falling short of analyst expectations—primarily because of the company's dependence on Facebook and in-game revenue. As with LinkedIn, Zynga will likely try to diversify its revenue streams to focus more on providing advertising and partner services.

Tactics:

Profit Model

FREEMIUM
Offer basic services for free while charging a premium for advanced or special features.

LinkedIn's basic accounts include a personal profile, networking, email, and other features. These are free for any user. Premium users pay for additional services, such as the ability to send messages to members to whom they are not connected, or the ability to see more information on who's been viewing their profile.

+

Profit Model

SWITCHBOARD
Connect multiple sellers with multiple buyers. The more buyers and sellers who join, the more valuable the switchboard becomes.

In this case, jobs are the goods that are bought and sold. 50% of LinkedIn's revenue comes from its "Hiring Solutions" offerings, which connects headhunters and staffing services with the company's database of potential candidates. Recruiters pay an annual subscription fee to build out job and career portals and manage talent acquisition pipelines.[7]

+

Profit Model

MEMBERSHIP
Charge a time-based payment to allow access to locations, offerings, or services that non-members don't have.

Premium users pay a monthly fee for access to these exclusive features. The site offers a tiered paid membership service, including "Business," which in 2012 was a lower option of about $20 a month and included perks such as premium search and the ability to request an introduction to a company. Top tier choice, "Executive," was a higher cost option of about $80 a month, and it included the ability to message anyone on the network—response guaranteed, or your money back.

+

Profit Model

AD-SUPPORTED
Provide content or services for free to one party while selling listeners, viewers, or "eyeballs" to another party.

"Marketing Solutions amount to your basic display advertising business, but there's a kicker," wrote Adam Clark Estes in *The Atlantic* of LinkedIn's profit model.[7] "Because LinkedIn is built around people's professional profiles, companies are able to create or sponsor custom groups around specific careers and build pages with deeper offerings than places like Facebook."

+

Product Performance

ENGAGING FUNCTIONALITY
Provide an unexpected or newsworthy feature that elevates the customer interaction from the ordinary.

Any free-based gameplan depends on providing an offering that attracts users and engages them over time. LinkedIn accomplishes this by making it easy to create a profile and develop a personal network. It also provides updates about individuals in your network and suggests other people to connect with.

INNOVATION PLAY
RADICAL OPTIMIZATION

THE PLAY AT WORK
CEMEX

Shift:
BUSINESS MODEL

Ambition:
CHANGE THE BOUNDARIES

Industry:
CONSTRUCTION

8 See Richard Pascale's
book, *Surfing on the Edge
of Chaos*, for an insightful
investigation of Cemex's
system. Thomas Petzinger
Jr. also tells this story in
more detail in an article for
Fast Company. See Part
Seven for links.

**MOVE BEYOND STANDARD OPERATIONAL EFFICIENCIES TO
MAKE IT PAINFUL FOR OTHER FIRMS TO COMPETE WITH YOU.**
Sometimes efficiencies become so radical that
they not only establish new benchmarks in the
value delivered to customers — they reset the bar
at a height that competitors struggle to reach.
What constitutes "radical" optimization will vary
by industry and context, but think about how
standardizing procedures and adding IT connectivity
and intelligence to parts of your business could
change the basis of competition.

Many cities in Mexico are notorious for traffic jams, which last for hours and can
turn a 15-minute trip into a five-hour ordeal. This is rather problematic for cement
trucks. At some point, despite spinning furiously, that load of wet cement in the
truck will cease to be either wet or cement; instead, you will have a large rock and
a broken truck. In the mid 1990s, Cemex solved this challenge by studying both
FedEx's hub in Memphis, and ambulance and EMS dispatchers in Houston. They
realized that while cement needs were individually unpredictable, in aggregate
there were discernible (and somewhat predictable) patterns.[8]

ANOTHER BUSINESS USING THE RADICAL OPTIMIZATION PLAY
ARAVIND EYE HOSPITAL
Aravind Eye Hospital was founded in Madurai, India, in 1976. Its mission: to
"eliminate needless blindness." Beginning as an 11-bed hospital manned by four medical
officers, the non-profit has since expanded throughout India. In 2012, 2.8 million
outpatients were treated and over 340,000 surgeries were performed. What's really
interesting about Aravind, however, is that aggressively streamlined procedures kept
costs low (Process Standardization) while it started its own manufacturing operation
to provide affordable lenses and supplies (IT Integration, Process Automation).

Tactics:

Structure		Process		Process
IT INTEGRATION	+	**PROCESS AUTOMATION**	+	**PROCESS STANDARDIZATION**
Integrate technology resources and applications.		*Apply tools and infrastructure to manage routine activities in order to free up employees for other tasks.*		*Use common products, procedures, and policies to reduce complexity, costs, and errors.*

Cemex equipped most of its fleet of concrete mixing trucks with global positioning satellite (GPS) locators and computers. These allowed managers to optimize scheduling, calculate travel times, and oversee the efficiency of the entire fleet. Mixers in certain areas even had technology to ensure an even distribution of the cement in the truck — this in turn helped to preserve the often under-maintained roads in those countries.

Cemex focused on designing a delivery service that was unparalleled in its efficiency. Instead of depending on one truck to connect to a single delivery site, the system constantly optimized routing and trucks were dispatched based on shifting traffic patterns and where they were in a city. Cemex also helped its customers by offering so-called "SmartSilo" technology to monitor cement usage — and had trucks available to make a delivery when stocks were running low.

The system only worked if multiple trucks were available at any given moment to respond to changing traffic patterns — and if those trucks were networked and communicating where they were. Thus, almost all of Cemex's trucks had a GPS-enabled IT system installed, and cement deliveries were scheduled from a central hub that oversees all of a city's operations.

Service

GUARANTEE

Remove customer risk of lost money or time from product failure or purchase error.

The system worked so well that in a program known as "Garantia 20x20," Cemex guaranteed cement deliveries within 20 minutes of their scheduled time. If a load arrived later than that, the customer was entitled to a discount of 20 pesos off every cubic meter. At the time, this was a promise the firm's competitors couldn't match.

INNOVATION PLAY
PREDICTIVE BUSINESS

GE AVIATION

Shift:	Ambition:	Industry:
BUSINESS MODEL	**CHANGE THE GAME**	**COMMERCIAL AVIATION**

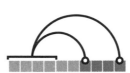

MINE DATA TO MODEL BEHAVIORS AND BREAKDOWNS, ALLOWING YOU TO MAKE PROMISES, PREDICT OUTCOMES, AND DRIVE EFFICIENCIES FOR CUSTOMERS.

The increasing ubiquity and connectivity of data, combined with the plummeting costs associated with accessing, storing, and mining them, allow more and more firms not only to improve their products or services — but to predict how these offerings might be used. In certain cases, it's even possible to determine the specific outcomes they'll deliver to customers. Consider how you could use such insights to offer compelling new guarantees to customers — and maybe even transform the economics of your industry.

GE Aviation revolutionized the aircraft engine industry with OnPoint Solutions, a service that integrates maintenance, material, and asset management services, along with GE Capital's financing capabilities (if the customer needs them) into an offering that guarantees engine uptime — all priced by the flight hour. There are many types of innovation afoot here, but the four tactics shown opposite are at the core of the breakthrough.

ANOTHER BUSINESS USING THE PREDICTIVE BUSINESS PLAY
JOHNSON CONTROLS

Johnson Controls exhaustively models the cost and performance of its building management solutions, which include climate control, sensor-driven automation, and other facility management tools that are bundled into comprehensive solutions (Product Bundling, Predictive Analytics). Remarkably, if the company doesn't provide a client with the promised savings, it will refund the difference between what was guaranteed and what was achieved (Risk Sharing, **Guarantee**).

Tactics:

Profit Model

RISK SHARING
Waive standard fees or costs if certain metrics aren't achieved, but receive outsize gains when they are.

+

Process

PREDICTIVE ANALYTICS
Model past performance data and predict future outcomes to design and price offerings accordingly.

+

Product System

PRODUCT BUNDLING
Put together several products for sale as one combined offering.

+

Engines are priced and guaranteed by the flight hour—which means that if an engine goes offline unexpectedly, GE Aviation bears the cost instead of the customer. By the same token, if costs are lower than expected, it captures that margin.

GE Aviation obsessively measures, monitors, and models the performance of its engines to predict when they need service, to forecast future costs, and to structure its service system appropriately. The "myEngines" digital service allows fleet managers to monitor maintenance even while on the move, while the optimized "ClearCore" engine wash system helps GE engineers to service the planes to improve fuel consumption and extend their "time-on-wing."

OnPoint bundles together formerly disconnected offerings such as engine trade-in programs, line maintenance, and technology upgrades into a seamless service. This is further integrated with GE Capital's financing capabilities to underwrite the engine lease via flexible financing options.

Service

GUARANTEE
Remove customer risk of lost money or time from product failure or purchase error.

OnPoint is backed by a worldwide system of rapid response service teams available 24/7 to guarantee uptime. As the service's marketing blurb puts it, "Airlines operate 24 hours a day, 365 days a year. Having the ability to make real-time decisions can truly impact customer satisfaction and drive down operating costs."

INNOVATION PLAY
FRANCHISE

HARRY POTTER

Shift:
PLATFORM

Ambition:
CHANGE THE KNOWN

Industry:
PUBLISHING

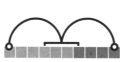

9   Imagine that—school
    kids desperate to read
    a book. Thank you,
    Ms. Rowling.

10 See also *50 Shades of
    Grey* (shudder).

11 The films have grossed
    $7.7 billion at the box
    office worldwide, while the
    Harry Potter experience
    has been such a draw in
    Orlando that, in 2011,
    Universal announced
    plans to build another
    Hogwarts in its
    Hollywood resort.

DEVELOP SIGNATURE OFFERINGS AND EXPERIENCES THAT YOU—AND OTHERS—USE TO DEVELOP ECOSYSTEMS OF EXTENSIONS.

Sometimes a story, an idea, or a technology is so captivating that it can't be contained; it finds surprising and unexpected utility and relevance in multiple places, and loyal audiences demand more. This is the heart of a Franchise play—identifying something that you do or deliver that's amazing, and finding ways to expand it through sequels, expansions, extensions, and complements.

The boy wizard and his chums captured the world's imagination and had school-children and adults alike breathlessly waiting to read the next installment.[9] Like most popular properties today, Harry Potter quickly evolved into a trans-media franchise, with movies, video games, candies, toys, and other offerings bringing the wizard school Hogwarts to fans in many different manifestations. Even after the publication of the final installment in the series, the platform continues to grow, and made over $1 billion for its author, J.K. Rowling.

ANOTHER BUSINESS USING THE FRANCHISE PLAY
FEBREZE

Franchises aren't the sole province of media firms. Launched in 1998, P&G's odor-killer, Febreze, has become a featured component in a wide array of products. Its patented cyclodextrin technology binds smelly molecules, limiting their release into our environment (Superior Product). P&G has integrated that technology into a host of smell-good products, from room sprays to cleaners to car fresheners (Complements). The Febreze brand and technology has also worked its way into related but separate product lines, such as P&G's laundry products Tide, Gain, and Bounce (Brand Extension). Mintel reported that Febreze was featured in 37 new product releases in the first nine months of 2010.

Tactics:

Product Performance	Product System	Brand
SUPERIOR PRODUCT	**COMPLEMENTS**	**BRAND EXTENSION**
Develop an offering of exceptional design, quality, and/or experience.	*Sell additional related or peripheral products or services to a customer.*	*Offer a new product or service under the umbrella of an existing brand.*

+ between Product Performance and Product System; **+** between Product System and Brand.

The core of a franchise has to capture our attention, and Harry Potter and company certainly did that. The novels were written in engaging and approachable prose and featured characters and worlds that appealed to children while being rich enough for adults. Sure, the series had its literary detractors — but the many fans who lined up overnight whenever a new title was due and the 450 million books sold worldwide showed how little that mattered.[10]

Though the main story arc was finished with the publication of *Harry Potter and the Deathly Hallows* in 2007, new complements continue to emerge. Rowling continues to publish new Harry-related content on *Pottermore*, a website the author created to keep the magic alive. Rowling has also penned shorter "in-story" books such as *Fantastic Beasts and Where to Find Them* (one of Harry's textbooks) and *Quidditch Through the Ages*.

Careful extension choices made by J.K. Rowling and her team really turbo-charged the franchise. The films are the most obvious manifestation of this — but there are also over 400 authorized products, ranging from "The Wizarding World of Harry Potter" attraction at Universal Orlando to Bertie Bott's jellybeans to action figures to toy wands. All of these extensions have stayed true to the characters and their worlds while continuing to make the human world of "muggles" a little more magical. Revenues from the films, DVDs, video games, and theme park attractions alone have easily eclipsed $10 billion.[11]

INNOVATION PLAY
EXCHANGE

THE PLAY AT WORK
KICKSTARTER

Shift:
PLATFORM

Ambition:
CHANGE THE BOUNDARIES

Industry:
MICROFINANCE

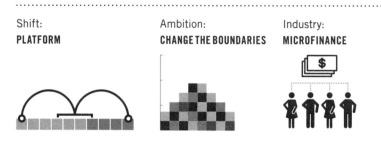

ESTABLISH HUBS OF ACTIVITY AND COMMERCE FOR ANY GIVEN RESOURCE, INTEREST, MARKET, OR INDUSTRY.

As humans, we seem wired to organize ourselves around the exchange of common interests and needs — from the market squares at the center of almost every Babylonian city to the first financial market in 16th century Antwerp[12] to the dizzying array of electronic interchanges that span the world today. Thanks to the networked nature of our digital lives, we can now connect with unprecedented ease and speed. But the trick to making an Exchange play work is both to identify which specific communities need a way to connect and figure out how to get paid for bringing its people together.

Launched in 2009, Kickstarter quickly became *the* place for independent product developers, artists, writers, and creators of almost any type to find an audience and funding for projects. Creators developed a pitch and offered a clear outline of how much money they needed, how long they would work on the project, and what donors could receive for contributing funds. Rewards could be small (say, a "thank you" on a website) or expansive (for instance, a one-off signed piece of artwork). What started as a way for relatively unknown fund-seekers to get started became a popular platform for celebrities looking to show off their indie cred, too: the likes of film-maker Charlie Kaufman and science fiction writer Neal Stephenson used the platform to fund their work.[13]

12 As you might expect, many writers have tackled the history and evolution of the stock market. One excellent, sobering account of real life on Wall Street is Michael Lewis's *Liar's Poker* (W. W. Norton & Company, 2010).

13 Fans pledged $406,237 towards the making of Kaufman's animation film, *Anomalisa*. Stephenson was promised $526,125 to revolutionize sword-fighting games.

14 Amazon takes another 3–5% for processing the payments. Yes, Amazon really is everywhere.

ANOTHER BUSINESS USING THE EXCHANGE PLAY
CRAIGSLIST

Started as an email distribution list to highlight interesting events in San Francisco, Craigslist blossomed into *the* local classified ad site on the Internet. Today, it serves 700 cities in 70 countries. Craigslist provides a majority of its services for free, but charges a fixed fee for things like job searches or real estate postings. It costs $75 to post a job in a single category in San Francisco (Switchboard). Users create the classified placements themselves, using simple and relatively low-tech tools and interfaces (User-Generated). The highly engaged Craigslist community is largely self-moderated; skilled users serve as "experts" to help others when issues emerge (**User Communities/Support Systems**).

Tactics:

Profit Model		**Process**		**Service**
SWITCHBOARD	**+**	**USER-GENERATED**	**+**	**USER COMMUNITIES/ SUPPORT SYSTEMS**
Connect multiple sellers with multiple buyers. The more buyers and sellers who join, the more valuable the switchboard becomes.		*Put your users to work in creating and curating the content that powers your offerings.*		*Provide a communal resource for product and service support, use, and extension.*

Exchanges have to make money by connecting individuals and parties—and taking a cut. Kickstarter accomplishes this by taking 5% of the funding committed to each project.[14] Within three years, over $400 million had been raised on the site. Most projects raise less than $10,000 though several projects raised millions of dollars, including OUYA, a new kind of video game console, and the Pebble E-Paper Watch, a smart-watch that communicates with Android and iOS devices.

The beauty of Exchanges is that once they achieve critical mass, they become largely self-sustaining. In the case of Kickstarter, project creators power the site, developing all of the descriptions, imagery, and videos to pitch projects; all the company does is offer tools to facilitate their creation, index them for searching, and host their content. By the beginning of 2013, over 80,000 unique projects had been launched via the site.

Kickstarter found a gap in the funding market and filled it smartly, highlighting the "indie" nature of the projects and connecting interested consumers and investors with exciting entrepreneurs. The community offers valuable feedback and insights on the desirability of projects—which can be just as valuable as the funding itself.

INNOVATION PLAY
COLLABORATIVE CREATION

THE PLAY AT WORK
THREADLESS

Shift:
PLATFORM

Ambition:
CHANGE THE BOUNDARIES

Industry:
APPAREL

CONNECT COMMUNITIES WITH CANVASES AND TOOLKITS THAT ENCOURAGE THEM TO CREATE OFFERINGS FOR YOU.
Open source communities such as Apache and Linux epitomize collaborative creation, with thousands of experts around the world working together to create a software product that's then often distributed for free.[15] But Collaborative Creation is not always technology-based; it is possible to find ways to take the incredible energy of a networked, like-minded community and put it to work on all sorts of problems. These plays equip communities with smart tools that support and amplify their efforts, and ensure contributors are appropriately recognized and rewarded.

Threadless is a fashion company without any fashion designers. Instead, it sources designs from its online community, which consists of both buyers and intrigued contributors. Design ideas are posted online, and the community votes using an automated system; top-rated submissions are then produced (and users who voted for the design are asked if they want to buy the item). This platform has helped Threadless solve one of the most vexing problems for any apparel company: how to predict what often-fickle fans might want to buy?[16] More recently, Threadless has moved into mass channels through collaborations with retailers such as Bed Bath & Beyond — and opened a real-world store in Chicago.

15 Netcraft surveyed nearly 666 million websites in July 2012 to determine the world's top web servers. Apache had 61.45% market share: http://tentyp.es/QZUK9x.

16 "I think of it as common sense," company founder Jake Nickell said in an interview in 2008. "Why wouldn't you want to make the products that people want you to make?"

ANOTHER BUSINESS USING THE COLLABORATIVE CREATION PLAY
WIKIPEDIA
Wikipedia gathers information on a wide range of topics from a dispersed network of contributors (Crowdsourcing). The template and web architecture for Wikipedia entries is standardized, simple, and highly automated, making it easy for users to contribute (Process Automation). Quality and accuracy are fundamental to the success of any website purporting to offer information; Wikipedia manages this through peer reviews and community moderation, with clear editing guidelines and policies (User Communities / Support Systems). A 2005 study in *Nature* magazine concluded that Wikipedia's accuracy was similar to that of Encyclopedia Britannica. In general, contributors seem to be motivated by a desire to collect, develop, and share educational content (Values Alignment).

Tactics:

Process
CROWDSOURCING
Outsource repetitive or challenging work to a large group of semi-organized individuals.

+

Process
PROCESS AUTOMATION
Apply tools and infrastructure to manage routine activities in order to free up employees for other tasks.

+

Service
USER COMMUNITIES/ SUPPORT SYSTEMS
Provide a communal resource for product and service support, use, and extension.

+

Threadless sources the designs for T-shirts and other products from its community of artists—who often interact with other users, seeking feedback and promoting designs to spur votes and sales. If a design is produced, an artist receives a $2,000 check and $500 in store credit.

Threadless's voting and design ranking systems are simple and intuitive, asking users to rate designs via a numbered scale. Voters are automatically asked if they would like to purchase a design if it is produced. Threadless also equips its artists with digital submission kits that include HTML tools for creating online advertisements for their designs.

Artists engage with the Threadless community through discussion forums, asking visitors to critique their designs and offer suggestions and advice. Many of them further connect to audiences using Twitter, Facebook, and their own websites. By 2012, Threadless had attracted nearly 150,000 submissions from 42,000 designers, and received more than 80 million votes.

Brand
VALUES ALIGNMENT
Make your brand stand for a big idea or a set of values and express them consistently in all aspects of your company.

+

Customer Engagement
STATUS AND RECOGNITION
Offer cues that confer meaning, allowing users—and those who interact with them—to develop and nurture aspects of their identity.

Threadless consistently communicates that independent artists are at the core of everything it does. When Urban Outfitters approached Threadless with a collaboration idea in 2007, founder Jake Nickell pitched them right back with the idea of installing a computer kiosk in stores to allow shoppers to score designs and read about the artists responsible for the shirts. When Urban Outfitters refused, Nickell turned down the offer of working together.

The $2,000 that artists receive for produced designs isn't chump change, but some of the creators are also driven by a deeper desire to see their art put into the world—as well as the status and recognition of having their designs selected by Threadless's discerning critics. Reviewers don't receive money for their time, but are inspired by the sense of belonging to a meaningful community.

INNOVATION PLAY
COMPETENCY-DRIVEN PLATFORM

AMAZON WEB SERVICES

Shift:	Ambition:	Industry:
PLATFORM	**CHANGE THE GAME**	**IT SYSTEMS**

OPEN UP KEY ASSETS AND CAPABILITIES AND LET OTHERS USE THEM TO POWER THEIR OWN BUSINESSES.

Signature capabilities occasionally become the envy of others around you — including those who aren't direct competitors. Allowing other companies to piggyback off of your investments and capabilities (and profiting handsomely for it) lies at the heart of a Competency-Driven Platform play. It allows other companies to achieve much more than they can by themselves, while allowing you to reap the benefits from expertise that you already possess.

Building a data center is not really an option for most companies. The cost of servers and applications, not to mention upkeep and maintenance, is both fiendishly complex and prohibitively expensive. Not so for Amazon. Launched in 2006, Amazon Web Services (AWS) provided almost unlimited computing power through a virtual infrastructure and set of applications. This allowed just about any company to rent computing power cheaply, and built a lucrative new business from one of Amazon's core strengths.

ANOTHER BUSINESS USING THE COMPETENCY-DRIVEN PLATFORM PLAY
CATERPILLAR

In 1987, executives at the heavy equipment manufacturer Caterpillar realized that its expertise in supply chain management might also benefit other firms. And so, they developed CAT Logistics to help clients with their own supply chain issues (Superior Product, Diversification). Companies such as Bombardier, Hyundai, and Toshiba signed up for the service. CAT Logistics also collaborated with Ford Motor Company and software vendor SAP to develop a new Service Parts Management (SPM) solution to stay on the cutting edge of logistics services (Complementary Partnering, Intellectual Property). By 2010, CAT Logistics' total revenue was $3.1 billion; in 2012 the company was spun off as a separate venture, Neovia Logistics.

Tactics:

Network

COMPLEMENTARY PARTNERING

Leverage assets by sharing them with companies that serve similar markets but offer different products and services.

+

Process

INTELLECTUAL PROPERTY

Use a proprietary process to commercialize ideas in ways that others cannot copy.

+

Product Performance

SUPERIOR PRODUCT

Develop an offering of exceptional design, quality, and/or experience.

+

AWS partners strategically with companies such as Adobe, which supplies media delivery platforms, ESRI, which offers geographic information systems, and Salesforce.com, which provides development toolkits. Other technical collaborators include Oracle and Symantec.

Amazon has systematically protected its innovations in managing complex IT infrastructure. It filed an early patent application on "facilitating interactions between computing systems" in 2004, two years before the launch of AWS.

AWS challenges the physical infrastructure-heavy models of traditional IT departments by providing a flexible, agile, open, and secure offering. Companies can alter the amount of bandwidth they require on the fly, making it a great service for start-ups, small businesses, and companies looking to scale quickly.

Channel

DIVERSIFICATION

Add and expand into new or different channels.

By building a new business around what was previously an internal competency, AWS diversifies its parent company's income stream and expands its customer base. In short: AWS adds another powerful arrow to Amazon's already bristling quiver.

INNOVATION PLAY
EXPERIENCE ECOSYSTEM

THE PLAY AT WORK
APPLE iTUNES

Shift:
PLATFORM

Ambition:
CHANGE THE GAME

Industry:
MEDIA

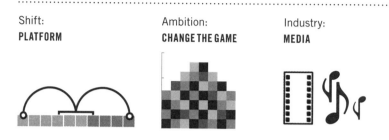

BUILD A SEAMLESS SYSTEM OF PRODUCTS, SERVICES, AND EXTENSIONS THAT INTEROPERATE AND CONNECT IN CONSISTENTLY ELEGANT AND BEGUILING WAYS.

In particularly complex arenas such as health care and technology, the winners are often the companies that deliver startling simplicity and coherence across their offerings. Such firms make it easy for customers and users to accomplish difficult and complicated tasks. Experience Ecosystems weave together a variety of offerings with elegance and by providing a consistently compelling experience. In doing so, they often attract other companies looking to expand and enrich the system with their own complementary capabilities and offerings.

What Apple has accomplished with its iTunes ecosystem is revolutionary and frankly unlike anything accomplished in history. This single platform has changed the music, media, software, mobile phone, and personal computing industries. While often criticized for providing more of a "walled garden" than a freely open ecosystem, Apple's various bets have paid off handsomely: in August 2012, its market capitalization made it the most valuable company in the world.[17]

17 Apple's market capitalization hit $623.5 billion on August 20th, 2012.

18 To see proof of this, watch young children around a flat screen television. Odds are that at some point, they will walk up to the screen and start pressing it. Then deal with their inevitable disappointment when it doesn't respond similarly to their parents' iPhone and iPad.

ANOTHER BUSINESS USING THE EXPERIENCE ECOSYSTEM PLAY
??? (A GREAT CONCIERGE)

No other company is currently executing this strategy with the same depth and rigor as Apple. The Android platform is probably closest, but Google made a strategic choice to be more open and flexible than Apple — making the operating system free to any hardware manufacturer and placing fewer controls on app development and distribution. This approach has enabled Google to take an overwhelming lead in the installed base of phones; in September 2012, 51.6% of smartphones in the US ran on Android versus 32.4% running on iOS. On the other hand, Apple handily dominated the tablet market with the iPad. Only time will tell which platform will win — but for now, Apple's remains the most coherent and integrated system. Perhaps the closest analogy is decidedly non-digital: a brilliant concierge at a great hotel. Connected to every restaurant, theatre, and sports team nearby, he or she is a miniature and very personal experience ecosystem — so do tip generously.

Tactics:

Profit Model

LICENSING

Grant permission to a group or individual to use your offering in a defined way for a specified payment.

+

Network

ALLIANCES

Share risks and revenues to jointly improve individual competitive advantage.

+

Process

STRATEGIC DESIGN

Employ a purposeful approach that manifests itself consistently across offerings, brands, and experiences.

+

Apple's iTunes Store and App Store offer the content that powers its collection of hardware devices. Both stores make money by taking a cut of every song, video, media subscription, or application sold. It's unclear how much money Apple actually makes from selling content, but its extensive library certainly serves as an enormously powerful driver of device sales.

Back when Napster and digital music were shaking the foundations of the industry, the major labels clung to their old business models. So enormous credit is due to Steve Jobs (and his army of lawyers) for convincing the labels to join in and sell their songs one at a time. As of September 2012, there were 26 million songs and more than 700,000 apps, 190,000 TV episodes, and 45,000 films in the iTunes Store.

Apple is famous for the primacy of design in its product development process. A core team of roughly 15 designers leads the design of all the company's products — literally sitting around a kitchen table to generate, critique, and refine ideas, and ultimately bring them to life.

Product Performance

PERFORMANCE SIMPLIFICATION

Omit superfluous details, features, and interactions to reduce complexity.

+

Product System

PRODUCT/SERVICE PLATFORMS

Develop systems that connect with other partner products and services to create a holistic offering.

+

Channel

GO DIRECT

Skip traditional retail channels and connect directly with customers.

Apple's iPod, iPad, and iPhone changed almost all existing notions of what personal electronics should look like and how we should interact with them. All three products dramatically reduced the number of buttons and input mechanisms that had been the norm on competitive products; iOS's intuitive touch-screen interface is so simple that even young children can use it.[18]

All of the devices and software in Apple's ecosystem interact seamlessly — syncing automatically with iTunes and with iCloud so that all of a user's content is available anywhere there is a cellular or WiFi connection. This slick interoperability is one of the primary reasons that Apple has stuck to its walled garden approach.

The desire to control the experience extends to Apple's channels, both online and in the real world. Establishing and managing the point of purchase not only helps Apple to ensure the quality of its customers' interactions, it also helps it to dictate terms to other companies looking to sell their products and services to Apple's vast audience.

INNOVATION PLAY
STATUS-BASED

FOURSQUARE

Shift:
CUSTOMER EXPERIENCE

Ambition:
CHANGE THE KNOWN

Industry:
SOCIAL MEDIA

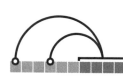

USE SUBTLE OR EXPLICIT CUES TO CONFER STATUS TO YOUR CUSTOMERS — CREATING ELITE GROUPS THAT ENGAGE RABIDLY WITH YOUR PRODUCTS AND SERVICES.
Everyone wants to be recognized for some aspect of his or her identity; something that tells the world that we are indeed one special snowflake. Status-Based experience plays are born from this innate desire. They spur customers to collect, compete, or invest time and money in return for recognition, special treatment, and a spotlight on their lives. This approach creates life-long mavens to celebrate and promote your offerings.

Foursquare is a free app for mobile phones that allows users to share what they're doing and where they are. As founders Dennis Crowley and Naveen Selvadurai explained in a blog post in 2011, the name of the game is "about discovering new places, connecting with friends, and forging new relationships with the places you visit. It's finding new ways to layer technology on the real world." The pair launched the app at South by Southwest Interactive in Austin in March 2009; as of September 2012, over 25 million members had checked in over 3 billion times.

ANOTHER BUSINESS USING THE STATUS-BASED PLAY
DISCOVERY

Discovery is a leading financial services company in South Africa. In 1997, it launched a wellness program called Vitality (**Loyalty Program**), which aimed to encourage members to improve their quality of life and reduce their long-term medical costs. Promoting wellness rather than care, members earned "Vitality points" for both learning about health and making smart choices. These were collected in a personal "Points Monitor" (**Personalization**). Members used them to work their way through four status levels, from "Blue" to "Diamond" (**Status and Recognition**). The higher the status, the better the rewards, all of which encouraged healthy living.

Tactics:

Service		**Customer Engagement**		**Customer Engagement**
LOYALTY PROGRAMS *Provide benefits and/or discounts to frequent and high-value customers.*	+	**PERSONALIZATION** *Alter a standard offering to allow the projection of the customer's identity.*	+	**STATUS AND RECOGNITION** *Offer cues that confer meaning, allowing users—and those who interact with them—to develop and nurture aspects of their identity.*

By 2013, nearly a million businesses had signed up to take advantage of Foursquare's Merchant Platform, by which companies could inform users who checked into their location about special offers, discounts, or free gifts. The idea: to encourage repeat visits and increased connection between venue and visitor.

Foursquare allowed users to see if any friends had previously checked in at any places in a particular neighborhood. That helped them to trust the feedback as coming from people they already knew rather than from random Internet denizens. Foursquare also developed a system whereby it gave users a list of places they might like based on signals such as prior check-ins, where friends have visited, and the time of day.

Foursquare badges are marks of achievement that could only be earned by checking in religiously. Examples included: "Gym Rat," given for 10 trips to the gym in 30 days; the "Hot Tamale," for visiting different Mexican restaurants, or "JetSetter," for checking in at airports. Meanwhile, "mayorships" were awarded to whomever visits a certain place the most times in the past 60 days—occasionally leading to fierce check-in battles between those vying for the title.

INNOVATION PLAY
IMMERSION

THE PLAY AT WORK
CABELA'S

Shift:
CUSTOMER EXPERIENCE

Ambition:
CHANGE THE KNOWN

Industry:
OUTFITTING

CREATE ENVIRONMENTS THAT CAPTIVATE AND MESMERIZE CUSTOMERS, FOSTERING NEW LEVELS OF ENGAGEMENT AND COMMITMENT.

Transformative experiences drive Immersion plays. They surprise, transport, or engage customers in ways that open them to new behaviors and help them see the world differently. But the approach is not just the domain of film, theater, museums, or theme parks (although these industries are typically quite good at it). Today, Immersion is increasingly a key factor within successful retail, restaurants, and interactive contexts, and many other industries are experimenting with this play.

Founded in 1961, Cabela's sells hunting, fishing, and outdoor goods—and its 40 stores are at the heart of its experience-focused strategy. "For many hunting and fishing enthusiasts in Minnesota, a trip to Cabela's means trekking to Owatonna, Rogers, or East Grand Forks for a daylong experience that is a mix of mercantile and museum," wrote Janet Moore in the *Star Tribune*.[19] The outfitter's showrooms include natural history displays, aquariums, gun museums, and in some locations, shooting galleries, mountains, and waterfalls.

19 "Cabelas, Other Outdoor Retailers Take Aim at Twin Cities," by Janet Moore, *Star Tribune*, February 9, 2013: http://tentyp.es/12ucBdi.

20 Cabela's came in at number 69. See the full Retail Customer Experience report at http://tentyp.es/WHoihl.

ANOTHER BUSINESS USING THE IMMERSION PLAY
ALINEA

The brainchild of chef Grant Achatz, the Chicago-based restaurant Alinea has received worldwide acclaim for its innovative, futuristic approach to food and dining. A years-long collaboration with Martin Kastner and the design studio Crucial Detail means that food is served on an elaborately sculptural set of dishes and servers (Strategic Design), some of which are now even available to buy. The restaurant was designed by Tom Stringer to be both hypermodern and comfortable, with programmable LED lighting that allows the mood of the dining room to be changed at the touch of a button (Flagship Store). The restaurant includes one set menu at one price; every piece of food is created to heighten the sensory experience of eating (Experience Enabling).

Tactics:

Process		**Channel**		**Customer Engagement**
STRATEGIC DESIGN	**+**	**FLAGSHIP STORE**	**+**	**EXPERIENCE ENABLING**
Employ a purposeful approach that manifests itself consistently across offerings, brands, and experiences.		*Create a retail outlet to showcase quintessential brand and product attributes.*		*Extend the realm of what's possible to offer a previously improbable experience.*

As Janet Moore wrote in the *Star Tribune*, traditional Cabela's stores are large, spanning up to 250,000 square feet. But even smaller stores are consistent in style and include a range of facilities that will appeal to outdoor enthusiasts, such as indoor archery and museum-quality dioramas of the natural world.

The investment made in these showrooms also extends shoppers' loyalty outside of the store, too: more than a third of Cabela's 2011 revenue came from catalog and Internet sales.

"Cabela's takes the concept of in-store experience to new vistas," wrote editors at Retail Customer Experience, who included the store in their "Top 100 of 2012."[20] Cabela's continually looks to find ways to extend its shoppers' experience—from iPhone apps that help hunters track and log their trips to branded video games, magazines, and television shows that celebrate life outdoors.

INNOVATION PLAY
CONNECTED
COMMUNITY

**LEVERAGE THE POWER OF SOCIAL TIES TO DEEPEN
EXPERIENCES AND ENCOURAGE CONSUMERS TO SHARE
COMMON INTERESTS, ACTIVITIES, AND THE OFFERINGS
THAT SUPPORT THEM.**

As humans we are predisposed to connect with others
who are similar to us. Groups of like-minded people
amplify our own sense of identity while connecting us
to a larger whole. Connected Community plays take
advantage of this, leveraging the power of social ties
to reinforce a company's authenticity and increase
the enterprise's scope and scale of impact.

THE PLAY AT WORK
HARLEY-DAVIDSON

Shift:
CUSTOMER EXPERIENCE

Ambition:
CHANGE THE BOUNDARIES

Industry:
MOTORBIKES

William S. Harley, Arthur Davidson, and Walter Davidson built their first single
cylinder motorcycle in 1903. They made three motorcycles that year. In 2011,
the company—now known by the founders' last names—had revenues from
motorcycles and related products of $4.66 billion. That's a lot of motorbikes.
Harley-Davidson remains popular with its devoted clientele and works hard to
keep connected to them, whether through regular meetings, "garage parties," or
events thrown throughout the world. The iconic motorcycles are the top choice
among communities such as women, young adults, and Hispanics, while the
brand is active in virtual worlds too, with 3.2 million Facebook friends.

ANOTHER BUSINESS USING THE CONNECTED COMMUNITY PLAY
WEIGHT WATCHERS

In the 1960s, Weight Watchers founder Jean Nidetch began inviting friends over so
they could share tips on how best to lose weight. The informal meetings soon evolved
into a company that's the market leader in weight loss management (Focus, Values
Alignment). Having developed its sophisticated "PointsPlus" system to break down
each food group, the company holds more than 45,000 meetings each week at which
members can meet, discuss, and weigh in (User Communities/Support Systems). More
recently, the firm started Weight Watchers Online for Men, a service for men looking
to shed a few pounds (Community and Belonging). This includes tailored content for
men, including cheat sheets for popular guy foods such as pizza and beer.

Tactics:

Product Performance

FOCUS

Design a product or service for a particular audience.

+

Service

USER COMMUNITIES/ SUPPORT SYSTEMS

Provide a communal resource for product and service support, use, and extension.

+

Brand

VALUES ALIGNMENT

Make your brand stand for a big idea or a set of values and express them consistently in all aspects of your company.

+

Harley-Davidson motorcycles are instantly recognizable, even to those who don't know an exhaust pipe from a handlebar. The bikes have both a signature look and sound; the roar of the engine is an integral part of their appeal. The company remains focused on making an iconic product. "We hold onto the values that have made Harley-Davidson motorcycles what they are, while modernizing the methods we use to build them," reads a blurb on the company website.

Harley-Davidson's Women Riders community was started as a way to encourage ladies to take up the motorcycle habit. Mentors are made available to give confidence and share advice, while "garage parties" are held to teach motorcycling basics and give women a chance to compare tips. Additional groups include Harlistas, for Latino riders, and the Iron Elite, for African American bikers.

Using popular slogans such as "Ride to Live — Live to Ride," Harley-Davidson has woven its bikes into the fabric of America. Communicating the thrill of the open road and the joy of motorcycle riding, the company's mission statement includes this explanation of its approach: "We are fueled by the brand loyalty and trust that our customers place in us to deliver premium quality and the promise of a fulfilling ownership experience."

Customer Engagement

COMMUNITY AND BELONGING

Facilitate visceral connections to make people feel they are part of a group or movement.

More than 1,400 Harley Owners Group, or "H.O.G." chapters around the world give nearly a million members the chance to meet and ride with other like-minded Harley motorcycle owners in their area. Other perks include roadside assistance and a regularly published magazine for enthusiasts.

INNOVATION PLAY
VALUES-BASED

THE PLAY AT WORK
PATAGONIA

Shift:
CUSTOMER EXPERIENCE

Ambition:
CHANGE THE KNOWN

Industry:
OUTDOOR PERFORMANCE GEAR

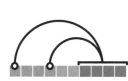

MAKE YOUR PRODUCTS STAND FOR SOMETHING AND FOSTER A MOVEMENT — FOCUSING ON A PARTICULAR CONSTITUENCY, CAUSE, OR REASON FOR EXISTING.

We all have beliefs, principles, or causes. These individual motivations connect us to larger issues in the world at large, and can confer additional meaning to otherwise run-of-the-mill behaviors and activities. Values-Based plays connect with these intrinsic motivations, prompting customer action and driving engagement and loyalty.

In 1957, Yvon Chouinard began making hard-iron pitons solely for himself, so that he wouldn't litter the rocks he was climbing with the soft-iron spikes that were commonly used. When his friends saw his designs, they wanted in, and before he quite knew what was happening, Chouinard Equipment was in business. Patagonia emerged from this firm to sell clothing created in a sustainable way from replaceable resources. It now sells its products in dedicated retail stores (and through partners) all over the world.

ANOTHER BUSINESS USING THE VALUES-BASED PLAY
WHOLE FOODS MARKET

Tony supermarket Whole Foods has gained a devoted following through its commitment to healthy deliciousness (Focus). The retailer sells more than 2,400 natural or organic products. Dubbing its local producers "rock stars," the company goes to great lengths to promote these small businesses — even supporting them through a Local Producer Loan Program (Values Alignment). In 2011, the supermarket rolled out the Global Animal Partnership's 5-Step Animal Welfare rating system to grade meat production, and an Eco-Scale Rating System for cleaning products (Transparency). Its social media presence was bolstered in 2012 by the launch of *Dark Rye*, an online magazine "exploring food, art, health and sustainable living" (Whimsy and Personality).

Tactics:

Product Performance
FOCUS
Design a product or service for a particular audience.

+

Brand
TRANSPARENCY
Let customers see into your operations and participate with your brand and offerings.

+

Brand
VALUES ALIGNMENT
Make your brand stand for a big idea or a set of values and express them consistently in all aspects of your company.

+

Patagonia's mission states that the company will "build the best product and cause no unnecessary harm." As such, the company works closely with suppliers to design effective and responsible fabrics including "Synchilla" fleece and "Regulator" insulation. In 1996, the company switched over to using organic cotton exclusively in its clothing.

Patagonia shares details of its entire supply chain for two reasons: first, to ensure that it remains as environmentally sensitive as possible, and second, to try to inspire other companies to follow its lead and reduce their own environmental impact. "The Footprint Chronicles" is an online service that provides information on the factories and textile mills Patagonia uses, including details such as the number and gender mix of employees who work on the company's goods.

The Common Threads Initiative is a joint commitment from the company to build useful things that last and from consumers to buy only what they need, uniting company and clientele in a shared mission. Meanwhile, Patagonia has over 75 brand "ambassadors," from each of the company's seven main sport lines (including fly fishing, trail running, and alpine climbing). These top athletes work directly with the design department to develop and test the best new clothing for their sport.

Customer Engagement
WHIMSY AND PERSONALITY
Humanize your offering with small flourishes of on-brand, on-message ways of seeming alive.

The *Cleanest Line* is Patagonia's blog, on which employees and brand ambassadors tell stories about what they've been up to (anyone for surfing in Russia or fishing in British Columbia?). Sharing candid photographs and uncensored opinions about various exploits, the blog communicates the passions of the company (environmental sensitivity; political activism) in a way that is accessible and not heavy-handed.

INNOVATION PLAY
SIMPLIFICATION

WII

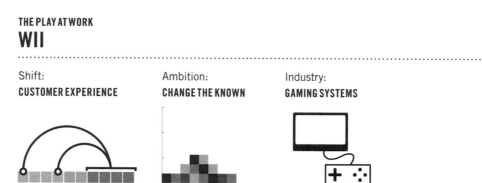

Shift:
CUSTOMER EXPERIENCE

Ambition:
CHANGE THE KNOWN

Industry:
GAMING SYSTEMS

RADICALLY EASE THE COMPLICATED, NAGGING, OR ARCANE FOR CUSTOMERS — ALLOWING THEM TO ACCOMPLISH THINGS THEY SIMPLY COULDN'T HAVE DONE BEFORE.

The promise of technology is to make our lives easier, more secure, and more productive. Yet despite its startling sophistication and ubiquity today, technology often only makes our lives more complicated and challenging — confronting us with a never-ending slew of features and options that demand too much of our time and attention. Simplification transforms this complexity into seamless elegance. It makes it easy to do hard things, and delivers great experiences in ways that require minimal effort from customers.

Launched in 2006, the Wii initially seemed unlikely to trouble the dominance of platforms such as Sony PlayStation or Microsoft Xbox. Those high-quality gaming machines offered terrifyingly realistic imagery and superior game play with superior resolution. But with its simple graphics and motion-sensitive controller, Nintendo had a hit. The system brought in $190 million in its first week on sale in the US.

ANOTHER BUSINESS USING THE SIMPLIFICATION PLAY
MINT.COM

Mint.com's mission is to help people understand and do more with their money by streamlining the accounting process (Experience Simplification). Launched in September 2007, the website featured patent-pending technology that identified and organized transactions from almost all US banks. Collecting banking information in one place and displaying it in a way that was easy to parse and organize (Engaging Functionality, Ease of Use), Mint.com identified savings opportunities based on a user's history. The site won more than 10 million members, attracted by the friendly approach to the daunting world of personal finance (Whimsy and Personality). Intuit was certainly taken with its appeal, purchasing the site for $170 million in 2009.

Tactics:

Product Performance

EASE OF USE
Make your product simple, intuitive, and comfortable to use.

+

Product Performance

ENGAGING FUNCTIONALITY
Provide an unexpected or newsworthy feature that elevates the customer interaction from the ordinary.

+

Customer Engagement

EXPERIENCE SIMPLIFICATION
Reduce complexity and focus on delivering specific experiences exceptionally well.

+

The console's interface was streamlined so that anyone could play video games "whether you're five or 95." It did away with multi-button controllers that require players to press buttons in increasingly complex patterns simply to shoot fireballs at aliens, instead relying on a simple wand with minimal buttons and no cords.

A new type of interaction between player and game was fundamental to the Wii, allowing players to play tennis against one another, box, or practice golf swings with lifelike actions enacted on the screen. (A wrist-strap was included so that over-zealous activity didn't end in tears or broken possessions.)

With simple games providing family and social fun, the Wii tapped into a new, enthusiastic market of previous non-gamers that hadn't been attracted to more difficult and complex gaming platforms. The Wii even became a feature in some nursing homes, as the elderly got their game on. In doing so, Wii made the gaming experience more about what was happening in the room than what was happening on the screen.

Customer Engagement

WHIMSY AND PERSONALITY
Humanize your offering with small flourishes of on-brand, on-message ways of seeming alive.

When players started out with the Wii, they created a digital avatar to represent their in-room activity on the screen. Known as "Mii"s, these characters added a whole layer of cute to the gaming platform.

WHAT TO ASK; WHERE TO FOCUS

Depending on the size of your organization, you may find
yourself applying multiple different plays in different areas of
your business simultaneously. Be conscious about the decisions
you're making—and understand the way they may evolve over
time. After all, innovation should never be static; even the best
innovations must evolve over time.

INSIGHTS

**Rethink what your customers need, understand what
they hate about an existing industry, and reimagine how
your business might actually change their lives.**

1

RETHINK

What novel activities can you add that are not the
norm within your industry now? How can you integrate
these smoothly and painlessly (for both your
organization and your customers)?

2

REIMAGINE

What about the status quo is just stupid at the core?
What baffles customers, wastes their time, or is just
so insanely difficult that they don't do it?

3

REFRAME

How might you enlarge or reinvent the category?
It's often the case that (paradoxically) by making
the problem bigger you can usefully make it more
elementary, simpler, and important in fresh ways.

ACTIVITIES

All businesses use a system of activities — some set of assets, processes, offerings, and channels. Innovation demands that you imagine, develop, and sustain new capabilities.

4

ENGAGE

What bold customer promise would be startling and newsworthy? Think of providing something no competitor now offers, and then figure out how you can deliver it with a guarantee.

5

EXTEND

Who are your ideal participants? Be as expansive as possible. Ideally your ecosystem should make it possible for many players to prosper. How can your way become the easiest way for anyone to operate in this industry in the near future?

6

EXPAND

Who will do what? Modern business ecosystems engage many players living on different margins, but they tend to have asymmetric power structures. What gives you the right to be the central player?

PART FIVE: IN SUMMARY
GO DEEP

These three tools provide a strong foundation for any initiative. Together, they provide a smart set of methods to help you think deeply and strategically about innovation.

1. THREE SHIFTS

Explore how you could use the business model, platform, or experience as the focal point of your work. This provides you with a helpful starting point to ensure the innovation you're developing is sophisticated, sustainable, and defensible.

2. TEN TYPES INNOVATION TACTICS

Crosscheck your project against the list of tactics and identify those that clearly apply. Cycle these in and out of your design to test different ideas and quickly gauge which ones might be worth building into your offering.

3. PLAYS AND GAMEPLANS

Break down the components of successful innovations to learn why they worked. Use the archetypal plays as inspirations and starting points for your own breakthroughs. Build them with smart combinations of innovation tactics for the best results.

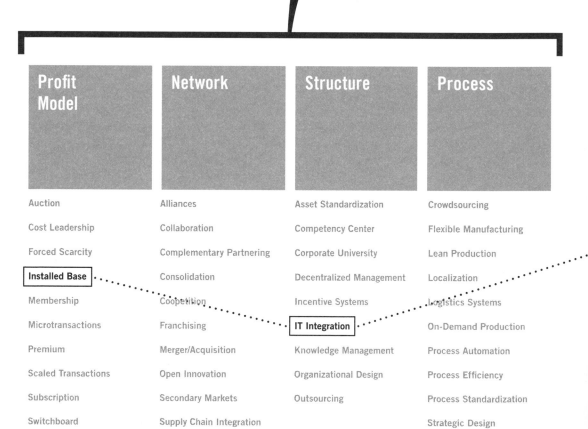

Profit Model	Network	Structure	Process
Auction	Alliances	Asset Standardization	Crowdsourcing
Cost Leadership	Collaboration	Competency Center	Flexible Manufacturing
Forced Scarcity	Complementary Partnering	Corporate University	Lean Production
Installed Base	Consolidation	Decentralized Management	Localization
Membership	Coopetition	Incentive Systems	Logistics Systems
Microtransactions	Franchising	IT Integration	On-Demand Production
Premium	Merger/Acquisition	Knowledge Management	Process Automation
Scaled Transactions	Open Innovation	Organizational Design	Process Efficiency
Subscription	Secondary Markets	Outsourcing	Process Standardization
Switchboard	Supply Chain Integration		Strategic Design

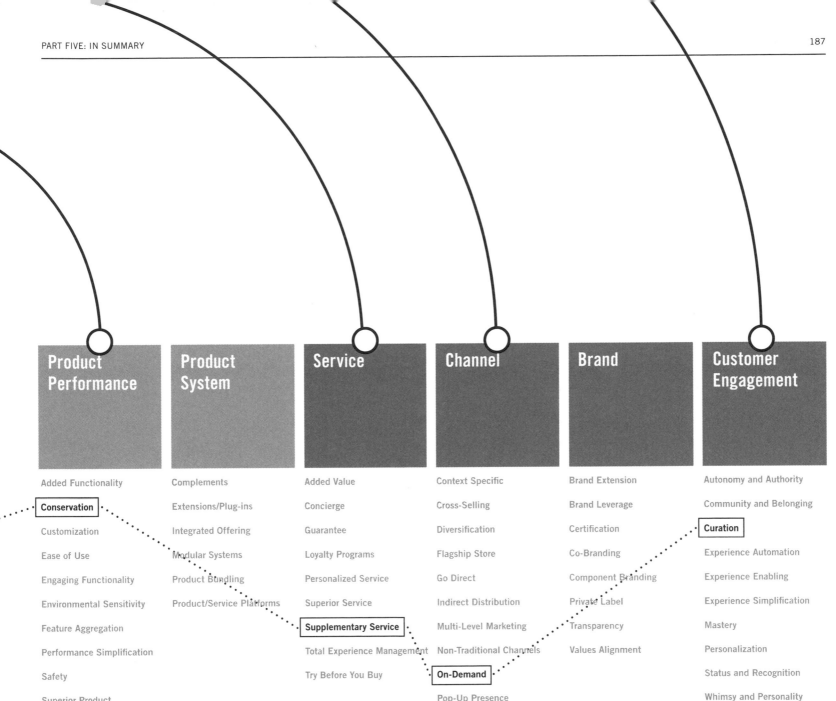

Product Performance

Added Functionality
Conservation
Customization
Ease of Use
Engaging Functionality
Environmental Sensitivity
Feature Aggregation
Performance Simplification
Safety
Superior Product

Product System

Complements
Extensions/Plug-ins
Integrated Offering
Modular Systems
Product Bundling
Product/Service Platforms

Service

Added Value
Concierge
Guarantee
Loyalty Programs
Personalized Service
Superior Service
Supplementary Service
Total Experience Management
Try Before You Buy

Channel

Context Specific
Cross-Selling
Diversification
Flagship Store
Go Direct
Indirect Distribution
Multi-Level Marketing
Non-Traditional Channels
On-Demand
Pop-Up Presence

Brand

Brand Extension
Brand Leverage
Certification
Co-Branding
Component Branding
Private Label
Transparency
Values Alignment

Customer Engagement

Autonomy and Authority
Community and Belonging
Curation
Experience Automation
Experience Enabling
Experience Simplification
Mastery
Personalization
Status and Recognition
Whimsy and Personality

PART SIX

FOSTERING INNOVATION

INSTALLING EFFECTIVE INNOVATION INSIDE YOUR ORGANIZATION

Everyone is in favor of innovation. Yet nearly every organization conspires to kill it. Here are principles on how to build an enterprise innovation system that fosters, rewards, and delivers results.

CHAPTER 21

GET CRACKING

EVERYONE IS AFRAID OF THE UNFAMILIAR. HERE'S HOW TO INNOVATE ANYWAY

It is natural to be suspicious of the unfamiliar. Actually, it's *entirely* natural. We're wired that way as humans; it's a protective self-defense mechanism that makes us alert and on guard when the normal patterns of the world are suddenly abnormal. We hear a rustle behind us in the bush; adrenaline floods our system; anxiety floods our brains and we flee. Over time, we learn to discern which rustles are harmless and which ones present real harm. As historian and humanist Michael Shermer put it, "Humans are pattern seeking, story-telling animals trying to make sense of our world." This wiring is how we've managed to avoid being eaten by lions, tigers, and hyenas for millennia.

But this same wiring tends to provoke anxiety about *anything* that's new and unfamiliar. If in principle we are all in favor of innovation, in practice we try to make our world safe and certain. Think about your own behavior. When the weekend rolls around, you wear the clothes that are most familiar; you watch the sports teams you like; you wade through whatever is stored on your DVR to catch up on your favorite shows. This is the dominant condition you will face within your organization, too. If you want to help people to innovate more—and become better at innovating—you have to get individuals and teams to embrace rather than resist the unfamiliar.

As a leader, you need to help your organization understand that innovation *is not optional*. Most companies are now interconnected—to other companies, to services, systems, and customers. This increased connectivity accelerates cycles of change, and blurs the boundaries between markets, governments, and industries. Just think: nearly 40% of the companies listed in the Fortune 500 in 1999 were no longer there 10 years later. Facebook founder Mark Zuckerberg was a billionaire by the age of 23. For any enterprise to remain relevant and vibrant today, it must innovate.

You must also help your organization to see that innovation is a discipline. Our position is that innovation is not an arcane art that can only be practiced by a handful of creative wizards. *Anyone* can innovate, and *any* company can build the approaches, management structures, resources, and tools necessary to help people to become better innovators. Your job is to catalyze that change.

So when you're faced with reasons and excuses for not innovating, listen patiently. Try to empathize with the anxiety and fear that lie underneath these explanations. Then explain why even someone's reasonable-sounding reasons must be overcome.

REASONABLE-SOUNDING REASONS
NOT TO INNOVATE

Here are some of the most common excuses we hear from people who aren't yet convinced that they too can innovate — and how to get past them.

"WE'RE TOO INWARDLY FOCUSED. WE LOOK AT EVERYTHING THROUGH OUR COMPANY LENS, ALL THE TIME."

Break free of this myopia by forcing your organization to look outside for inspiration. One way to challenge the orthodoxies of your business is to use the Ten Types to illustrate where and how your competitors have historically innovated. Look at both current and potential rivals and assess their work to see if they are innovating in different ways. By studying how others are innovating differently, you open up a new sense of possibility for your own activities.

"WE KNOW OUR INDUSTRY BETTER THAN ANYONE. WE KNOW WHAT THE BIG PROBLEMS ARE — AND THEIR ANSWERS."

As Joy's Law states, "No matter who you are, most of the smartest people work for someone else."[1] A key blind spot in most well-run firms is that they hyper-focus on their best and most demanding customers, steadily improving the known instead of inventing the new. Particularly in a hyper-connected world that is upended by technological advances on a regular basis, there's simply no room for this attitude — particularly when the firm that will disrupt you almost certainly isn't in your industry today.

1 That's Bill Joy, the legendary technologist and cofounder of Sun Microsystems.

2 We have discovered that customers tend to find the boldest ideas easy to grasp and endorse—they will usually be quick to accept that something hard and remarkable can be done. It's a different story with your own colleagues, who instead focus on all the obstacles. This is a key reason to make business ideas tangible, quickly: this helps to bring the doubters on board.

"OUR CULTURE IS TOO RISK AVERSE AND ANTI-BREAKTHROUGH."

The urgent always displaces the important. The pressure companies face today to deliver quarter-to-quarter earnings is real, and that can lead companies to focus too much on incremental innovation, to steadily improve existing products. It's not that it's a mistake to develop core innovations; in fact, we suggest that most of an organization's innovation efforts should focus on it. But it's important to make sure you *also* drive a handful of more sophisticated, higher-ambition efforts. Effective innovators manage innovation like an investment portfolio composed of many reliable performers but also spiked with a few bold bets.

"WE FIND IT DIFFICULT TO BRING IDEAS FROM CONCEPT TO MARKET."

Quite right. It *is* difficult to bring ideas from concept to reality; it's a hard, grueling journey with lots of headwinds and bumps. But there are methods to make this journey routinely successful. For instance, prototype the entire new business end to end, and do so visually so that internal stakeholders *and* customers can see the same future you do.[2] Use these visualizations not only to drive fast and cheap iteration of an idea, but also to build emotional commitment to the concept throughout your organization. Bite off the smallest viable part of the idea to bring to market first, and use that as a beachhead to grow and scale the business. All of these principles and approaches help to de-risk the journey to market.

"WE DON'T KNOW HOW TO BE CREATIVE OR GENERATIVE, ONLY ANALYTICAL AND EVALUATIVE."

This view is often held by executives within well-established, large companies that have embedded management sciences such as Six Sigma and stagegate processes throughout their organizations. Let's return to our contention that creativity is rarely the scarce resource in innovation. What most organizations need is discipline, not more creative ideas. One of the fastest ways to overcome this obstacle is to bring in different types of thinkers. Designers aren't just for the design department anymore; they can help surface provocative ideas to change the way you work. Social scientists can also help to surface fascinating insights into what customers are really seeking.

"INNOVATION IS EASIER IN A SMALL COMPANY OR A START-UP."

Many people believe that innovation is easier in a small company. They also often believe that innovation is easier in a technology or engineering firm than it is within other companies. These beliefs are wrong and only serve to reassure people in larger organizations that they don't have to innovate. They do. You do. Every single employee of every single company needs to stand in the future and embrace it—no matter how difficult or scary it feels or how impossible a goal seems to achieve. And every single employee and every single organization can become better at innovating. The trick is to start, and to be precise about the methods and tools you are using.

BALANCING ESSENTIAL TENSIONS (AND RESISTING FALSE TRADE-OFFS)

Some qualities innovators need to master seem to contradict one another. How can I be creative *and* disciplined? Is it really possible to be practical *and* ambitious? Yet designers and scientists typically have no particular problem embracing these seeming dilemmas. Many great advances involve deeply appreciating and resolving the essential tension in a challenge: "How can a device be smaller, lighter, *and* more powerful?" Or "How can a car be comfortable *and* fuel-efficient?" Or even "How can the health care system produce better outcomes *and* cost dramatically less?" Any great innovation system respects and resolves these seeming conflicts. The key is to see them as tensions to be managed rather than trade-offs that must be made.

INNOVATION REQUIRES

CREATIVITY + DISCIPLINE

Creativity is not the scarce resource in innovation efforts. Discipline is. This is mastery of the methods and tools needed to identify, sequence, and solve all the problems of an innovation challenge. Just as musicians practice scales and arpeggios regularly, innovators must be disciplined about their craft to maximize their impact. Constraints amplify creativity; they never hamper it. It is fair, reasonable, and responsible to expect anyone to innovate, creative or not — *and* to pursue that mission with rigor.

PRAGMATISM + AMBITION

An essential (and often uncomfortable) part of innovation is committing to solving bold and complicated challenges—especially when you don't know precisely *how* you'll solve them. Make sure you don't let the natural anxiety of that moment reduce your ambition; first, trust in using better methods and tools, and over time, trust in your talent. Make sure you are tackling challenges that are relevant to your firm and your customers, and look for every opportunity to de-risk your effort. Use prototyping and piloting to drive iterative development, and consider how you will deliver the hardest part of your big challenge.

TOP-DOWN + BOTTOM-UP

Senior leaders cannot be immersed in every detail of every project—but they can articulate an inspired and inspiring innovation focus, and hold teams accountable for delivering results. The best innovation leaders remain open to the work taking surprising turns and producing unexpected outcomes. As the innovation develops, the intended customer or user may change; the solution may involve radically different types as the work evolves. It's also critical for leadership to give teams the support they need to be successful—and to encourage ownership at all levels of the organization.

ANALYSIS + SYNTHESIS

Analysis (solving problems by breaking down and examining their component parts) and synthesis (solving problems by creating new solutions from disparate parts) are very different processes. Both are needed in successful innovation and they are most powerful in combination. Our approach to innovation demands both: analyzing powerful innovations and industry patterns, and synthesizing new innovations from great building blocks. For too long, there has been an unhelpful divide between the two sides; creative types dismissing MBAs as dull drillbits and vice versa. Happily this gap is dissolving, and strong teams use both of these skills recursively and in abundance.

CHAPTER 22

SPONSORS AND AUTHORS
GREAT FIRMS MAKE SURE THAT INNOVATION IS NOT OPTIONAL

Leaders play an indispensable role in catalyzing and driving innovation. Given that most people (and organizations) innately resist change, the job of an innovation leader is to overcome this inertia and drive a path to the future. There are many different ways to foster this momentum, but the same fundamental behavior underlies the following examples, taken from iconic companies such as Amazon, General Electric, and IBM. Great leaders make innovation obligatory instead of optional; they sponsor the change they want to see, and they set the conditions for their organizations to author and drive initiatives from concept to market successfully.

INNOVATION LEADERS MAKE BOLD
AND COMMITTED CHOICES

In 1997, the year he took his fledgling company public, Jeff Bezos wrote a few words to Amazon's new shareholders. In this letter, he referred to their collective environment as "Day 1" of the Internet. "Because of our emphasis on the long term, we may make decisions and weigh tradeoffs differently than some companies," he wrote, proceeding to outline his precise vision for his organization. Bezos outlined his beliefs in making investment decisions to drive toward sustainable market leadership rather than chasing short-term profitability, and his commitment to the aggressive management of every internal program. "We will make bold rather than timid investment decisions where we see a sufficient probability of gaining market leadership advantages. Some of these investments will pay off, others will not, and we will have learned another valuable lesson in either case," he wrote.

Despite media skepticism at some of his decisions over the years, Bezos has rarely wavered. Amazon's more recent pursuit of the high-end fashion market with MyHabit.com is a great example of this. Despite fierce competition from companies such as Yoox.com and Gilt, Amazon is pursuing the market with typical long-term commitment—with three women hired full-time to try on size eight shoes, and a fashion studio using patented technology to shoot 3,000 images every day. Bezos's commitment to driving Amazon his way—making long-term decisions and inexorably expanding an empire—has been effective: where Amazon enjoyed revenues of $147.8 million in 1997, that figure had grown to just over $48 billion in 2011. And yet, alongside his 2011 note to shareholders, Bezos included his original letter, writing, "Our approach remains the same, and it's still Day 1!"

Innovation always feels obvious in retrospect. Yet the journey from idea to implementation is anything but; it is fraught with doubt and danger, and as a leader you will be second-guessed by analysts, shareholders, and employees alike. Your job is to sustain the effort. As Bezos explained in a shareholder meeting in 2011, "Any time you do something big, that's disruptive, there will be critics… You listen to them, because you want to see, always testing, is it possible they are right? But if you hold back and you say, 'No, we believe in this vision,' then you just stay heads down, stay focused and you build out your vision."

INNOVATION LEADERS TRUST THEIR TALENT —
AND HOLD THEM ACCOUNTABLE

Maintaining a growth trajectory becomes challenging as an enterprise increases in scale. Consider this: General Electric made roughly $147 billion in revenues in 2011. So for the company to grow 5% annually requires it to create the equivalent of a Fortune 500 company every year. CEO Jeff Immelt seized this challenge by holding his managers accountable for innovation. The "Imagination Breakthroughs" program, launched in 2003, was specifically designed to engage and commit managers and employees to innovation throughout the vast organization, and to harness, protect, and promote their bright ideas.

Every year, the heads of each business unit from within the corporation submit their biggest ideas for driving organic growth. These proposals are reviewed by a leadership team (including Immelt) and each year, a number are given the "Imagination Breakthrough" imprimatur. Note: It's not a meaningless badge of honor. The so-called "IB projects" are designed, nurtured, and implemented within the individual business units, but each month senior leadership takes the time to review the current status of a selection of them. This provides the projects and their participants greater visibility, commercial expertise, and sometimes, supplementary funding.

"Ultimately, I'd like to see the concept morph so that we have 1,000 imagination breakthroughs and the focus is less on these big elephants and more on creativity throughout the businesses," Immelt commented back in 2006.[1] The results have been promising: in the ensuing years, Immelt has committed billions of dollars to over 100 Imagination Breakthroughs, ranging from distributed energy to advanced software and services.

Think back for a minute, if you will, to the beginning of your career. Do you remember a time when someone took a risk on you and gave you a chance? Did you have a mentor who trusted you to step up and do well, despite a near total lack of evidence that you were capable of doing any such thing? We believe the best innovation leaders do this routinely: they charge young, high-potential individuals with the expectation that they will innovate, and trust them to pull off tough initiatives. At the same time, you must hold your organization accountable for innovation with smart metrics and incentives. This is how you give innovation teeth.

1 "I knew if I could define a process and set the right metrics, this company could go 100 miles an hour in the right direction," Immelt said in that same interview with *Harvard Business Review*.

INNOVATION LEADERS STAND IN THE FUTURE
AND HELP OTHERS SEE IT

2   IBM has 12 Research Labs worldwide, so it is literally true that the sun never sets on IBM's R&D.

3   For a fascinating account of this history—including the tale of Steve Jobs visiting Xerox PARC in 1979—see Malcolm Gladwell's "Creation Myth," published in The New Yorker (May 16, 2011).

In the 1990s, Lou Gerstner famously diverted IBM away from making products toward providing services. It was a bold move, one that by now has been dissected and documented in many places. Less noted are the huge bets made by Gerstner's successor Sam Palmisano, who became the company's CEO in 2002, to double and triple down on that shift to services.

It was Palmisano who made the call to dump Big Blue's ThinkPad unit, selling it to the Chinese firm Lenovo. He also oversaw the acquisition of nearly 100 firms, including PricewaterhouseCoopers Consulting and Cognos, to move aggressively into global consulting and data analytics. This was the beginning of the true watershed shift in the nature of the firm, and a true reinvention of an enterprise that once led an industry.

All told, Palmisano induced IBM to spend $50 billion on acquisitions and R&D. The company has a $6 billion annual R&D budget, and the department churns out thousands of patents every year—it is nearly always the top global recipient of annual patents.[2] IBM's consultants find, package, and leverage the resulting "repeatable assets"—think of them as problem-solving technologies that can work in various settings. The result is that IBM has deep expertise in a huge array of diverse subjects. And now it can offer consulting that is not low-margin enterprise software implementation, but instead provides high-margin concepts that stem from rich research discoveries.

History is littered with cautionary tales about companies that missed fundamental shifts in their markets—from Xerox developing but then ignoring many of the integral components of personal computing, including the mouse and graphic user interfaces,[3] to Blockbuster failing to respond to the existential threat that Netflix and video-on-demand posed to its business model. Your job as a leader is to stand in the future and embrace it bravely, regardless of its implications for today's business—and then to help your organization stand there as well.

CHAPTER 23
INSTALLING INNOVATION
DON'T WORRY ABOUT CULTURE. BUILD A SYSTEMIC CAPABILITY

Many leaders believe building an innovative organization relies on culture. They look at innovation giants like Apple or Google and think, *"If only we had a culture like theirs. The halls must hum with innovation. They have beautiful offices, fabulous cafes, great perks…"* Lots of time and millions of dollars later, the company sports a gleaming new innovation center, festoons its walls with pretty posters, runs corporate innovation fairs to enhance creativity, and proudly displays the company ping pong tables. Just one problem: it's very rare indeed for actual innovations to make it to market following all of that hoopla.

The problem with trying to change the culture of an organization is that it's a bit like trying to hug a cloud — you can see and feel it, but it's hard to get a grip on it. That's why we encourage companies to focus instead on building innovation capabilities.

We define an innovation capability as an institutional ability to innovate reliably and repeatedly over time — meaning it doesn't depend on luck or the talent of any single employee. Instead, it relies on an orchestrated set of organizational behaviors. It turns out that when your people act and think differently over time — and when they see different and better results emerge from these behavioral shifts — culture takes care of itself. Put simply, nothing spurs innovation across an organization like actually bringing a few hot concepts to market. After that, you can hang all the posters you want.

THE FOUR COMPONENTS OF AN INNOVATION CAPABILITY

To shift the behaviors of your organization, you need to define and drive the change from multiple angles. It isn't enough just to hire more innovative individuals. Without a clear approach to guide and coordinate their efforts, the right place in the organization to house them, and appropriate metrics and incentives to guide them, they will fail. In our experience, shifting the behaviors of an organization and building lasting capabilities requires four distinct components — carefully designed to reinforce one another and work in concert to drive innovation reliably and repeatedly.

APPROACH

Clear definitions for the work to be done in creating innovations — the phases, activities, deliverables, and decision rights — as well as any specific methods and tools that should be used.

ORGANIZATION

The units that house the innovation capability — teams, divisions, leadership — along with the interfaces that connect it to the broader enterprise and the world.

RESOURCES & COMPETENCIES

The individuals who perform the work of innovation; the skills and training they need to do it capably, as well as the funding and time to fuel it.

METRICS & INCENTIVES

The targets to guide performance, the measures to evaluate progress, and the incentives (monetary and otherwise) to drive supporting behaviors.

INNOVATION CAPABILITY:
THE FOUR COMPONENTS IN GREATER DETAIL

Almost every business has some existing function for producing simple innovations — typically within R&D, marketing, or product development. But highly sophisticated innovation doesn't fit neatly within a typical organizational structure. It depends on multidisciplinary teams that include everyone from engineers to marketers to brand strategists to finance experts. The most common mistake we see from executives trying to build an innovation capability is they assume that both simple and sophisticated innovations can come from the same system. They can't. "Improving the known" and "inventing the new" demand and deserve different handling. The job of an innovation leader is to understand the differences, and then design and implement the right system for each.

APPROACH

Core innovation approaches tend to be fairly linear and predictable: they're typically grounded in technology and execution, and managed using firm, normalized stagegate processes (we need x number of ideas at stage one, which will narrow to y number of ideas in stage two, and so on). More ambitious innovation requires a different approach—one that prizes experimentation and iteration, and gives teams the space to explore left turns, discover startling surprises, and follow a non-linear path. This doesn't give teams a license to make things up as they go along—effective firms use rigorous protocols, with clear phases, methods, and tools, to help teams pursue bold innovation with discipline.[1]

MAYO CLINIC'S BREAKTHROUGH APPROACH

Mayo Clinic uses a five-phase process to vet innovation projects: "Scanning and Framing" to identify opportunities; "Researching and Experimenting" to develop insights; "Synthesizing" to turn those insights into concepts; "Prototyping" to develop the concepts iteratively; and finally, "Implementing" to launch them into the world at large. Each of those phases is designed to diverge and explore a wide range of new possibilities before converging on an opportunity, concept, and then prototype. As ideas progress, they steadily increase in tangibility and are awarded more development dollars—helping to de-risk the investment that the world-renowned clinic makes in building breakthroughs.

1   See the website tentypesofinnovation.com for other useful ways to build a smaller number of bigger ideas—and de-risk them enough so that they are more likely to succeed than fail.

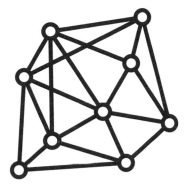

ORGANIZATION

Almost all companies have some structure in place to coordinate core innovation and ongoing product development. Driving adjacent and transformational innovation often requires new and distinct organizational structures and interfaces. Not every firm has dedicated structures for developing new markets and businesses. There are a variety of organizational options: "greenhouses" that both house innovation knowledge and create and develop innovations; "service centers" that use unique expertise to support the innovation efforts of different business units, and even highly distributed systems where most employees have some innovation responsibility. The one constant is that the innovation organization must foster collaboration across functions and divisional silos without being impeded by internal bureaucracy or politics, and it must interact well with the existing business units. At some point, a fledgling innovation concept or emerging business needs to join its brothers and sisters in the existing enterprise—and survive and thrive during that transition.[2]

VALVE'S FLAT ORGANIZATION, DESIGNED FOR INNOVATORS

Gaming company Valve started out in 1996 with a clear mission: to make great games its players would enjoy. Its secret sub-mission: to design an internal environment that would foster greatness from its employees. Today, Valve has an entirely flat management structure, a place where not even the founder has any more say than anyone else. Not only can employees select every project they work on (here, there's no such thing as "20% time"; it's "100% time"), but all desks have wheels so that people can easily relocate to work with a new team. (Of course, teams do form, and leaders do emerge, but these are short-term, temporary arrangements.) No employee is fired for making a (single) mistake, while working long hours is seen as a sign that something's wrong. Meanwhile, all are reminded to spend time and effort thinking about the company's long-term goals as well as more immediate objectives. The deliberate lack of formal organization seems to be working: Valve games such as Half-Life have sold millions of copies.[3]

RESOURCES & COMPETENCIES

Adjacent and transformational innovation need diverse individuals with a range of competencies, training, and skills, and a range of abilities in analysis, synthesis, and user empathy. We recommend convening a mix of designers, user researchers, and business strategists, and complementing them with market researchers, technology experts, and engineers. At a minimum, ensure that these teams are multidisciplinary, staffed with high-potential employees, and that they represent different stakeholders and interests in the organization. The initiatives they undertake are typically nurtured and managed directly by senior or corporate leadership, and are often paid for via discrete sources such as a venture fund or protected corporate innovation budget. These teams must be granted the time and space to understand the future needs of the market and should be protected from being crushed by the always urgent (but sometimes less important) needs of the present business.

HYATT'S LAB HOTELS EMPOWER EMPLOYEES

"The next time you visit a Hyatt hotel, you may be part of one of its experiments to improve the customer experience, perhaps without even knowing it," wrote Stacy Collett.[4] Hyatt has 488 hotels, operating under seven brand names, spread all over the world. And its so-called "laboratory hotels" act as crucibles for innovation; areas where staff members can quickly test ideas that might then be rolled out more broadly to the rest of the hotel portfolio. Collett reported that the lab hotels experiment with between seven and nine unique projects at a time: employees are encouraged to come up with new ways to solve old problems, looking to see what works and what doesn't without agonizing over the details. Funding depends on the size and scope of the project; sometimes an individual hotel will pay for experiments; sometimes this support will come from broader corporate innovation dollars. Ideas tested to date include equipping employees with mobile check-in tools, and dispensing with the front desk altogether.

4 "Ready, Set, Compete: The Benefits of IT Innovation" by Stacy Collett takes a look at the "fail fast and move on" trend, *Computerworld*, January 14, 2013: http://tentyp.es/XHSveu See also the profile of Hyatt's CEO, Mark Hoplamazian: "Hyatt's Travelin' Man," featured *Barron's*, July 14, 2012: http://tentyp.es/VT3AH

METRICS & INCENTIVES

Incremental innovation metrics tend to call for reliability; projects need to get through the pipeline efficiently and are measured primarily by forecasted and actual economic returns. Given the inherent uncertainty of something that's entirely new to a market or the world, breakthrough innovations must be measured in different ways. Use a combination of input and output metrics, and leading and lagging indicators. Even fairly loose measures such as "the percentage of customers who expressed interest in buying the prototype," or "the mix of core versus breakthrough innovation initiatives in our portfolio" can be more meaningful and useful than estimates of future revenue or profit. Get the metrics right first—then make sure you connect them tightly to employee incentives. While financial rewards matter, most employees are driven to innovate for other reasons—ranging from company recognition to personal satisfaction to the meaning drawn from creating something new. So be sure to include both monetary and other incentives, such as company awards, personal development time, and leadership attention.[5]

PROCTER & GAMBLE DRIVES BREAKTHROUGHS

"The hardest thing for a company is to change its thinking," said P&G CEO Edwin Artzt in 1994. "You have to have rules that give us intellectual permission to make changes." Among his new rules: a move to value pricing; a stripped-down bureaucracy, and "SGE," or "Strengthening Global Effectiveness." The four rules of SGE: change the work; do more with less; eliminate "rework"; and reduce costs.

Realizing that too much innovation was incremental, P&G eliminated 25% of its product extensions. Meanwhile, leadership figured out a new management structure whereby brand managers could take a promising idea to a superior—who had the authority to fund it quickly with as much as $1 million per project. Artzt's successors have continued to embrace his policies and focus. "If we spend our time working on small modifications to something, we won't have time to work on the big new stuff," acknowledged John Pepper in 1996.[6]

5   At Apple, Steve Jobs met annually with the "Top 100," a group he convened to discuss the company's future strategy.

6   *Fortune* magazine ran several articles covering P&G in this era. In particular, see Brian Dumaine's "P&G Rewrites the Marketing Rules," November 6, 1989: http://tentyp.es/TjEPID; Bill Saporito's "Behind the Tumult at P&G," March 7, 1994: http://tentyp.es/UTCVtm; and Ronald Henkoff's "P&G New and Improved!" October 14, 1996: http://tentyp.es/Q2o6mj.

PUTTING IT ALL TOGETHER: DESIGNING YOUR CAPABILITY BLUEPRINT

When designed and implemented well, the four components support and reinforce one another. Each is critical in driving the right organizational behaviors that power innovation. Be clear about how the capability will work before you implement; otherwise, you risk stumbling out of the gate and reinforcing many of your organization's worst fears about its inability to innovate.

The Capability Blueprint is one tool we use with our clients to help them be thoughtful and intentional in designing an innovation capability. The simplified example shown here is illustrative only—after all, one size does not fit all. Some organizations will work well with a concentrated and centralized innovation function; others will demand the agility and self-direction of de-centralized models. There is no one design that suits all enterprises; figure out which one will work for yours.

CAPABILITY COMPONENTS

APPROACH
The work to be done and methods to use in developing innovations

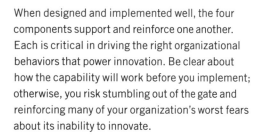

ORGANIZATION
Where this work happens, and how it connects to the broader enterprise

RESOURCES & COMPETENCIES
The people, skills, funding, and other assets we need to fuel the work

METRICS & INCENTIVES
How we'll measure our progress, track success, and reward the right behaviors.

ILLUSTRATIVE EXAMPLE

We need to charter and drive an initiative to develop a breakthrough new diabetes diagnostic business, bringing it to pilot by next year.

Our Innovation Center will lead this work until it is ready for pilot; it will then slowly transition to management by our existing diagnostic business.

The leader of the diagnostic business will sponsor the initiative. We'll staff the team with a mix of innovation specialists from our Center and high-potential employees from the diagnostic business, and fund it through our Innovation Fund.

We'll measure it with qualitative assessments in the concept stage, and then via projected sales and customer response in the prototype and pilot stages. Our leaders and the project team will have 20% of their compensation tied to the initiative's success.

These components *supply* and *support* new behaviors from the enterprise...

...This component *demands* and *pulls* the enterprise to exhibit the new behaviors.

We regularly use capability blueprints with firms looking to get better at breakthrough innovation. The page below shows an overview of the system for the entire process, from identifying opportunities and chartering initiatives through to prototyping, piloting, and launching innovations. Additional pages elaborate on each of these different components and stages.

	APPROACH How will we develop innovations?	**IDENTIFY & PRIORITIZE OPPORTUNITIES** Consider changing user needs, shifts in industry structure, and unchallenged orthodoxies to identify potential opportunities.	**DEVELOP CONCEPTS** Produce tangible new business concepts by designing innovative business models, platforms, and customer experiences.	**BUILD & TEST PROTOTYPES** Iterate and refine concepts by identifying key problem areas and creating prototypes (of all kinds) to test them with customers and users.	**CONDUCT PILOTS** Validate your idea by building parts of the new businesses and bringing them to market—carefully gauging the response from clients.	**START-UP** Build and launch the businesses, focusing on scaling rapidly and attracting customers to drive growth.
ORGANIZATION Where does innovation happen? Who's in charge?	Innovation Council					
		Executive Leader & Portfolio Management Group				
	Innovation Center of Excellence (COE)					
			Development Teams		Commercialization Teams	
RESOURCES & COMPETENCIES Who and what do we need to fuel our innovation efforts?	Competitive analysis Technology strategy Scenario planning		Ethnography Secondary research Visual design Business strategy	Design planning Evaluative user research Competitive analysis Visual design Business strategy	Pilot management Business development Vendor management UX design and management	Sales strategy Operational scaling
	Funded and Staffed by Innovation COE				Funded and Staffed by Individual Business Units	
METRICS & INCENTIVES How will we know we are succeeding?	Make sure you have a balanced portfolio including simple, category-changing, and game-changing kinds of innovation.		How many concepts and prototypes are currently in development? "Balanced Breakthrough" assessment: how desirable your idea will be to customers, how feasible it is to make, and how viable it might be from a business and strategy perspective.		How many customers engage with the pilot?	Revenue Operating income Return on invested capital

METRICS MOVE MOUNTAINS
(BUT ONLY IF YOU PICK THE RIGHT ONES)

What gets measured, gets done. This old chestnut has been kicking around management theory for decades, and lies at the heart of "management by objective" (MBO)—the principle that if you set a target and measure progress toward it, your organization will inexorably move to achieve it come hell or high water.

Unsurprisingly, then, what you measure turns out to be pretty important. 3M has long prided itself on innovation, and has an admirable record of repeatedly developing innovative new products. In 1988, executives put in place an incentive system to help drive innovation. One of its core metrics was the "Freshness Index," which measured the percentage of revenue that came from new products. The company target: 25% of revenue over a four- to five-year span should come from new introductions.

At first glance, this seems sensible. It takes a goal of repeatedly developing innovative new products—and attaches it to an easily defined and observable measure. However, when the target was raised to 30% in 1992, the organization's product managers began to make up the difference by developing ever more incremental innovations, until many of its "new" products were merely new package sizes or different colors.[7] These multiplied the number of products that 3M was making, alright—but also increased the costs of complexity and marketing, caused channel management problems, and drove little incremental revenue. Since then, 3M has refined this metric by clarifying what constitutes a new product. Clearly it has worked; 3M is a feature in any list of top innovators, and its revenue has nearly doubled over the past decade.

Most organizations tend to pursue many small, incremental innovation initiatives and not enough breakthrough initiatives. The Freshness Index can amplify this problem because it disproportionately rewards a shorter (and less risky) time to market—and breakthrough initiatives are inherently riskier and take longer to develop. For this reason, we tend to avoid using a metric like the Freshness Index.

Instead, your goal should be to develop a balanced system of metrics that can nurture bold initiatives instead of rejecting them. This requires using a mixture of indicators that look backward and ahead, grounded in both internal and external measures such as value for the company or value for customers. Critically, you must measure both the success of individual initiatives and the impact of your collective portfolio of initiatives.

7 This tale is explored in *Corporate Creativity* by Alan G. Robinson and Sam Stern, and deepened in Robert B. Tucker's *Driving Growth Through Innovation*.

There is no set prescription or formula for developing the metrics that will work for your organization, but here are some principles to help you get started:

CREATE A BALANCED SET OF MEASUREMENTS
You should have at least one measure from each of the four quadrants—looking back and looking ahead, internal and external.

AVOID METRIC OVERLOAD
Organizations rarely need more than six metrics to drive and guide innovation effectively.

METRICS MUST BE MEANINGFUL
In some firms, a metric that isn't attached to hard numbers is meaningless; in others, qualitative measures are entirely valid. Choose metrics that speak the language of your organization.

USEFUL INNOVATION METRICS

	LOOKING BACK	LOOKING AHEAD
EXTERNAL	■ Innovation hit rate for initiatives across the portfolio (the number of them that return their cost of capital) ■ Economic value created by innovation ■ Firm's Net Promoter Score ■ Customer satisfaction ■ Brand perception—for both individual initiatives and the overall portfolio ■ Number of positive media and analyst mentions the firm receives regarding innovation	■ Economic value estimates (EVE) of individual initiatives and the overall portfolio ■ Percentage of initiatives in the portfolio that are clearly motivated by compelling customer insights ■ Percentage of initiatives in the portfolio that involve cocreation with suppliers, customers or partners ■ Percentage of innovation costs borne by you versus cocreators—for individual initiatives and the innovation portfolio
INTERNAL	■ Net Present Value (NPV) created by innovation ■ Growth in NPV across the innovation portfolio ■ Percentage of innovation initiatives taken to market ■ Percentage of innovations that have survived three or more years in the market versus the number of initiatives in the portfolio ■ Revenue generated by innovation initiatives	■ NPV estimates across initiatives and portfolio ■ Growth in project NPV estimates across the portfolio ■ Size, speed, and efficiency of the pipeline across the portfolio ■ Degree of alignment of the innovation portfolio with other strategic growth platforms ■ Ratio of incremental to game-changing innovation in the portfolio, measured in the number of initiatives and/or expenditures

CHAPTER 24
EXECUTE EFFECTIVELY
PRINCIPLES FOR BRINGING YOUR INNOVATIONS TO MARKET ON TIME AND ON BUDGET

If you find yourself in the exhilarating and occasionally terrifying role of overseeing an innovation initiative—or even just participating in one—here are the most important principles to keep in mind.

INNOVATE WITH A MISSION—DON'T BE RANDOM

Many innovation initiatives fail before they begin. Their desired outcomes are unstated or vaguely defined, their connection to the strategy and purpose of the enterprise is unclear, and the underlying opportunities are hazy and diffuse. Great innovators know what they are trying to achieve; they focus on fewer, bolder ideas and execute them with care. They have a clearly defined intent and desired outcomes, married to an equally clear strategy for achieving them.

FOCUS ON THE HARDEST PARTS TO GET RIGHT

The dumbest way to simplify a tough problem is to throw out all the hard parts. And yet this is precisely what many leaders urge their teams to do. Faced with a list of possibilities, they trot out their tired clichés: "What can we do differently next Monday?" or "Where are the low-hanging fruit?" The thing with innovation is that the hardest parts are often the only ones that really matter. If you don't crack the tough core of a problem, your ideas are simply ordinary and easy to copy. Instead, identify the truly critical parts of the innovation concept.[1] Work on them relentlessly until they're solved. The easy bits you can usually do *en passant*.

SET GUARDRAILS TO KEEP THE TEAM ON TRACK

Constraints amplify creativity. As Charles Eames said in 1969, "Design depends largely on constraints"—and so does the success of your innovation initiative. In the absence of such parameters, teams drift and drown in possibilities, veering from option to option—because without guidelines, everything is essentially optional and no one can tell you you're barking up the wrong tree.

RESOLVE DILEMMAS BOLDLY AND HAVE PATIENCE FOR THE ANSWERS

Throughout the innovation process, trade-offs and dilemmas arise at every turn. "Surely an offering can't have superior service *and* be low cost?" Or, "No way it can come with a guarantee *and* offer flexibility and choice to the customer." Faced with such challenges (often amid increasing time pressure and decreasing resources), innovators often pick one side of the challenge and ignore the rest. This leads to incomplete answers and partial solutions. Great innovators find ways to develop new options that resolve the problems and deliver the impossible. Demand holistic solutions instead of ideas that merely filigree around the edges of a gnarly problem.

1   The experience at the iTunes Store depends, in large part, on being able to go there and buy a single song. We hear it took 200 lawyers working for Apple round the clock for two years to negotiate the rights to do this. Talk about getting the truly critical part of the innovation right. It was also a key factor in the company becoming the most valuable firm in the world by mid-2012.

2   Atul Gawande's terrific book, *The Checklist Manifesto*, surveys the importance of protocols. Historically, look at the *Betty Crocker Cookbook*. General Mills (there never was an actual Betty Crocker) helped people reliably and repeatedly prepare home meals.

3 In the movie *Barbarians at the Gate*, the former CEO of RJR Nabisco comments on an initiative to develop a smokeless cigarette: "We've spent 350 million dollars and we come up with a turd with a tip?... We put enough technology in this project to send a cigarette to the moon and we come up with one that tastes like it took a dump?" This kind of response does not suggest a project is going well.

4 It's worth noting that DARPA — which has no shortage of legitimate concerns over letting secrets slip — has used open innovation spectacularly well to develop new offerings and engage its network of suppliers, customers, and collaborators.

USE "HIGH-PROTOCOL" INNOVATION, AND KNOW WHICH METHODS WORK

One of the cruelest things done to smart people is to ask them to innovate, lock them in a small room, and equip them with nothing but expectations — no principles, no methods, no tools to fulfill their mission. It's akin to asking a novice to perform brain surgery. It's patently unfair and it rarely works. "High-protocol" innovation means that you equip your teams with smart tools (including the Ten Types) and augment them with step-by-step instructions about what to do, in what sequence, to get a good outcome.[2]

VISUALIZE EXPERIENCES FROM END-TO-END

Make your concept as tangible as possible by illustrating it as though it already existed in the world. Use paper prototypes first; they're cheap and easy to change. Be sure to illustrate the whole concept, showing how the entire business will work, not just some product or gadget at its center. This level of narrative helps you communicate your concept to others and test it with customers, and it ensures that everyone in your team fully subscribes to the same vision. Visualizations also help to clarify what your team will ultimately need to build, averting costly delays or course corrections.

NEVER INNOVATE IN A VACUUM

Any team can get stuck in an endless loop as they discuss the technology, features, and functionality they might use some day. Such teams are starving themselves of inspiration and insight. Get outside of the conference room. Observe customers and end users, and study other initiatives that tackled similar problems. Without these insights, you'll only spin your wheels until you run out of time and end up committing to some groupthink consensus. Then you'll rush to implement a concept that is fundamentally disconnected from market and customer realities. Ten million dollars later, you discover your idea sucks and the dogs won't eat the dog food.[3]

COCONSTRUCT INNOVATIONS WITH CUSTOMERS, SUPPLIERS — EVEN COMPETITORS

Executives often fall into the trap of believing that everything must be done in-house. For projects where capabilities don't exist, teams may try to trust a supplier or (more likely) just drop the project altogether. The excuses cited are numerous: "Hey, it's a secret. We can't tell strangers about our idea!" Or, "Our intellectual property will be compromised!"[4] In today's hyper-connected world, no firm should do everything solo. Embrace open innovation and find ways to work with friends or rivals to design, build, and deliver ideas.

TOOLS TO HELP YOU INNOVATE EFFECTIVELY: PROTOTYPES AND PILOTS

It's a bumpy road from concept to commercialized new offering or business. Despite all of your careful work, your first version of an innovation concept is unlikely to be your best. If you've done your work well, you'll have a strong articulation of the idea, including clear visualizations, an understanding of why customers will want it, how it will make money, and what's needed to bring it into the world. However, at this stage, these are almost always informed but untested hypotheses. You have every reason to believe they're true, but you haven't confirmed them with customers and other stakeholders yet. Inevitably, there will be gaps and uncertainties; certain parts of the concept will be less defined than others.

The worst mistake you can make at this point is to jump ahead to full commercialization. Consider how many prototypes automobile manufacturers move through before committing a new design to production: they typically start with sketches, move to CAD drawings, then perhaps build foam-core or clay physical models, or even one-off "concept cars" for the auto shows. They build these prototypes both to elicit customer reactions and to learn more about the vehicle they intend to build. Most importantly, however, they move through these successive prototype stages to de-risk development. It's a lot faster, cheaper, and easier to figure out a

design is ugly and won't appeal to drivers by modeling it in clay than manufacturing an entire car. After all, the amount of risk can increase exponentially when you contemplate building an offering or an entire business that's new to the world. Satellite phones sounded like a great idea until — 15 space rockets, 66 satellites, and more than $5 billion later — it turned out nobody wanted a phone the size of a brick that didn't work well indoors.[5]

This is where prototyping and piloting come in. What's the difference between the two? Well, it's all about the stage of a concept's development and where and how it's being worked on. Prototypes are tested in "lab" conditions (including the likes of interviews and user groups) and typically rely on mock representations of the offering or business. Pilots are in-market experiments, engaging real customers with your real offering and enterprise. Both are fundamentally grounded in continuous iteration and testing of hypotheses. By moving through a cycle of building, testing, and learning, innovation concepts steadily increase in both strength and tangibility and decrease in risk and uncertainty. Good innovators know how to prototype and pilot effectively.

5   Yep, that's Iridium. Conceived by three engineers at Motorola in 1987, Iridium forecast it would have 42 million satellite phone users by 2002. It finally launched in 1998, only attracted about 20,000 users and went bankrupt nine months later. The space-age technology that would make a phone work anywhere on earth overlooked a crucial detail: satellite phones needed line of sight to their satellites. Which meant they needed big antennas and didn't work all that well indoors or on cloudy days. Bummer.

INNOVATION PROTOTYPES:
MORE THAN PRODUCT MOCK-UPS

Traditional prototypes create a mock-up showing how something might look. They're three-dimensional, rough sketches of an idea. Innovation prototyping has much in common with this approach, but there's a big difference. Just as you need to think about more than products when developing an innovation initiative, you need to do the same when it comes to prototyping. Prototype and test *the entire business*— including how you will develop the system surrounding your product or service, as well as how you will bring it to market and deliver it to customers. Doing this helps you to test not only the entire value proposition with customers, but also to be sure you understand what's really needed to build your innovation and any implications around how it connects with other parts of your enterprise.

There are many different prototyping methods out there. Here are some of the ones we regularly use, loosely mapped to the three categories within the Ten Types framework.

❓

WHEN TESTING AND ADDRESSING UNCERTAINTIES RELATED TO THE CONFIGURATION **OF AN INNOVATION CONCEPT, ASK YOURSELF:**

Which parts of the business model will have the greatest impact on our profitability?

What are the exchanges of value (money, information, expertise, and so on) between us, our partners, vendors, and customers?

What additional capabilities and assets will we need, and will we buy, build, or partner to obtain them?

SAMPLE PROTOTYPING METHODS

VALUE WEB
Draw a diagram of all of those involved in producing, delivering, purchasing, and using your innovation—including suppliers, collaborators, channel partners, customers, and end-users—and visualize the flows of value across that system (monetary and otherwise).[6]

PROCESS DIAGRAMS AND SIMULATIONS
Put together a more focused and deeper analysis of the processes that are either directly or indirectly involved in creating the innovation. These can take the form of flow charts, but can also be developed as interactive simulations to use internally and with external partners to test the process.

6 See Michael E. Porter's *Competitive Strategy* (Free Press, 1998) for his examination of the value chain—the primogenitor of value web analysis.

②

WHEN TESTING AND ADDRESSING UNCERTAINTIES RELATED TO THE OFFERING **OF AN INNOVATION CONCEPT, ASK YOURSELF:**

What does it look and feel like?

How does it compare with and connect to other products and services that are currently in the market?

Which features or services must we absolutely include? Which ones could we leave out?

②

WHEN TESTING AND ADDRESSING UNCERTAINTIES RELATED TO THE EXPERIENCE **OF AN INNOVATION CONCEPT, ASK YOURSELF:**

What is the best way to engage our target customers?

Which channels and touchpoints will provide our users with a singular experience?

What is the core promise of our innovation idea, and how should we communicate it?

SAMPLE PROTOTYPING METHODS

PRODUCT AND SERVICE ILLUSTRATIONS
Create visualizations of the offering itself, with some attention paid to marketing and brand issues, to help an audience understand and evaluate the offering and its overall value to them, as well as its individual features and functionality.

FEASIBILITY ANALYSIS
Often done in close collaboration with experts from inside and outside the organization, put together a technical assessment of the tools, technologies, and other factors that will be needed to bring an innovation to market.

SAMPLE PROTOTYPING METHODS

EXPERIENCE VIGNETTE
Depict how customers or users will interact with an innovation, and how the new offering might fit into their lives more broadly. This prototype often consists of a series of illustrations demonstrating changes in behavior prompted by context (when someone is on the move versus when they're eating at a restaurant, for instance).

VALUE PITCHES
Mock up brochures, sales collateral, promotional websites, and ads that convey an innovation's brand, message, and values, often in concert with depictions of the service and purchase experience.

INNOVATION PROTOTYPES:
DE-RISK DEVELOPMENT

The typical journey of a prototype...

GREATER UNCERTAINTY

GET THE
RIGHT IDEA

LESS INVESTMENT

There are two main reasons to use innovation prototyping. The first is to reduce risk and uncertainty. To accomplish this, focus your efforts on the things you *have* to get right for the innovation to succeed. Starting with the easy problems is a recipe for disaster in commercializing innovations—it shoves all of the critically important work to the end of the process, when accumulated expense and exposure to customers is at its greatest. Instead, ask yourself which elements of the innovation idea matter most—without which your concept will simply crumble. Is it an aspect of customer behavior, the feasibility of the offering, or the viability of the business model? These central elements should be the focus of your prototyping efforts.

The second reason to use prototypes is to evolve and improve your innovation iteratively. This means that prototypes are fundamentally transitional and ephemeral; much like a lost wax mold or a miniature model, they will be consumed and discarded in the development process. Start with cheap methods—paper, digital visualization, and simple models—and transition toward higher-fidelity and higher cost methods only as uncertainty declines and validation of your concept emerges. Otherwise, you risk wasting money on prototypes you will need to discard—or worse, have cost and effort bias your judgment and lock you into flawed designs.

CONCEPT VISUALIZATION

Cut cubes out of fog

This is the first type of prototype that we use in our work, and one of the first methods to use to convey the essence of an innovation. Concept Visualizations aim to depict a concept holistically, across the entire business system, at a relatively low level of fidelity. They help stakeholders and potential customers grok the intention of the idea, and how it will look, feel, and work conceptually. They almost always have some narrative form, often committed to paper or using fairly inexpensive video or digital animation. The specifics of the narrative can vary by context, but it must always show the offering or business as though it already existed in the world. The trick is to make sure you're contemplating and dramatizing the broader system—and glossing some of the more detailed components for the moment. In concert with financial analyses, these help people to grasp the strategic value of an innovation not only logically, but also emotionally. Use them internally to help decision makers build the confidence needed to take action and commit to the next phase of development. Use them externally to engage suppliers, partners, and customers to elicit feedback and entice them to codevelop the concept with you.

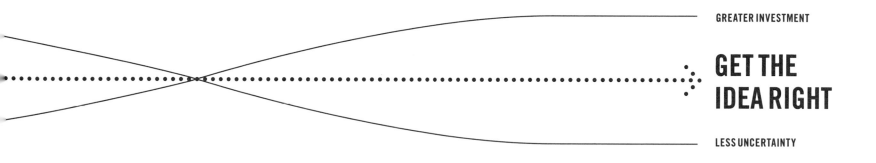

GREATER INVESTMENT

GET THE IDEA RIGHT

LESS UNCERTAINTY

FOCUSED PROTOTYPES

Resolve uncertainty and evolve the design

As you pivot from designing an innovation concept to considering how to bring it to market, new uncertainties will emerge. How much will it really cost to develop that online portal? What types of interactions and transactions does it need to support? How will it connect to the manufacturing and logistics systems you envision? This is where designing and testing focused prototypes helps. Depending on the uncertainties you need to resolve, you may develop a narrative about how customers will access, purchase, and use an offering, or you may focus on value networks and process diagrams that map out how the organization will work and interact with other players to produce an offering. You may mock up parts of the offering with limited functionality to observe how customers behave and interact with it; alternatively, you may develop design and brand studies that imagine how the offering will look and what message it communicates. Many of these prototypes can still be developed quickly and cheaply on paper or using digital visualization tools. The key principle: concentrate on the aspects of the innovation that are most important and most uncertain, and address them by building and testing focused prototypes that iteratively evolve in refinement and fidelity.

FUNCTIONAL PROTOTYPES

Integrate multiple elements and invest in fidelity

At some point in the prototyping process, uncertainty declines and a clear validation of the innovation emerges. There will still be uncertainties about how the market will actually respond to it and a few nagging questions about what's required from your organization to deliver it — but they can only be resolved by building the sucker and bringing it to market. This is the moment to invest in greater fidelity and functionality; to build working prototypes that you can eventually test through pilots. Here, the focus shifts to getting the details right. However, remember that you aren't in launch mode; there is still a possibility that you'll realize you *shouldn't* scale up your innovation. It's a balancing act — build elements of the business with enough fidelity to give them a fair shake in the market, but preserve flexibility and adaptability. This often requires some manual processes — building a website that has a fully functional front-end but some hacked and kludged back-ends, products that require significant shop time to produce, and service experiences that demand some of your best customer-facing people and moments of improvisation as they interact with users. These are the right trade-offs to make at this stage; although your innovation has undoubtedly come a long way, it still has several tests to pass before it earns its launch wings.

INNOVATION PILOTS:
DE-RISK LAUNCH

The typical journey of a pilot...

GREATER UNCERTAINTY

TEST THE
MARKET

LESS INVESTMENT

The same spirit of iteration and experimentation that guided your prototypes should continue in your pilots. Remember—innovation pilots are not market launches. Instead, they are focused, in-market tests designed to resolve uncertainties surrounding your innovation and de-risk its development. They are typically conducted within a limited geography or market segment. In fact, firms often use early pilots to engage their best customers in a focused and exclusive manner—giving them a sneak peek at what's next and ensuring they feel heard and valued. In building the assets and systems you need to bring your innovation to market, always prize flexibility and agility over scalability. You have to remain open to the possibility that a pilot may teach you not to launch the business.

EARLY-STAGE PILOTS
Early-stage pilots often feel jury-rigged. You likely have a reasonably developed offering, but other elements of the business system feel slapped together with spit and duct tape. That's as it should be. At this stage, you are simply trying to validate the value proposition of the innovation—its desirability to customers and its financial viability for you and your enterprise. So start small. Build and test the smallest, most discrete form of the innovation that still fulfills your promise to customers. This may mean you don't incorporate all of the types of innovation that you envision, but only those critical to your design. And you may start with small, short-term, or somehow limited pilots that maximize rapid learning. Pick a single geography or market, and depending on your context, even consider engaging customers by invitation only. If you are innovating within a larger enterprise, these pilots should help inform and validate which elements of your innovation can draw on existing assets and infrastructure, and which elements will need to be kept separate or built new (for example, can the existing sales force really push the innovation?).

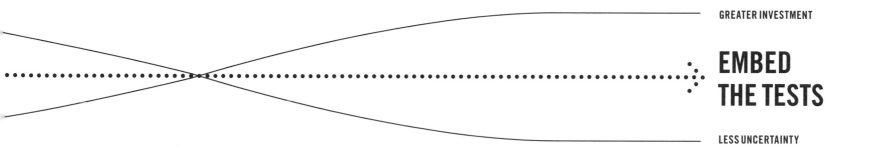

GREATER INVESTMENT

EMBED THE TESTS

LESS UNCERTAINTY

LATE-STAGE PILOTS

As your early-stage pilots succeed and further validation emerges for your idea, you can expand the scope and scale of your pilots. The focus then turns to ironing out the feasibility of your innovation—thoroughly testing and refining what is needed from you and your organization to deliver it to customers. Invest in making elements of the business system more scalable and automated (for example, build out a more robust service infrastructure, add additional sales representatives, convert your quick and dirty data architecture into an enterprise-level system, and so on). Pressure-test operations by expanding the scope and scale of the pilot, inviting more customers and adding additional markets and geographies. If you are innovating within a larger enterprise, this is the moment to begin connecting and transferring the elements of your innovation that will draw on existing systems and infrastructure.

LAUNCH

At some point, the line between a late-stage pilot and a soft launch gets blurred. If you're innovating within a larger enterprise, this is now the time to secure commitment from your organization and its leadership—recognition that the innovation is on its feet, succeeding in the market, and that it deserves continued resources (in terms of people, capital, and leadership attention). If you're an entrepreneur and your pilots have been successful, congratulations. Keep going. Remember that no value proposition lasts forever; you must continually refresh and expand your innovation over time. Your job at this moment is to think about how to learn from and adapt your innovation with customers and partners. These days this nearly always involves applied social media (and in digital contexts, constant A/B testing)—so you consistently improve every nuance and detail.

TOOLS TO HELP YOU INNOVATE:
FINANCIAL MODELS FOR INNOVATION

Finance wizards on innovation teams are often palpably relieved once the time comes to suss out the financial viability of a concept (and we suggest starting this process as early as possible).[7] Laptops open, spreadsheets launch, pro-forma models are called up, and knuckles crack. The MBAs and financial analysts in the room smile— "Finally, it's time to put some real numbers to all the pretty pictures and words. *This* is something I know how to do."

Financial analysts are indeed vital for this work. But sometimes, their prior experience in business development or perhaps all of that pent up energy waiting for the numbers to come sends them hurtling in the wrong direction. They build financial models that grow like weeds, sprouting supplemental sheets, side-analyses, and elaborate back-ends. They agonize over overhead configurations and depreciation schedules. They develop seven-year forecasts, tweaking the assumptions until revenue in year five looks just right.

All of this detailed work is useful and will be required at some point— but it is a mistake to invest in too much detail too early. Remember our principles of prototyping: use prototypes to resolve uncertainty, and invest in fidelity iteratively and over time. The same principles should guide your financial modeling. So when you're first exploring the financial viability of an innovation concept, ask yourself a simpler and far more important question: "*What would have to be true for our concept to make money?*"[8] Determining an accurate weighted average cost of capital for your fledgling enterprise is useless if revenues seem unlikely ever to exceed costs.

Here are some principles and approaches you should keep in mind when determining the financial viability of an innovation concept:

REVERSE-ENGINEER THE FINANCIAL REQUIREMENTS OF THE BUSINESS
Typical financial analysis focuses on point estimates and projections. But, as ever, predicting the future is tough—and even harder when you're predicting the future of something that doesn't yet exist. Instead, flip the analysis on its head. Rather than trying to project how much revenue the business will generate in the third year, ask how much it *has* to generate in year three to be viable. This approach will shortcut useless forecasting; it will also identify the key sensitivities and hypotheses you need to test in subsequent work.

DITCH THE STANDARD FINANCIAL MODELS AND FOCUS ON THE BASICS
The standard project investment or prospective pro-forma models you or your company have in hand are almost certainly too detailed.

7   We typically start at the very beginning, right as we frame the innovation initiative. As we define the users and markets we hope to serve and the problem we want to solve, we can also examine the flows of money involved—including revenues paid for existing offerings, total economic value generated, costs incurred, and adjacent markets. Thinking expansively—and early—about the potential profit pools helps us to imagine novel ways for innovations to be viable.

8   If you're working in a non-profit context, ask yourself, "What would have to be true for us to sustain this innovation over time?"

9   This is true even for
    businesses, like Google
    or Facebook, that rely on
    digital and/or network
    economies; while variable
    costs often approach
    zero per user, hosting
    isn't free and development
    costs must be amortized.
    Similarly, advertising
    revenue, micro-
    transactions, and
    secondary data streams
    all depend on attracting
    individual users (hopefully,
    lots of them).

Just as concept visualizations grow in fidelity through successive iterations, so should your modeling. Focus on developing the barest sketch of the financials first. This can often be done on a sheet of paper or white board instead of as an Excel model. This work can always be ported to more detailed models when the time is right.

UNDERSTAND UNIT ECONOMICS FIRST

Unit economics are the heart of almost any business.[9] These comprise the cost of producing an offering, the revenue a company can earn from it, and how that changes with volume. Focus the bulk of your early modeling work here, because nothing else matters if you can't see a way to make unit economics profitable. Understand how they change as units scale; this will help you to identify the key inflection points in growth (for example, how many units do you need to sell to break even?).

MODEL MULTIPLE REVENUE STREAMS

Consider each and every way that your offering or business can make money — which should include not only a variety of different profit models, but also a variety of different revenue sources. For example, in any US health care innovation project, we consider how patients, physicians, private insurers, the Center for Medicare and Medicaid Services, and other suppliers could *all* somehow become paying customers. Modern business models always rely on multiple revenue streams. Consider how you could make money by not only selling a product to a customer, but by attracting other suppliers to serve them, adding complementary services, and so on. This work generates lots of additional options in case your initial profit model proves insufficient, and creates a roadmap for future growth.

CASH (CONVERSION) IS CRITICAL

There is one part of the balance sheet you need to pay attention to early, and that's working capital — how much you'll need on hand, and how quickly it converts to cash. This is the "cash conversion cycle." Investors use it to gauge management effectiveness, but you can use it to consider how quickly your new business can scale and how much capital it will need to do so. The shorter the cycle, the less capital you will need to grow the business. This is particularly vital if you are innovating in industries with significant asset requirements (such as heavy manufacturing) or valuable inventory (such as medical devices). It can also become a source of advantage: besides its virtual store, which cost less than physical spaces, Amazon's management of the cash conversion cycle helped it offer books at lower prices than retail competitors when it launched back in 1995.

WHAT TO EXPECT WHEN YOU'RE EXPECTING INNOVATION

Given all of the uncertainty involved in bringing an innovation concept to life and to market, it's reasonable to feel anxious about the journey. At multiple points along the way, everyone in the organization will need to take leaps of faith and invest more and more money in something that can't be guaranteed to succeed.

We call this a journey through the "Valley of Doubt." Along the way, you're likely to encounter predictable emotional responses from your people that will weigh down a new project, bending the curve and casting it deeper into unproductive doubt. You can counter them and help prevent the curve from dipping too violently with the following responses:

HOW TO CROSS THE VALLEY OF DOUBT

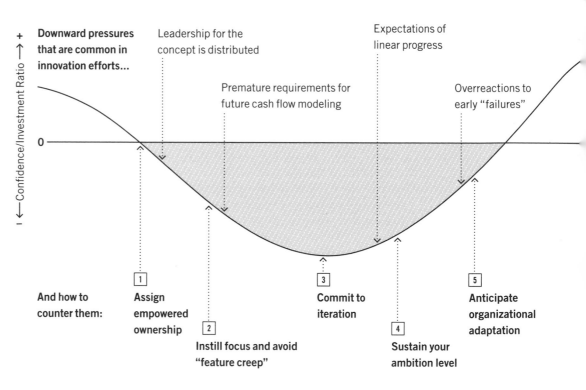

← Confidence/Investment Ratio →
− ← 0 → +

Downward pressures that are common in innovation efforts...

Leadership for the concept is distributed

Premature requirements for future cash flow modeling

Expectations of linear progress

Overreactions to early "failures"

And how to counter them:

1 Assign empowered ownership

2 Instill focus and avoid "feature creep"

3 Commit to iteration

4 Sustain your ambition level

5 Anticipate organizational adaptation

time $\longrightarrow$

This and any visualization of the journey of innovation is wrong in detail but right in spirit. Fostering innovation is inherently emotional. As a leader you must expect and encourage strong points of view. On any healthy innovation team, the level of discord and ambiguity should settle down over time and the shared excitement should build steadily. If you do not see both parts of this pattern, there is something wrong. No disagreement at the beginning means the ideas aren't bold or scary enough. No excitement near the end means everyone knows the result has been compromised to death.

1. ASSIGN EMPOWERED OWNERSHIP

To counter the confusion that arises when working on an entirely new idea, each initiative must have a clear central owner. This individual must have organizational credibility and heft to marshal internal support and work across functions, must be able to interact confidently with senior executives, and on occasion, act as an external representative.

2. INSTILL FOCUS AND AVOID "FEATURE CREEP"

Encourage teams to focus and to resist the habit of adding too much complexity or too many features initially. Take several weeks to create a more detailed view of the system elements, and begin to evaluate and refine those before adding new ones. You want to launch with the smallest viable version of your big idea, use it to establish a beachhead, and then add complexity and sophistication.

3. COMMIT TO ITERATION

Don't fall into the trap of trying to "prove" a concept first. You'll have more luck putting together a pilot and cycling quickly through the options to test and experiment. This will be quicker and more efficient than traditional analysis techniques.

4. SUSTAIN YOUR AMBITION LEVEL

A team can naturally get disheartened as clarity refuses to emerge from the fog. Creating new offerings and forms of value for new audiences will necessarily stretch your organization both collectively and individually. Figure out how to remain calm in the face of early "failures" by recasting them as important and useful lessons. Sustain the appropriate ambition levels and challenge colleagues to resist the rapid gravitational pull toward the familiar.

5. ANTICIPATE ORGANIZATIONAL ADAPTATION

Your current structure is probably not going to provide the right home for some of your new concepts. You don't have to create a new formal organization immediately, but you do have to be prepared to adapt. Don't let your management practices and systems become too rigid; instill a spirit of flexibility within your teams by changing things up regularly.

IN CLOSING:

BIG SHIFTS AND FAST MOVES...

Nearly everywhere in this book we have urged you to manage the minutiae of innovation. *Eradicate lore, substitute logic. Root out myths, bring in methods. Know that there are ten types of innovation; use more of them. Find orthodoxies and slay them. Expect people to give you excuses; make them innovate anyway. Get leaders to sponsor innovation from the top; get high-potential people to build innovation from the bottom. Get the details right.* Fundamentally this is a book filled with tradecraft — practical, real-world ways to ensure that innovation actually happens.

1   Just to be clear, this is a metaphor. We dislike real pirates as much as anyone. Please read this not literally but for the idea that you need to think and act unconventionally whenever you develop, pilot, or launch bold innovation efforts.

2   Brilliant idea, by the way. Micronutrient foods save lives and vastly advance health. Gates Foundation is partnering with the World Food Programme and several huge food companies to do this for real, and has reportedly invested as much as $100 million in the program. So far.

We're proud of our minutiae, of course. The tradecraft wc have shared is hard won over decades of work with clients. It is born of painful failures, hardened in battle, annealed in the furnace of urgent deadlines, and tested on the hardest of user groups, including three year olds and generals. Most people do innovation in ways doomed to fail. It is actually hard to cram even the basics of what you need to know to innovate effectively in just one book.

But here's the thing. You can do all the tradecraft brilliantly and still miss the mark. Real innovation mixes science and art. If you've made it this far, you've endured a couple hundred pages about the part of innovation that is an emerging science. But it would be a huge error of omission on our part to miss telling you about one key piece of the art.

It has to do with your *mindset*. Tradecraft tells you what to *do*. Mindset tells you how to *think*.

THINK LIKE A PIRATE

Every innovation initiative can be helped by thinking like a pirate. By being scrappy and undaunted, by improvising something from nothing, by being dogged, committed, and unconventional. More than likely you expect and plan to startle and defeat a stronger, better equipped, and far richer target. If there are rules, don't play by them. Indeed, you should take special delight in undermining them. These are qualities every innovator must possess.

Think of building your initiative as you would a pirate ship. Make one that is stealthy, maneuverable, lightning fast, and more than a little terrifying. Once your ship is seaworthy, set sail under cover of foggy darkness late on a moonless night, and head straight into your competitor's protected harbor. From there, just before dawn, at a moment calculated to be maximally disruptive, wage a savage war. Use whatever tactics and skills you need. Do not take prisoners.[1]

This mindset turns out to be fundamental, no matter what you are building. You may be trying to solve world hunger, creating the world's most sophisticated micronutrient fortified foods, and finding ways for farmers in Bangladesh or sub-Saharan Africa to grow and formulate them.[2] You'll achieve any noble goal more ably when you *think like a pirate*.

Khan Academy is on a mission to change education. But look at Salman Kahn's approach: his non-profit organization offers lessons online, for free, to everyone. Six years after the first video was uploaded to YouTube, students were completing more than 2 million exercises every day. Khan Academy, meanwhile, is now working with existing schools to figure out how best to use the video lessons with students. *Nota bene*: he's not interested in integrating the videos into the existing curriculum; savvy schools use them to provide an entirely different type of education. Khan's radical way of thinking and his willingness to take on a deeply entrenched educational system are already impacting the world more broadly: the videos are being distributed in India, Ethiopia, and Latin America. He is a modern-day, global pirate.

Dr. Dean Ornish has focused on one research question for over three decades: "*What do we need to do to enjoy longer, healthier lives?*" He founded the Preventive Medicine Research Institute to develop clinical evidence about the effects of different lifestyle choices. If his research led to a pill you could take, it would be worth billions. Instead, he published his principles, helping to develop a system to reverse the four most costly health care conditions in the world. The dogged mindset of this extraordinary pirate doctor led to the development of the first lifestyle program ever covered by Medicare— so that doctors would learn to use it.

Or take Paul Farmer, MacArthur Genius and founder of Partners in Health. Farmer had a simple goal, to use all the means available to help people get well. His organization's mission statement declares that it will do "Whatever it takes. Just as we would do if a member of our own family—or we ourselves—were ill." By culturally adapting basic health practices so they would work in places such as Lesotho, Malawi, and Haiti, Farmer has ended up with an organization employing more than 11,000 people in health centers and hospitals in 12 countries. His fiery, uncompromising piracy has had incredible results.[3]

3 Tracy Kidder's book *Mountains Beyond Mountains* is a beautiful book about the earliest days of this journey. More recently, Farmer and Partners in Health built Mirebalais Hospital, a full-scale teaching hospital in Haiti and the biggest reconstruction project in that country since the devastating earthquake of 2010.

In 1993, Milwaukee farmer Will Allen teamed up with a local organization to offer work to chronically unemployed urban teenagers—with the goal of teaching them to become organic farmers. Since then, Growing Power has expanded to Chicago to build urban farms such as Altgeld Gardens, which employs 150 adults and 40 at-risk youth from local neighborhoods. All of the Growing Power sites are focused on creating a closed loop, sustainable future that delivers both great produce and better lives for young people. This idea is so compelling and scalable that every urban area the world over could adapt it. But it was Allen's courageous spirit that made it happen in the first place.

Tradecraft helps you to do the tasks right. A bold mindset helps you to do the right tasks.

Innovation is too damned important to leave to the faint-hearted. When you do it right, it will reverberate in stunning ways. It will solve tough problems on which dozens of good teams before you broke their picks. It will stun competitors, delight your customers, and reinvent entire fields. We hope you find the tradecraft in this book to be an indispensable aid. But see yourself as a pirate, and build yourself the most awe-inspiring ship you can possibly handle. Then set sail.

You may discover that it is the hardest work you ever loved.

PART SEVEN

APPENDIX

PUTTING THESE PRINCIPLES INTO PRACTICE

Go beyond the book to create your own innovation revolution.

ACKNOWLEDGMENTS

Our colleagues at Doblin have been obsessed with finding the frontiers of effective innovation for three decades. Ten of us are adjunct professors at Chicago's famed Institute of Design, a leading global graduate design school. This helps us select and cultivate a steady stream of talented young colleagues. Collectively through the years more than 400 people have worked at Doblin, far too many to mention here, and many of them made important contributions to the emerging science of innovation effectiveness. We are indebted to them all, and grateful for their work.

Several individuals were particularly important in developing the original Ten Types of Innovation discoveries in 1998. Vijay Kumar, one of the world's leading methodologists in design, who recently published an important book of his own, used several of his robust methods to lead the research.[1] Other disciplined and talented key contributors were Jeff Barr, Ewan Duncan, John Pipino, Tomoko Ichikawa, and Peter Laundy; the latter two led the important design work that made the ideas compelling and understandable.

We have reinvested in the analytics around the Ten Types of Innovation at many critical junctures. In particular, some brilliant library scientists helped develop the search algorithms that would allow us to use the Ten Types diagnostically, such as the Innovation Landscapes in Part Four, including Marilyn Brda, Tracey Lemon, and Matthew Robison. Others such as Ben Jacobson, Kim Erwin, Katie McGlenn, Tom Mulhern, and Todd McCullough helped us to adapt the Ten Types to client programs.

Also as a part of this work we have developed an important algorithm not described in this book that reveals the base levels of innovation effort across the Ten Types in any field. This work, led by Henry King and Matt Locsin, produced the Innovation Intensity Index (I³), an amazing tool that we expect will become important to industry and financial analysts over time.

Since Doblin became part of Monitor and, most recently, a part of Deloitte, there has been a significant investment in 21st century analytics for the work. Bansi Nagji, then in a role as head of Monitor's innovation unit, saw the value of The Ten Types framework and encouraged deeper analysis and development. Three of us, Ryan Pikkel, Brian Quinn, and Helen Walters, led an internal design competition to refine, test, deepen, and graphically redesign the framework in 2011. Among the contributors to this most recent version are Steven Babitch, Clint Barth, Audrey Clarke, Colin Drylie,

1 *101 Design Methods* is a thorough and sophisticated compilation of design methods. A long-awaited and important book, it is also published by Wiley.

Jessie Gatto, YiLeng Lee, Tom Nassim, Samantha Ruiz, Ruth Schmidt, Hillary Schuster, and Eli Weinberg.

A handful of individuals helped to produce analysis that has advanced our understanding of what drives innovation success, especially how it works inside an organization, including Jarrod Cady, Amelia Dunlop, Angelo Frigo, Darrel Hayes, Dustin Kress, and Eli Robinson.

Still other colleagues helped us in the intense efforts to produce the book in your hands, including Jenny Collins, Jonathan Copulsky, Jeanne Gatto, Jesse Goldhammer, Katie Joyce, Eamonn Kelly, Erik Kiaer, Sarah King, John Leach, Matt Lopez, Melissa Quinn, Amar Singh, Harpreet Singh, Geoff Tuff, Jeff Tull, Erik van Crimmin, and Jeff Wordham. We are also grateful to the many individuals at all of the companies that have allowed us to reproduce imagery and stories; to Richard Narramore and his team at Wiley for helping to plan and publish the book; and to Natasha Jen, Jeffrey Waldman, Jin Kwang Kim, and the gifted design team at Pentagram for making the book aesthetically refined and easy to understand.

At the hands of all these talented and dedicated colleagues, innovation is finally giving up its secrets and being reinvented as a robust science. As teachers and students we ask gnarly questions, and then work to answer them with facts, methods, and research. But a very large part of what makes Doblin a special laboratory is our remarkable clients. It is the client work, in the real world, with urgent deadlines and the imperative of producing concepts that succeed in the maelstrom of competitive markets, which keeps us from being academic eggheads.

With so many skilled people flooding the field, one pattern is clear: this book is just one of the signs that innovation is now a deep professional discipline, with all the classic hallmarks — history, criticism, and theory, plus a wealth of academic and applied frontiers. If you found the book useful, please join us. We are at the very beginning of profound shifts in the innovation field directly, and scores of additional fields where effective innovation is catalyzing and precipitating accelerated rates of change. Throughout the world the problems are real, the stakes are high, time is short, and abstract academic answers are fundamentally unsatisfying. So...

We're gonna have to innovate.

INNOVATION BIBLIOGRAPHY

Scores of books about innovation are published every year (or does it only feel that way?).
Some of them are even worth reading. Here are some of our favorites from over the years.
The ones marked with stars should be in the personal library of any serious innovator.

INNOVATION CLASSICS: USEFUL BASICS

★ Thomas S. Kuhn,
The Structure of Scientific Revolutions
(University of Chicago Press, 1962)
http://tentyp.es/PZHbre

★ Everett M. Rogers, *Diffusion of Innovations*
(Free Press of Glencoe, 1962)
http://tentyp.es/T6MMjx

Peter F. Drucker, *Innovation and Entrepreneurship*
(Harper & Row, 1985)
http://tentyp.es/Rgnfjx

★ Clayton M. Christensen, *The Innovator's Dilemma*
(Harvard Business School Press, 1997)
http://tentyp.es/RgmLdb

Harvard Business Review on Innovation
(Harvard Business School Publishing, 2001)
http://tentyp.es/VBiYL6

Clayton M. Christensen, Michael E. Raynor,
The Innovator's Solution
(Harvard Business School Press, 2003)
http://tentyp.es/PZHxhL

Henry Chesbrough, *Open Innovation*
(Harvard Business Review Press, 2003)
http://tentyp.es/WqOyut

★ Roger L. Martin, *The Opposable Mind*
(Harvard Business School Press, 2007)
http://tentyp.es/TG9BJj

Roger L. Martin, *The Design of Business*
(Harvard Business School Press, 2009)
http://tentyp.es/RgnoTW

★ Steven B. Johnson, *Where Good Ideas Come From*
(Riverhead, 2010)
http://tentyp.es/OG7MNj

INNOVATION STRATEGY: FRAMING, PATTERNS, AND CHOICES

★ James M. Utterback,
Mastering the Dynamics of Innovation
(Harvard Business School Press, 1994)
http://tentyp.es/UHJLIM

Andrew Hargadon, *How Breakthroughs Happen*
(Harvard Business School Press, 2003)
http://tentyp.es/SAss8E

Jamshid Gharajedaghi, *Systems Thinking*
(Butterworth-Heinemann, 2005)
http://tentyp.es/PBBPjJ

Michael J. Mauboussin, *Think Twice*
(Harvard Business School Press, 2009)
http://tentyp.es/R1gGAM

★ John Mullins, Randy Komisar, *Getting to Plan B*
(Harvard Business Review Press, 2009)
http://tentyp.es/OG7K7Y

INNOVATION IN DISCOVERY: SOCIAL AND COMPUTING SCIENCES   **INNOVATION IN MARKETING: BUILDING BRANDS AND MARKETS**

Matt Ridley, *The Rational Optimist*
(Harper, 2010)
http://tentyp.es/Rgq4B6

Vijay Govindarajan, Chris Trimble,
The Other Side of Innovation
(Harvard Business Review Press, 2010)
http://tentyp.es/T4jz3e

★ Joshua M. Epstein, Robert L. Axtell,
Growing Artificial Societies
(The MIT Press, 1996)
http://tentyp.es/REvLL8

Joshua M. Epstein, *Generative Social Science*
(Princeton University Press, 2006)
http://tentyp.es/QUMkTK

Dan Ariely, *Predictably Irrational*
(HarperCollins, 2008)
http://tentyp.es/SAtq4w

Richard H. Thaler, Cass R. Sunstein, *Nudge*
(Penguin, 2009)
http://tentyp.es/QK2nmW

Albert-László Barabási, *Bursts*
(Dutton Adult, 2010)
http://tentyp.es/Sva82z

★ Michael Nielsen, *Reinventing Discovery*
(Princeton University Press, 2011)
http://tentyp.es/SLI1aW

Chip Heath, Dan Heath, *Made to Stick*
(Random House, 2007)
http://tentyp.es/R1p1Va

Kevin Maney, *Trade-Off*
(Crown Business, 2009)
http://tentyp.es/SLuQWc

★ Youngme Moon, *Different*
(Crown Business, 2010)
http://tentyp.es/Wr3NUg

INNOVATION NETWORKS: PLATFORMS, MODELING, AND CONNECTION EFFECTS

★ James Surowiecki, *The Wisdom of Crowds*
(Doubleday, 2004)
http://tentyp.es/QLPky4

Henry Chesbrough, Wim Vanhaverbeke, Joel West
Open Innovation: Researching a New Paradigm
(Oxford University Press, 2006)
http://tentyp.es/RgDzR2

Jeff Howe, *Crowdsourcing*
(Crown Business, 2008)
http://tentyp.es/REx3G1

Len Fisher, *The Perfect Swarm*
(Basic Books, 2009)
http://tentyp.es/OG2Bgl

★ Clay Shirky, *Here Comes Everybody*
(Penguin, 2009)
http://tentyp.es/O8BKrJ

★ Kevin Kelly, *What Technology Wants*
(Viking, 2010)
http://tentyp.es/T4jvR6

★ Clay Shirky, *Cognitive Surplus*
(Penguin, 2010)
http://tentyp.es/UjzyBo

★ David Weinberger, *Too Big to Know*
(Basic Books, 2012)
http://tentyp.es/S99ZNu

INNOVATION METHODS: TECHNIQUE, IP, AND EFFICACY

★ Lawrence Lessig, *The Future of Ideas*
(Random House, 2001)
http://tentyp.es/QLXypS

Carl Franklin, *Why Innovation Fails*
(Spiro Press, 2003)
http://tentyp.es/VBDMCn

C.K. Prahalad,
The Fortune at the Bottom of the Pyramid
(Wharton School Publishing, 2005)
http://tentyp.es/SLA9oJ

Henry Chesbrough, *Open Business Models*
(Harvard Business Review Press, 2006)
http://tentyp.es/O8FoSk

Lawrence Lessig, *Code 2.0*
(Basic Books, 2006)
http://tentyp.es/T4hS5P

David Silverstein, Philip Samuel, Neil DeCarlo,
The Innovator's Toolkit
(Wiley, 2008)
http://tentyp.es/Wr70TH

★ Atul Gawande, *The Checklist Manifesto*
(Metropolitan, 2009)
http://tentyp.es/O8FgSU

★ Alexander Osterwalder, Yves Pigneur,
Business Model Generation
(Wiley, 2010)
http://tentyp.es/QLVtKS

★ Peter Sims, *Little Bets*
(Free Press, 2011)
http://tentyp.es/O8GEF7

★ Vijay Kumar, *101 Design Methods*
(Wiley, 2012)
http://tentyp.es/TndbIH

INNOVATION IN PHILANTHROPY: SOCIAL SECTORS

Jim Collins, *Good to Great and the Social Sectors*
(HarperCollins, 2005)
http://tentyp.es/SGiXjO

Paul Polak, *Out of Poverty*
(Berrett-Koehler Publishers, 2008)
http://tentyp.es/UHPA2x

Katherine Fulton, Gabriel Kasper, and Barbara Kibbe,
What's Next for Philanthropy
(Monitor Group, 2010)
http://tentyp.es/SGjxOq

★ Abhijit V. Bannerjee, Esther Duflo,
Poor Economics
(PublicAffairs, 2011)
http://tentyp.es/VzswU8

Salman Khan, *The One World Schoolhouse*
(Twelve, 2012)
http://tentyp.es/TkhnnX

NOTES AND RESEARCH DATA

Stories in the book were sourced directly from the originating company, sometimes via media sites and press information, and also via contemporary articles in national and international media. We have organized these notes by chapter, relating back to the book's main text by highlighting the relevant topic in blue. This is not an exhaustive catalog of the many sources we consulted while researching this book. Rather, it is intended to give you additional interesting resources and reference material. We have included links where possible, knowing that sadly many of them will die out over time. Still, our hope is to provide you with a strong starting point for your own reading, so you can go forth and create your own innovation revolution.

PREFACE

In August 2012, 10 percent of Americans approved of the job being done by Congress; 83 percent actively disapproved: http://tentyp.es/WEj5rv.

The American Diabetes Association has all the stats and figures about the disease you could ever wish to read: http://tentyp.es/SenGgB.

Esther Duflo is the director of J-PAL Global, the Abdul Latif Jameel Poverty Action Lab. Read more about her work: http://tentyp.es/Uzw4dC.

David Weinberger is a senior researcher at Harvard University's Berkman Center for the Internet and Society. *Too Big to Know* was published by Basic Books in 2012: http://tentyp.es/T7f7R2.

Read more about Doblin — including writing by Jay Doblin from 30 years ago that can seem almost eerily prescient today — at our website: http://tentyp.es/WElr9K.

PART ONE
CHAPTER 1: RETHINK INNOVATION

Clayton Christensen noted that each year 30,000 new consumer products are launched — and 95% of them fail. "Clay Christensen's Milkshake Marketing" by Carmen Nobel, *HBS Working Knowledge* (Harvard Business School, February 14, 2011): http://tentyp.es/QjZd7x.

Jack Welch was quoted in the book, *Jack Welch & the G.E. Way: Management Insights and Leadership Secrets of the Legendary CEO* by Robert Slater (New York; McGraw-Hill, 1998): http://tentyp.es/Pdy2c3.

Details of Kodak filing for Chapter 11 business reorganization are at http://tentyp.es/SuOZn7.

"Any technology that is going to have significant impact over the next 10 years is already at least 10 years old," wrote Bill Buxton in "The Long Nose of Innovation," *BusinessWeek*, January 2, 2008. http://tentyp.es/Syt3TI.

For a lovely description of work by various scientists, including Dmitri Mendeleev, on the periodic table, see Oliver Sacks's article "Best Invention; Everything in Its Place," *The New York Times*, April 18, 1999. http://tentyp.es/SyxbTG.

PART TWO
CHAPTER 2: THE TEN TYPES
You can, of course, read more about the Ten Types framework and its initial development and evolution (as well as get more information about our other work and thinking) at our website: http://tentyp.es/SBQrX1.

CHAPTER 3: PROFIT MODEL
"A main object of my invention is to provide a safety-razor in which the necessity of honing or stropping the blade is done away with," wrote King C. Gillette in his 1904 application for a patent for his razor design: http://tentyp.es/13aVEER.

Find more details on Geisinger's ProvenCare procedures at http://tentyp.es/XgEiYE.

"Taking control of your tools helps protect your business from hidden costs," promises the online blurb for Hilti's Tool Fleet Management program: http://tentyp.es/Y3nce2.

"By eliminating no-shows, requiring pre-payment, and varying the price by time and day we are able to create a predictable and steady flow of patrons," reads the answer to a Frequently Answered Question on Next's website: http://tentyp.es/PECnW6.

"We weren't afraid to cannibalize ourselves," said Rolv Erik Ryssdal, chief executive officer (CEO) of Schibsted Media Group about the decision to spin off FINN.no. "Norway's Schibsted: No. 3 in Online Classifieds," *Bloomberg BusinessWeek*, October 14, 2010. http://tentyp.es/SOWVvW.

CHAPTER 4: NETWORK
The $10 million Ansari X-Prize was awarded to Scaled Composites on October 4, 2004: http://tentyp.es/OtJAfy. Netflix gave $1 million to the team "BellKor's Pragmatic Chaos" on September 21, 2009: http://tentyp.es/Wcfz5D.

Target features a rather nifty online, interactive timeline on its website, which tracks the firm's evolution from its roots in the early 1900s to the present day: http://tentyp.es/UykN8a.

Find the 2011 press release announcing GSK joining WIPO Re:Search at http://tentyp.es/QkM4id.

Read more about Natura's initiatives to develop collaborative networks with colleges around the world at http://tentyp.es/Yu4Bba.

For details of the partnership between Toshiba and UPS Supply Chain Solutions, see Geoffrey James's "The Next Delivery? Computer Repairs by UPS," *Business 2.0 Magazine*, July 1, 2004. http://tentyp.es/T5zzC8.

Theresa Howard gives some useful background to the growth of Howard Johnson's franchises in "Howard Johnson," *Nation's Restaurant News*, 1996.

CHAPTER 5: STRUCTURE
John Mackey published the blog post, *Creating the High Trust Organization*, March 9, 2010, http://tentyp.es/VF6z98. For an in-depth (if somewhat dated) look at Whole Foods's radical structure, read Charles Fishman's "Whole Foods Is All Teams," *Fast Company*, April 30, 1996. http://tentyp.es/VF6Dpj.

Read more about W. L. Gore's internal organization at http://tentyp.es/SS1JoO.

Southwest added 88 Boeing 717 planes to its fleet with its acquisition of AirTran in May 2011. For more facts and figures on the airline, see http://tentyp.es/OYAcCi.

Through its "Unified Clinical Organization" work to integrate its technology and services, Trinity Health reported a reduction in patients' length of stay in hospital and readmissions. Costs related to sepsis cases were reduced by more than $3 million in the first eight months of the 2011 financial year. See the company's 2011 annual report for more details: http://tentyp.es/WuSwCr.

A good story on Fabindia's structure was written by our colleagues, Nikhil Prasad Ojha, Parijat Ghosh, Sarah Stein Greenberg, and Anurag Mishra: "Weaving Scale into Handicrafts," *Business Today*, May 30, 2010. http://tentyp.es/UITDvD.

CHAPTER 6: PROCESS
"The production process, from start to finish, takes only two to three weeks," wrote Suzy Hansen in her

article about Zara written for the *New York Times Magazine*. "How Zara Grew Into the World's Largest Fashion Retailer," November 9, 2012: http://tentyp.es/12bPkkU.

The late C. K. Prahalad wrote beautifully about Hindustan Unilever in *The Fortune at the Bottom of the Pyramid* (Wharton School Publishing, 2009): http://tentyp.es/Rioq1H. Also worth a look, by Sumantra Ghoshal, Gita Piramal, and Sudeep Budhiraja: *World Class in India: A Casebook of Companies in Transformation* (Penguin Books Australia, 2001): http://tentyp.es/QVZqjb.

FastFleet by Zipcar saved the city of Washington, DC, $1 million and enabled the manager to rid the fleet of 300 cars. See more information at http://tentyp.es/Riouia.

The classic book on Toyota and its "lean" production system is James P. Womack, Daniel T. Jones, and Daniel Roos's *The Machine that Changed the World* (Free Press, 2007): http://tentyp.es/RSY3PU.

IKEA was founded by Ingvar Kamprad in Sweden in 1943. Read more about the company's evolution at http://tentyp.es/VyZecZ.

CHAPTER 7: PRODUCT PERFORMANCE

Sam Farber picked the name OXO for its symmetry: "whether it's horizontal, vertical, upside down or backwards, it always reads 'OXO.'" http://tentyp.es/UITRTq.

"A lot of people give up when the world seems to be against them, but that's the point when you should push a little harder," James Dyson commented on his years-long struggle to bring his vacuum to market: http://tentyp.es/PXhSVW.

You can choose up to three colors of M&M's to customize, while Mars helpfully supplies a whole library of clip art from which to choose images: http://tentyp.es/R3uwCO.

TurboTax guarantees to search a tax return for more than 350 tax deductions and credits, as well as do thousands of error checks before you file. Along with QuickBooks and Quicken, TurboTax is now a flagship product owned by Intuit, which reported revenues of $3.9 billion in 2011: http://tentyp.es/Q1lgjl.

The process of making Corning® Gorilla® Glass involves ion exchange and salt melted to a temperature of about 400°C. The fascinating story of its development (and the company's exchanges with Apple's Steve Jobs over its inclusion in the iPhone) is featured in Bryan Gardiner's "Glass Works: How Corning Created the Ultrathin, Ultrastrong Material of the Future." *Wired*, September 24, 2012. http://tentyp.es/SHPxBV.

CHAPTER 8: PRODUCT SYSTEM

"We know that we are not the biggest car brand and we don't want to be. What we do want is to provide a unique and better alternative that is right for today's new car buyers." So ran the thinking behind a brand campaign for Scion in September 2012. To customize the cars online: http://tentyp.es/Q1ll6Z.

Firefox is free and open source software, with approximately 40% of its code written by volunteers: http://tentyp.es/Unw9S7.

Lunchables options include chicken strips, deep dish pizza, sandwiches, chicken nuggets, and what are known as *cracker stackers*. There are even adult lunch combos, featuring steakhouse cheddar subs or roast beef and honey ham and crackers: http://tentyp.es/PEE3yW.

Elfa has supplied goods to The Container Store since the 1970s; the giant retailer formally acquired the business in 1999. More on how the system works is at http://tentyp.es/WcgMKg.

CHAPTER 9: SERVICE

"Happy Feet" is a fascinating look at Zappos' culture, written by Alexandra Jacobs, *The New Yorker*, September 14, 2009: http://tentyp.es/QP5dUy. On June 1, 2010, *Inc.* magazine published "Why I Sold Zappos." In it, the company's founder Tony Hsieh wrote of the firm's commitment to service: "At Zappos, we *want* people to call us. We believe that forming personal, emotional connections with our customers is the best way to provide great service": http://tentyp.es/QA8QPI.

Some 350 people took advantage of the Hyundai job-assurance offer during the program's two-year tenure, according to a story by Peter Valdes-Dapena that ran in *CNN Money* on March 30, 2011: http://tentyp.es/PeVFH4.

"You're going to like the way you look. I guarantee it." A catchphrase for all time, courtesy of Men's Wearhouse founder George Zimmer. For more details on the store and its services: http://tentyp.es/Oangrk.

Find out more about 7-Eleven's history in Japan at http://tentyp.es/RRnlNH.

Sysco also offers other services to its customers, including an online nutritional analysis tool known as Sysco eNutrition: http://tentyp.es/SBVXqu.

CHAPTER 10: CHANNEL
The actor George Clooney was selected by Nespresso Club members as their ideal brand ambassador in 2005. For more on the company's brand efforts, see http://tentyp.es/T9Rddo.

In 2012, Nike updated its store in Chicago, rebranding it as Nike Chicago. *The Chicago Tribune* ran an article by Corilyn Shropshire about the makeover, "Nike Gives Its 2-Decade-Old Chicago Flagship a Makeover and New Name," September 27, 2012: http://tentyp.es/Trjmga.

In 2012, M-Pesa looked to rebrand itself from money transfer service to more of a lifestyle choice. "Customers with M-Pesa need not queue at ATMs or to pay their bills," said Safaricom CEO Bob Collymore. "We have established strategic partnerships that make it possible for you to access your finances from the comfort of your home or office, at the touch of a button": http://tentyp.es/PEErND.

One of the best things about Amazon's Whispernet? It's independent of WiFi, meaning you never have to try to find a hotspot: http://tentyp.es/R3v1MZ.

Find out more about Dow Corning's Xiameter brand at http://tentyp.es/U7OQEB.

CHAPTER 11: BRAND
Richard Branson is a prolific author, having written various entertaining but insightful business books that are worth a read. Titles include *Like a Virgin: Secrets They Won't Teach You at Business School* (Portfolio Trade, 2012), http://tentyp.es/VKHU4n, and *Screw Business As Usual* (Portfolio Hardcover, 2011): http://tentyp.es/RNIkoy.

Trader Joe's supermarkets eschew the usual PA systems. Instead it has a system of "island-style" alerts: One bell to signal that someone needs to open a new register; two bells that a customer has questions at the checkout; three bells that a manager is required: http://tentyp.es/UnwPqx.

Intel marketing manager Dennis Carter was a key figure in developing the "Intel Inside" marketing strategy, including the five-tone melody that first sounded in 1995. For more of the back story, see http://tentyp.es/RGvHdK.

The American Heart Association surveyed in-store sales data and found that the Heart-Check mark "boosted incremental sales an average of five percent when certified products were highlighted with a shelf hang-tag promotion along with messages distributed at check out": http://tentyp.es/QP5QNV.

Method's blog is regularly updated with content that reflects the company's friendly, quirky attitude. As one of the writers put it, the company's philosophy is all about "presenting your weekly dose of weird": http://tentyp.es/PXiDym.

CHAPTER 12: CUSTOMER ENGAGEMENT
John Seely Brown gave a great presentation that featured some of his thinking on the deeper meaning of World of Warcraft at the Strategy Conference hosted by IIT Institute of Design in 2011: http://tentyp.es/PXiHyb.

One of the best reasons to start a company is to scratch an itch that no one else is reaching. That's what Aaron Patzer did in 2005, when realizing he was in for an afternoon of mind-numbing accounting. Two years later, he launched mint.com; two years after that, Intuit snapped up the service for $170 million. Patzer's own account of the journey can be found at http://tentyp.es/SyDj4M.

As of 2013, Fab had more than 11 million members in 26 countries and had already worked with more than 10,000 design partners. In 2012, it sold 4.3 million products at a rate of 5.4 products per minute. For more Fab facts and figures see the company's press kit: http://tentyp.es/PEEI3I.

According to Foursquare lore, mayorships came about after a friend teased the company cofounders for camping out at the Think Coffee shop in Manhattan: http://tentyp.es/VF8E4R.

The rapid sale of all Apple WWDC tickets led several people to scalp tickets on eBay and Craigslist. In 2011, *Computerworld* reported that some were priced as high as $4,599—nearly triple the regular sticker price: http://tentyp.es/SOZM81.

PART THREE
CHAPTER 13: GO BEYOND PRODUCTS

"While there is a role for continually keeping a product fresh, brand managers appear to be reluctant to try something genuinely new. And when they try something new, they often fail to generate significant incremental revenue and profits because the product may not have a redefined or new value proposition." So wrote Pat Conroy, Anupam Narula, and Siddharth Ramalingham of the failure of Product Performance-focused innovation in *A Crisis of the Similar: Consumer Products* (Deloitte, 2011). Register for the report at http://tentyp.es/OaGE7I.

Benjamin Klein and Joshua D. Wright took an incredibly wonky look at supermarket slot fees in "The Economics of Slotting Contracts," *The Journal of Law & Economics*, August 2007: http://tentyp.es/Q1Ciy3.

The International CES is held each year in Las Vegas, catering to the global consumer technology industry. In 2013, this was estimated to reach $209 billion in the US alone: http://tentyp.es/117LB89.

Before becoming Apple's CEO, Tim Cook was the company's chief operating officer (COO), "responsible for all of the company's worldwide sales and operations, including end-to-end management of

Apple's supply chain, sales activities, and service and support in all markets and countries," as his corporate bio puts it. http://tentyp.es/PFaAVv.

"Apple's position in selling tens of millions of iPods gives it the ability to cherry pick components at prices many competitors can't match. Apple has specifically noted favorable component pricing as a key factor in the company's profitability over the last several quarters." Prince McLean, "Apple Buying up Available Flash RAM Supplies for Next iPhone," *Apple Insider*, February 18, 2009: http://tentyp.es/PFaEVl.

The 25 billionth song bought at Apple's iTunes store was "Monkey Drums" (Goksel Vancin Remix) by Chase Buch. It was purchased by one Phillip Lüpke from Germany: http://tentyp.es/11RksqC.

Aktion Plagiarius estimates that 10% of worldwide commerce is fake, at an annual worldwide loss of EUR 200 to 300 billion. Jessie Scanlon wrote a great story on the issue: "And The Best Knockoff Is…" *BusinessWeek*, February 8, 2008. http://tentyp.es/RtL3QN. To see past winners and register for the annual Plagiarius award, go to: http://tentyp.es/QYhWaT.

During its first 30 days of business, Amazon.com fulfilled orders for customers in 50 states and 45 countries—all shipped from founder Jeff Bezos's garage. An Amazon overview is available at http://tentyp.es/OaGUnb.

In his book *Screw It, Let's Do It*, Richard Branson revealed that his nickname internally was "Dr. Yes,"

named for his inability to say no to people. "I have always tried to find reasons to do something if it seems like a good idea, than not to do it," he wrote: http://tentyp.es/VFLIm7.

"We start with the consumer, work back through the design and finally arrive at manufacturing. The manufacturing becomes a means to the end of service." Henry Ford, quoted in Steven Watts's *The People's Tycoon: Henry Ford and the American Century* (Vintage, 2006): http://tentyp.es/SPwy9i.

"Almost half a century before Ray Kroc sold a single McDonald's hamburger, Ford invented the dealer-franchise system to sell and service cars. In the same way that all politics is local, he knew that business had to be local. Ford's 'road men' became a familiar part of the American landscape. By 1912 there were 7,000 Ford dealers across the country." So wrote Lee Iacocca about his former boss, Henry Ford. Iacocca, of course, famously went on to revive Chrysler. "Driving Force: Henry Ford," *Time* magazine, December 7, 1998. http://tentyp.es/QYijSP.

Google's "Ten Things We Know to Be True" is still available at http://tentyp.es/S5YgDQ.

The story by Bharat Mediratta as told to Julie Bick about Google's 20% time policy is worth a read: "The Google Way: Give Engineers Room," the *New York Times*, October 21, 2007. http://tentyp.es/VFMYFD.

Visit the Search Engine Graveyard for a salutary look at how many were experimenting in the online search space in the 1990s: http://tentyp.es/ShjhG2.

"I'm incredibly excited to collaborate with Zagat to bring the power of Google search and Google Maps to their products and users, and to bring their innovation, trusted reputation and wealth of experience to our users," wrote then-Google vice president Marissa Mayer in 2011: http://tentyp.es/PXLBy8.

The first Google Doodle ran on the search engine's home page in 1998, designed to let visitors know that execs had gone to the Burning Man Festival. The company now has a team of doodlers to respond to news events and anniversaries: http://tentyp.es/RiMpxO.

Bill Gates's 1976 letter to hobbyists concluded, "I would appreciate letters from any one who wants to pay up": http://tentyp.es/RGPudd.

McDonald's corporate website has a slick interactive timeline to describe the launch of various menu items, characters, and advertising campaigns: http://tentyp.es/Pfbo93.

For an officially sanctioned version of the history of Lexus, see Jonathan Mahler and Maximilian Potter's *The Lexus Story* (Melcher, 2004): http://tentyp.es/ShvwCw. Eiji Toyoda is quoted in *Lexus: The Relentless Pursuit* (Wiley, updated version published in 2011), written by journalist Chester Dawson: http://tentyp.es/V5S51E.

CHAPTER 14: STRENGTH IN NUMBERS
Failure to consistently, relentlessly improve the known is one of the surest routes to failure. One hard-to-find

resource for more on this topic is Carl Franklin's *Why Innovation Fails: Hard Won Lessons for Business* (Spiro Press, 2003): http://tentyp.es/UT8VIM.

A fifth anniversary edition of *The Fortune at the Bottom of the Pyramid* by the late C.K. Prahalad was published in 2009 (Wharton School Publishing): http://tentyp.es/TaCTvx. Also worth a look is Prahalad's book (with M.S. Krishnan) *The New Age of Innovation* (McGraw-Hill, 2008): http://tentyp.es/RkazJ7.

Jonathan Byrnes looked at how Dell learned the secrets of just-in-time inventory in "Dell Manages Profitability, Not Inventory," *Harvard Business School Working Knowledge*, June 2003. http://tentyp.es/QYjyRY.

FedEx's other technological innovations include the Command and Control satellite to ground operations system, based in Memphis, which it describes as "the largest UNIX undertaking in the commercial world": http://tentyp.es/QL8Mhu.

The LEGO Group bought its first plastic injection-molding machine in 1946. It cost 30,000 Danish Kroner (about $5,000 in current money). The firm's revenues that year were 450,000 Danish Kroner (nearly $78,000). For more of the company's history and evolution: http://tentyp.es/PD59Mh.

More on the Method story is included in Steve Diller, Nathan Shedroff, and Darrel Rhea's *Making Meaning: How Successful Businesses Deliver Meaningful Customer Experiences* (New Riders, 2006):

http://tentyp.es/QvBPGj. Method also includes copious details about its processes and products on its own corporate website: http://tentyp.es/QL8PKs.

PART FOUR
CHAPTER 15: MIND THE GAP
We regularly use the Ten Types framework to conduct an internal analysis for our clients. We take client confidentiality very seriously, so while our illustrative analysis is derived from real work, we have renamed the initiatives. In a nod toward the enduring LOLcat web meme, we rechristened them after various breeds of cat. Did you notice?

CHAPTER 16: CHALLENGE CONVENTION
"Should we put shareholder money at risk in a market that's at best five years away from being commercial?" asked Blockbuster CEO Jim Keyes in the interview with Rick Aristotle Munarriz. "I don't think so." "Blockbuster CEO Has Answers," *Motley Fool*, December 10, 2008: http://tentyp.es/135t08i.

"While Blockbuster's business faces significant challenges, we look forward to working with its employees to reestablish Blockbuster's brand as a leader in video entertainment." So commented DISH Network EVP Tom Cullen at the announcement of DISH's acquisition of the bankrupt media company: http://tentyp.es/XJxpdP.

Founded in 1992, Palm was repeatedly bought, sold, split into pieces and reformed. In 2010, HP bought the firm for $1.2 billion (http://tentyp.es/UDSvyl) but shut down the division producing hardware that ran Palm's WebOS operating system. As of this writing, its latest incarnation seems to be as a subsidiary within HP called Gram. For a pithy recap of the firm's history, see Arik Hesseldahl's "Meet Gram, HP's New Name for the Company Formerly Known as Palm," *All Things D*, August 15, 2012: http://tentyp.es/QdeYfV.

Bluetooth was born in an Ericsson lab in Lund, Sweden. Within 10 years of its introduction, it had been incorporated into 2 billion devices. In 2012, its inventor Dr. Jaap Haartsen was nominated as Inventor of the Year by the European Patent Office: http://tentyp.es/Pb72AO.

Motorola's StarTAC was the smallest and lightest cell phone available in 1996. In 2010, *Time* magazine featured the phone in a list of the greatest and most influential gadgets from 1923 onward: http://tentyp.es/QQX9pk.

Bob Parks's story of Philippe Kahn, who sent the first mobile photograph of his newborn daughter in 1997 and who developed the LightSurf network infrastructure, is well worth a read: "The Big Picture," *Wired*, October, 2000: http://tentyp.es/PTu20G.

The "consumerization" of IT and its impact on the telecoms industry, especially on Research in Motion, is memorably detailed in James Surowiecki's article, "Blackberry Season," *The New Yorker*, February 13, 2012: http://tentyp.es/UDT3ok.

The Centers for Disease Control and Prevention included electronic medical record data in a report published in 2010 (http://tentyp.es/V5Xm9w). The other data points in this section were taken from

two papers published by IMS Institute for Health Informatics: "The Use of Medicines in the United States: Review of 2010," http://tentyp.es/NVmgHw, and "Searching for Global Launch Excellence," http://tentyp.es/PKNa3h.

See also "Transforming Commercial Models to Address New Health Care Realities," a white paper written by our colleagues, Jeff Wordham and Sheryl L. Jacobson, which looks at how fundamental changes in the health care system are transforming the ways in which pharma companies go about their work. *Monitor Perspectives*, November 2011: http://tentyp.es/WMTJVQ.

Eliel Saarinen quoted by, among many others, Anne D'Alleva in *How to Write Art History* (London; Laurence King, 2010): http://tentyp.es/RiMWQk.

"The beautiful indoor space looks nothing like a traditional hospital," Bill Taylor continued in his piece about the Henry Ford West Bloomfield Hospital for the Management Innovation Exchange. "More than two thousand live plants and trees line the curved "streets," which are decked out with various shops (selling products for sounder sleep, better diets, and so on) that feel like the world's healthiest vacation village." http://tentyp.es/VSJGNi.

CHAPTER 17: PATTERN RECOGNITION

If ever an innovation book deserved to be awarded the epithet "classic," it's Clayton Christensen's *The Innovator's Dilemma*. A new edition was published in 2011 by HarperBusiness: http://tentyp.es/QZnCPB.

The corporate website of American Girl has lots of useful facts and figures: http://tentyp.es/PTuzjg. Doris Hajewski wrote a charming account of the excitement engendered by American Girl: "Middleton, Wis., Doll-Maker Gets Makeover but Keeps Historical Roots," *Knight Ridder Tribune Business News*, January, 2004. http://tentyp.es/SJVHWv. Pleasant T. Rowland told her story in "A New Twist on Timeless Toys," an essay featured in *Success*, by Tony Zhou (2004): http://tentyp.es/ScGFby.

One of us, Larry Keeley, wrote a longer essay looking at Nike's strategy around its stores, published in *They Say They Want a Revolution: What Marketers Need to Know as Consumers Take Control* (compiled by Paul Matthaeus, iUniverse, 2003): http://tentyp.es/U72IIr.

Three Harvard Business School articles/case studies are extremely informative on all things Nike: "Nike, Inc. in the 1990s: New Directions" (April 25, 1995): http://tentyp.es/RF3Wjt; "Nike, Inc.—Entering the Millennium" (March 16, 2001): http://tentyp.es/S4NKL1, and "Knight the King: The Founding of Nike" (June 24, 2010): http://tentyp.es/T1SKRp.

Phil Knight shared his impressions of goings-on at Nike in "High Performance Marketing: An Interview with Nike's Phil Knight," *Harvard Business Review*, July–August, 1992: http://tentyp.es/Qdgfn3.

A mini case study of the Just Do It campaign was published by the Center for Applied Research: http://tentyp.es/RfVNSs. Do also see the company's website, which includes plenty of information on the company's history and evolution along with quotes from executives: http://tentyp.es/RcSGuL.

PART FIVE
CHAPTER 18: DECLARE INTENT
JFK's speech continued: "In a very real sense, it will not be one man going to the moon — if we make this judgment affirmatively, it will be an entire nation. For all of us must work to put him there," http://tentyp.es/RcT1O3. As you might imagine, NASA has tons of documents, interviews, and information on the dramatic decade that ensued after the President laid down his challenge: http://tentyp.es/RaBFT4.

Zipcar's mission is pretty simple: "We make life more rewarding, sustainable and affordable. We enhance urban lifestyles by maximizing our members' most precious resource — their time." For more on the company's philosophy, see http://tentyp.es/Wqr37u. For details of the company's acquisition by Avis Budget Group, see the press release from January 2, 2013: http://tentyp.es/Y31Ak6.

"Amazon Web Services provides a highly reliable, scalable, low-cost infrastructure platform in the cloud that powers hundreds of thousands of enterprise, government and startup customers businesses in 190 countries around the world," boasts the company's online overview: http://tentyp.es/OaGUnb.

In "The HBR Interview: 'We Had to Own the Mistakes'," Starbucks CEO Howard Schultz discussed returning to the coffee company in 2008 to, as writer Adi

Ignatius put it, "retake the reins in the middle of a crisis." *Harvard Business Review*, July 2010, http://tentyp.es/YkCOYN.

The study of managing a portfolio of innovation initiatives across ambition levels by our colleagues, Bansi Nagji and Geoff Tuff, was published in *Harvard Business Review* in May 2012. "Managing Your Innovation Portfolio," http://tentyp.es/PwOg3o.

Matthew E. May wrote compellingly about the goings-on at Toyota, including the company's quest to innovate continually and its vaunted Production System, in *The Elegant Solution* (Free Press, 2006), http://tentyp.es/TmKqat.

Alan Kay came up with the phrase "object-oriented programming" in 1967. As he explained in a later email, he thought of it as "an architecture for programming," http://tentyp.es/TdvtaP.

Lieutenant Grace Murray Hopper found a moth trapped in the Mark II Aiken Relay Calculator in 1947, leading computer scientists to joke of "debugging" their machines. See a photograph of her log entry (with the offending moth attached), now on show at the Naval Surface Warfare Center Computer Museum in Dahlgren, Virginia: http://tentyp.es/SKOV2e.

CHAPTER 19: INNOVATION TACTICS
To buy one of our packs of Innovation Tactics Cards, designed by Ryan Pikkel and containing the 112 discrete tactics identified at the time of writing, email us: tentypes@doblin.com.

CHAPTER 20: USING THE INNOVATION PLAYBOOK
Rachel Botsman and Roo Rogers's *What's Mine is Yours: The Rise of Collaborative Consumption*, HarperBusiness, 2010 (http://tentyp.es/TeBwvL) and the book's website http://tentyp.es/Tvo7Sq cite multiple examples of this play at work.

"An Expert Perspective on Open Innovation" is an interview by Wyatt Nordstrom with the former head of open innovation at GlaxoSmithKline (GSK) Consumer Healthcare, Helene Rutledge, Maven Research, http://tentyp.es/QZSGOK.

Robert Wolf of GSK was quoted in "A Prescription for Profit," published in *HQ* magazine: http://tentyp.es/RnTRK2. You can also search the list of current open topics at GSK's open innovation portal. In 2012, issues of interest included pain management for the elderly and a material that might protect teeth from food acid: http://tentyp.es/SqJTnA.

In her piece "P&G Asks: What's the Big Idea?" Jena McGregor also included details of Procter & Gamble's so-called technology entrepreneurs, "the more than 75 innovation scouts it has stationed in far corners of the globe." *BusinessWeek*, May 4, 2007: http://tentyp.es/XcReMZ.

For more on collaborative consumption, see Marcus Felson and Joe L. Spaeth's "Community Structure and Collaborative Consumption: A Routine Activity Approach," *American Behavioral Scientist,* March 1978: http://tentyp.es/PVOISw.

For more on Zipcar's philosophy and principles, take a look at the company's own website: http://tentyp.es/QvogGM. The company's 2011 annual report also has some useful information on the firm's internal approach and management setup: http://tentyp.es/QKtDPd.

More than 10 million nights had been booked through Airbnb by the beginning of 2013. For more details on the company's tactics and approach, see "Airbnb at a Glance," http://tentyp.es/WMVD90, and the company's online "Trust & Safety Center." http://tentyp.es/QaWBJv.

Chris Anderson's book *Free* is a foundational text on the free-based play. It was pubished by Hyperion in 2010: http://tentyp.es/TtLtWb.

"LinkedIn is a free service, but people pay premiums for things like access to anyone's professional information; these premium subscriptions brought in $23.9 million [in 2011]," wrote Quentin Hardy in "LinkedIn Wants to Make More Money From Job Recruiters." the *New York Times*, October 18, 2011: http://tentyp.es/WZGphb.

In the third quarter of 2012, Zynga had 311 million monthly active users. Download Zynga's full 2011 annual report, which has a ton of interesting insights into the world of online gaming, including CEO and founder Mark Pincus's admission: "We have a short operating history and a new business model, which makes it difficult to effectively assess our future prospects. Our business model is based on offering games that are free to play. To date, only a small portion of our players pay for virtual goods." http://tentyp.es/ShIyBc.

Richard Pascale's book *Surfing on the Edge of Chaos* was published by Crown Business in 2001: http://tentyp.es/RI9InK. Thomas Petzinger's story on Cemex's clever new system was published in *Fast Company* in March 1999: "In Search of the New World (of Work)," http://tentyp.es/RnV2cm. Meanwhile, Peter Katel's "Bordering on Chaos" for *Wired* magazine is also a good read on "seeing complexity theory in action" throughout Cemex's business: http://tentyp.es/SUp0Ie.

Aravind Eye Hospital's own site has a decent description of the goings-on at the organization: http://tentyp.es/UPAo3A. See also the white paper by Angel Diaz Matalobos, Juan Pons, and Stephan Pahls: "The McDonald's of Health Organizations: Lean Practices at Aravind," June 2010: http://tentyp.es/VKO7NH.

The company blurb describes GE Aviation's OnPoint Solutions as an offering "for customers who prefer a more customized, comprehensive and longer-term solution to meet business needs and cost of ownership objectives." http://tentyp.es/NVgh5t.

For more on Johnson Controls' smart systems, see details on its Performance Contracting service, http://tentyp.es/VUIs6u, as well as its dedicated website, Make Your Buildings Work (http://tentyp.es/UDVnMd), which includes an energy efficiency calculator to help customers assess potential savings.

J. K. Rowling gave more details about her writing process in a 2001 interview published by Scholastic. In particular, she described the design of the "in-story" books, which feature doodles by young wizards Harry Potter and Ron Weasley. "I always wrote all over mine," she says. "Teachers reading this will not be happy that I'm saying it but you do, don't you?" http://tentyp.es/OtDEEl. In 2008, Rowling was featured on *Forbes*'s list of "The World's Billionaires." http://tentyp.es/Sh91IF.

For details of just some of the Harry Potter paraphernalia that can be yours for a price, see Universal Orlando's store: http://tentyp.es/TemO8t. To see details of *Harry Potter* film grosses, check out Box Office Mojo: http://tentyp.es/PKGDp9.

P&G's patent for "Uncomplexed Cyclodextrin Solutions for odor control on inanimate surfaces" (the technology in Febreze) was filed in 1994 and granted on February 3, 1998: http://tentyp.es/OtDL36. *The Wall Street Journal*, meanwhile, ran the story, "Febreze Joins P&G's $1 Billion Club" in March 2011 to detail the product's popularity as a cross-branding entity: http://tentyp.es/TMxP7j.

For the raw data behind Kickstarter, including statistics on each of the funding site's 13 different project categories, see http://tentyp.es/V5HJyP. In line with the company's spirit of openness, the page is updated daily.

Craig Newmark wrote on his personal blog about starting Craigslist: "We're one of the 10 most-visited English language web platforms on the planet. Really not because of me, I'm really bad at business stuff, but because at least I was smart enough to hire Jim Buckmaster to run the biz and I mostly got out of the way." http://tentyp.es/SMIRda.

Netcraft surveyed nearly 666 million websites in July 2012 to determine the world's top web servers. Apache had 61.45% market share, Microsoft had 14.62%, and Google had 3.44%: http://tentyp.es/QZUK9x.

The story of Threadless is well told by Max Chafkin in "The Customer is the Company" for *Inc.* magazine, June 2008, http://tentyp.es/T24fZ5. Threadless stats are also featured in a case study in William C. Taylor's *Practically Radical: Not-So-Crazy Ways to Transform Your Company, Shake Up Your Industry, and Challenge Yourself,* HarperCollins, 2011: http://tentyp.es/SprVpR. The company was also the focus of a *Harvard Business Review* multimedia case study by Karim R. Lakhani and Zahra Kanji: "Threadless: The Business of Community," June 30, 2008. http://tentyp.es/RNnkgz.

Jim Giles analyzed both Wikipedia and Encyclopedia Britannica in detail in "Internet Encyclopedias Go Head to Head," *Nature,* December 15, 2005, http://tentyp.es/VUneoi. (*Nature* also rebutted Britannica's later complaint in a fascinating document: http://tentyp.es/RbbEVs.) See also Wikipedia's own mission statement: "to empower and engage people around the world to collect and develop educational content under a free license or in the public domain, and to disseminate it effectively and globally." http://tentyp.es/RnWg7t.

For examples of companies using Amazon Web Services (including NASA, Netflix, and News International), see http://tentyp.es/WMWO8q. More general information on AWS is available at http://tentyp.es/S631NU while details of Amazon's strategic partners are found at http://tentyp.es/TMzoC8. Information on one of the patents that goes into the service, "for providing a marketplace for web services" is available at http://tentyp.es/UyiwtE, along with the eventual patent awarded, in 2008, at http://tentyp.es/Qvsoqd.

For details and case studies of CAT Logistics, now known as Neovia, see http://tentyp.es/QjTY6m, and Jeneanne Rae, Carl Fudge, and Colin Hudson's "Growing B2B Services: Three Trends to Act Upon Now," *Innovation Management,* March 5, 2012, http://tentyp.es/PKHKFp.

To see just one report on Apple becoming the world's most valuable company, see David Goldman's piece for *CNN Money:* http://tentyp.es/OIqKaF. For Apple's own stats on innovation and job creation, see http://tentyp.es/S63NKE.

In a 2008 interview with the *Wall Street Journal*'s Nick Wingfield, the late Steve Jobs described Apple's phone strategy: "Phone differentiation used to be about radios and antennas and things like that… We think, going forward, the phone of the future will be differentiated by software." ("iPhone Software Sales Take Off," http://tentyp.es/PIL1yf.) The *Washington Post*'s Rob Pegoraro wrote "Apple's Taking 30 percent of App Store Subscriptions Is an Unkind Cut," February 20, 2011, http://tentyp.es/SIIwHQ.

Apple described the all-new iTunes in September 2012: http://tentyp.es/RnXnnF. Long-time Apple designer Chris Stringer described the team's working habits when he appeared as a witness in the Apple vs. Samsung trial of 2012, as detailed by Ina Fried in the piece "Apple Literally Designs Its Products Around a Kitchen Table," *All Things D*, July 31, 2012: http://tentyp.es/UT25wF.

For stats on the installed base of phones, including Android's current dominance in the United States, see analysis in Charles Arthur's "Android is Winning—if You're Writing Apps for China. Elsewhere, Though… ," August 16, 2012, http://tentyp.es/QKw98i.

All Foursquare data comes from the company itself. A good place to start is the "About" page of the website: http://tentyp.es/UDWv2j.

Answers to frequently asked questions about Discovery and its Vitality program are available at http://tentyp.es/XFmTod, along with details on the nuts and bolts of Vitality at http://tentyp.es/RNnJzA.

Janet Moore detailed the proposed opening of a 85,000-square-foot Cabela's store in Woodbury, Minn.: "Cabela's, Other Outdoor Retailers Take Aim at Twin Cities," *Star Tribune*, February 9, 2013: http://tentyp.es/12ucBdi.

In October 2012, the $210 Alinea menu featured items such as "scallop acting like agedashi tofu," "squab inspired by Miro," and "black truffle explosion": http://tentyp.es/SPBIkN. Achatz is also careful to acknowledge his collaborators, including

CookTek, which supplies equipment, and Martin Kastner of Crucial Detail, who's the restaurant's "designer and sculptor": http://tentyp.es/VKQ78X.

Harley-Davidson's own website has a lot of information about the company's growth: http://tentyp.es/UDWNGs. Harley also boasts its own $75 million museum showcase, designed in 2008 by Pentagram's James Biber with associate Michael Zweck-Bronner: http://tentyp.es/TrrrkT.

More information about Weight Watchers, its background, history, and continued quest to help people lose weight can be found at the corporate website: http://tentyp.es/RNnO6m. Particular details on the 2011 initiative targeting men can be found at http://tentyp.es/R4ecl1.

Patagonia's full mission statement reads: "Build the best product, cause no unnecessary harm, use business to inspire and implement solutions to the environmental crisis," http://tentyp.es/QaXMbQ. The story of the company's founding is available at http://tentyp.es/UPBn3H, while details on the Common Threads initiative is at http://tentyp.es/WMY37p. Meanwhile, the company's blog, *The Cleanest Line* is at http://tentyp.es/R4eo3x.

For details of Whole Foods Market's local sourcing, see its online declaration: http://tentyp.es/SJXdrN. A fairly detailed history of the company's milestones is available at http://tentyp.es/TrrT2q. Whole Foods also published the "5-Step Animal Welfare Rating" as a way to educate consumers on how meat is produced: http://tentyp.es/WMYjDC.

"We are trying not to increase the number of buttons the player has to manipulate," Nintendo president Satoru Iwata said in a company briefing in 2006. "We are trying not to be constrained by conventional rules. We are trying to make games so that anyone can enjoy playing easily," http://tentyp.es/PTxJ6F.

See notes on Chapter 12 for some useful sources on mint.com. Or, watch an interview by J. D. Lasica with the company's CEO Aaron Patzer: http://tentyp.es/WMYmz8. Belinda Luscombe analyzed the website's sale to Intuit in the *Time* magazine article, "Intuit Buys Mint.com: The Future of Personal Finance?" September 15, 2009. http://tentyp.es/UDXpvF.

PART SIX

CHAPTER 21: GET CRACKING

Joel Garreau quoted Michael Shermer, founding publisher of *Skeptic* magazine, in this piece in the *Washington Post*: "Science's Mything Links," July 23, 2001: http://tentyp.es/Spt7tt.

Fortune keeps archives of 50 years of America's largest corporations: http://tentyp.es/QRhk51.

Author Jim Collins also writes extensively and entertainingly about what makes great companies endure in books such as *Built to Last* (HarperBusiness, 2004): http://tentyp.es/T1R46L; and *Good to Great* (HarperBusiness, 2001): http://tentyp.es/QRhvOa.

Mark Zuckerberg first appeared on *Forbes*'s list of "The World's Billionaires" in 2008, the youngest of the 1,125 billionaires featured on the list that year.

See Ryan Mac's later story for the magazine, *The Evolution of Mark Zuckerberg's Wealth*, May 17, 2011: http://tentyp.es/RaA7qc.

CHAPTER 22: SPONSORS AND AUTHORS

For more on Jeff Bezos's innovation and investment philosophy, it's always useful to follow his statements to shareholders. Here's the link to Amazon's earnings calls and annual reports: http://tentyp.es/S65B6w. Bezos was also quoted in a transcript from the 2011 webcast: http://tentyp.es/Qvwcrm.

For details on Amazon's move into high-end fashion, see Stephanie Clifford's "Amazon Leaps Into High End of the Fashion Pool," *The New York Times*, May 7, 2012, http://tentyp.es/OZQFWA.

"Growth as a Process" features an extensive discussion of innovation and "Imagination Breakthroughs" with General Electric CEO, Jeffrey R. Immelt, *Harvard Business Review*, June 2006: http://tentyp.es/SptWCy.

IBM features many stories about its corporate evolution on its website: http://tentyp.es/UQOYgQ, while many facts and figures can be found in its annual reports. The 2011 version is here: http://tentyp.es/RTMhqA. IBM patent information is found at http://tentyp.es/QW1Vlz.

Details of IBM's innovation investments can be found in this concise piece from *Fortune* magazine by Jeffrey M. O'Brien: "IBM's Grand Plan to Save the Planet," April 21, 2009, http://tentyp.es/QvxFOQ. "Just a few years ago, IBM peddled PCs, disk drives, and other basic building blocks of computing. Now it's being sold as a kind of technology visionary able to reshape cities in a single bound through analytics software and the brainiest consultants on the planet," wrote Ashlee Vance in "How IBM Wooed Wall Street," *Bloomberg Businessweek,* March 6, 2012, http://tentyp.es/QKxZG7.

"Why aren't you doing anything with this? This is the greatest thing. This is revolutionary!" So spoke Steve Jobs after a visit to Xerox PARC in 1979, as told by Malcolm Gladwell in "Creation Myth," *The New Yorker,* May 16, 2011: http://tentyp.es/Y6CL6I.

See a chart showing Blockbuster's decline and fall at http://tentyp.es/PTyDjr.

CHAPTER 23: INSTALLING INNOVATION

"We cannot simply fine-tune current methods of health care delivery," wrote Dr. Nicholas LaRusso, Medical Director of the Mayo Clinic Center for Innovation (http://tentyp.es/OROYfQ). "It will require transformational innovation in virtually everything we do." Mayo also hosts an annual health care innovation-related conference, Transform, which is well worth checking out if that's your kind of thing. (Full disclosure: Larry Keeley sits on the external advisory board at the Center for Innovation.)

Valve's handbook for new employees is a joy to read: http://tentyp.es/QQYOvc.

"At the Hyatt Regency O'Hare in Chicago, mobile hosts are now stationed at the airport shuttle center, where they greet guests, check them in, and issue room keys," wrote Stacy Collett in "Ready, Set, Compete:

The Benefits of IT Innovation," *Computerworld,* January 14, 2013: http://tentyp.es/XHSveu.

Adam Lashinsky detailed much of Apple's way of working (in the Steve Jobs era, at least) in "How Apple Works: Inside the World's Biggest Startup," *Fortune* magazine, August 25, 2011, http://tentyp.es/UDYvHS.

"The company is providing American business with a case study of how a large and bureaucratic organization can change internally without totally destroying the culture that made it great," wrote Brian Dumaine of Procter & Gamble in "P&G Rewrites the Marketing Rules," *Fortune* magazine, November 6, 1989, http://tentyp.es/TjEPID.

The story of 3M, its Freshness Index, and its approach to innovation are well told in the books *Corporate Creativity,* by Alan G. Robinson and Sam Stern (Berrett-Koehler Publishers, 1998), http://tentyp.es/T1e8BQ, and *Driving Growth Through Innovation* by Robert B. Tucker (Berrett-Koehler Publishers, 2002), http://tentyp.es/RbdWE4. Details of 3M's past and current financial performance are, of course, documented by the SEC: http://tentyp.es/RVMO9U.

CHAPTER 24: EXECUTE EFFECTIVELY

An interview between Charles Eames and Madame L'Amic of the Musée des Arts Decoratifs is featured in *Eames Design* (Abrams, 1989), http://tentyp.es/TeoM8O.

Atul Gawande's *The Checklist Manifesto* (Picador reprint, 2011) is engaging and rewarding (as is most

of his writing): http://tentyp.es/PDundv. See also the doctor's own website for an updated list of his most recent articles: http://tentyp.es/Y6Mo5g.

For a list of projects for which DARPA is actively seeking external contributions, including in 2013 the call for "innovative multidisciplinary research proposals to rapidly develop and demonstrate non-contact methods to detect explosives embedded or packaged in opaque media with high water content (e.g., water, mud, meat/animal carcasses) at standoff," see http://tentyp.es/Y9qEUz.

David Barboza's piece "Planet Earth Calling Iridium: Can the Satellite Phone Service Achieve a Soft Landing?" looks at the woes of Iridium and was published in the *New York Times,* September 7, 1999, http://tentyp.es/TXqxgN. See also Steve Blank's blog post, "No Business Plan Survives First Contact With A Customer," http://tentyp.es/RsIKjD.

Michael E. Porter, a cofounder of Monitor, has written numerous books on strategy. *Competitive Strategy* (Free Press, 1998) is one of his most famous, now nearing 60 printings in English and translated into 19 languages and counting: http://tentyp.es/PbDHWf.

IN CLOSING...

Read more about the U.N. World Food Programme and its ongoing mission to fight hunger worldwide at http://tentyp.es/WQOAi6. And find out more about Bill and Melinda Gates and their foundation's philanthropic initiatives: http://tentyp.es/U5BUhI.

To learn more about the Khan Academy and its promise to provide "a free world-class education for anyone anywhere," see http://tentyp.es/PDuZ2T. Also see *The One World Schoolhouse* by the academy's founder, Salman Khan (Twelve, 2012): http://tentyp.es/TkhnnX.

The Preventive Medicine Research Institute is "a non-profit research institute that performs scientific research investigating the effects of diet and lifestyle choices on health and disease." For more information on the organization and its founder, Dr. Dean Ornish, see http://tentyp.es/PlMnsE.

Paul Farmer won his MacArthur Fellowship (aka the "Genius Grant") in 1993. He used the prize money to establish Partners In Health's research and advocacy arm, the Institute for Health and Social Justice. Partners in Health now directly cares for 2.4 million people: http://tentyp.es/Rbe9aw.

"Growing Power is a national nonprofit organization and land trust supporting people from diverse backgrounds, and the environments in which they live, by helping to provide equal access to healthy, high-quality, safe and affordable food for people in all communities." For more details on the organization and its founder, Will Allen, another MacArthur Genius, see http://tentyp.es/RtPv1Z.

IMAGE CREDITS

Images used throughout this book are either from the authors' personal collection or are copyrighted images from iStockPhoto and Shutterstock that have been used with permission. Exceptions include the following:

PART ONE
"Proteus growing on brilliant green agar in a petri dish" by Fancy Photography/ Veer.

PART THREE
"Supermarket aisle stocked with products" by Chuck Keeler/ Stone/Getty Images.

"Plagiarius Award Trophy" courtesy of Aktion Plagiarius e.v.

"Black 1914 Model T Ford (USA), side view" by Dave King/Dorling Kindersley/Getty Images.

"Ford Model T Assembly Line at Ford Motor Company Oklahoma City Plant," "Ford Automobile Dealership," and "Crowd of Applicants outside Highland Park Plant after Announcement of Five Dollar Day" are all from the collections of The Henry Ford.

Google Search Screen and Google Doodles: Google.

Microsoft Office packaging courtesy of the Microsoft Archives.

McDonald's restaurants and Hamburger University images courtesy of McDonald's.

"McDonald's Truck DSC00519" by William O. Slone.

Jim Hudson Lexus dealership exterior and lounge: Clear Sky Images.

"Lexus Elite Trophy" courtesy of Lexus.

"OpenRoad Lexus Cafe" courtesy of Kasian Architecture Interior Design and Planning Ltd.

"Overhead view of symphony orchestra" by Kevin Jordan/ Photodisc/Getty Images.

Ginger Hotels logo and cafe courtesy of Ginger Hotels.

Dell laptop and boxes courtesy of Dell © 2012 Dell Inc. All Rights Reserved.

FedEx truck courtesy of FedEx. FedEx service marks used with permission.

LEGO Minecraft Set courtesy of the LEGO Group. LEGO, LEGOLAND and MINDSTORMS are trademarks of the LEGO Group of Companies, used here by permission. © 2012 The LEGO Group, CUUSOO System and Mojang AB. All rights reserved.

Method hand soap courtesy of Method.

PART FOUR
"Birds on a wire and one all alone" by Dusty Pixel Photography/ Flickr/Getty Images.

Henry Ford West Bloomfield Hospital Atrium and Demonstration Kitchen courtesy of Henry Ford Health System.

"I screwed my camera. [apart]" by Kelly Hofer.

"Mother kissing baby daughter" by Photography by Bobi/Flickr/ Getty Images.

"Baby sleeping" by Floresco Productions/OJO Images/ Getty Images.

"Cute portrait of mother and her daughter" by Philippe Regard/ The Image Bank/Getty Images.

Niketown NYC and Nike+: Nike Inc.

PART FIVE
"The Full Moon" by NASA/courtesy of nasaimages.org.

Innovation Tactics Cards and Innovation Play Book by Amar Singh.

PART SIX
"Iron composition" by Yagi Studios/Digital Vision/Getty Images.

"First flight, 120 feet in 12 seconds, 10:35 a.m.; Kitty Hawk, North Carolina" courtesy of the Library of Congress.

INDEX

PEOPLE

TOPICS

ABOUT THE AUTHORS

Larry Keeley is a globally recognized leader in innovation effectiveness, a topic he tackles as a professor in design and business schools, and a speaker, writer, and researcher. Obsessed with understanding why innovation mostly fails, he has worked to grow the field as a science rather than an exercise in applied creativity. Along with his mentor Jay Doblin, he cofounded Doblin back in 1981 and since 2013 he has been a director in Monitor Deloitte, where he serves as thought leader for the firm's global innovation practice.

Larry has worked on innovation challenges in 55 different industries and with many of the world's leading firms and philanthropies. He is both a board member and adjunct professor at Chicago's Institute of Design—the first design school in the United States to offer a PhD in the topic. He lectures at executive education programs at Kellogg Graduate School of Management and is an adjunct faculty member in the core MBA program and in Northwestern University's McCormick School of Engineering, where he teaches in the Masters of Manufacturing Management program. Larry was a Senior Fellow of the Center for Business Innovation in Boston, serves on the external advisory council for the Mayo Clinic, and is also a board member for Chicago Public Radio, where he helped to develop shows like *This American Life* and other innovative programs.

Ryan Pikkel is a design strategist at Doblin. He is responsible for guiding clients and teams through innovation programs to articulate and develop solutions that will benefit both the client and the end user. In addition, Ryan makes significant contributions to developing Doblin's own tools and processes — including the Ten Types of Innovation framework, the Innovation Tactics, and associated Tactics cards. His work has spanned industries, while he has helped to establish innovation capabilities for clients in Seoul and Mumbai. Ryan is also a member of adjunct faculty at the Institute of Design at IIT, where he teaches innovation tools and techniques.

Brian Quinn is a leader at Doblin. He is responsible for designing and overseeing scaled innovation programs with some of our largest clients — working with them both to innovate and become more effective innovators. He helps advance the company's leadership in building innovation capabilities and implementing innovations for clients, and is a key member of the team that continues to evolve the Ten Types of Innovation framework. His work has spanned many industries, but he has particular experience in health care. Brian has also worked as a screenwriter for the film industry, and is fascinated by the power of narrative.

Helen Walters is a writer, editor, and researcher at Doblin. Previously the editor of innovation and design at *BusinessWeek* (and later at *Bloomberg BusinessWeek*), she joined the firm to help develop editorial strategy, including work on this book. She is also a member of the team that continues to work on the Ten Types of Innovation framework. Happy to observe the innovation process from within, Helen nonetheless sates her inner journalism junkie by writing and publishing the regular blog, *Thought You Should See This,* as well as tweeting incessantly (@helenwalters). She is also the live blogger for the TED conference.

ABOUT DOBLIN AND MONITOR DELOITTE

Founded in 1981 and headquartered in Chicago, Doblin is one of the world's leading design-driven innovation firms. As of 2013, Doblin became a central part of the innovation offering at the global strategy consultancy, Monitor Deloitte. The combination of broad strategy capabilities with sophisticated innovation methods provides virtually unparalleled value to clients.

With offices all over the world and a strong cadre of global practitioners providing a radically expanded set of innovation services to clients worldwide, Monitor Deloitte helps leaders to apply innovative and unconventional insight to make decisions in an increasingly dynamic world; take timely, effective action; and build lasting and sustainable advantage by creating leading edge internal capabilities.

Doblin and Monitor Deloitte continue to expand into new markets, and help firms and philanthropic organizations foster new growth and build bold breakthroughs. Together they aim to change the world for the better through long-term collaborations with organizations and leaders committed to producing bold innovation.